THE MARKETING MANUAL

FOR PERFORMING ARTS ORGANISATIONS

HEATHER MAITLAND

Commissioned and published by the Arts Marketing Association with
additional financial assistance from the Arts Council of England,
the Arts Council of Wales and the Scottish Arts Council

THE MARKETING MANUAL

Heather Maitland
© Arts Marketing Association

The Marketing Manual was first published in May 1990 as part of the then Arts Minister Richard Luce's marketing initiative for 1989/90 and was published on his behalf by the Arts Council of Great Britain. It was reprinted in June 1991 with an introduction by Minister for the Arts, Tim Renton.

This edition is published by the Arts Marketing Association
Bolton's Warehouse
23 Tenison Road
Cambridge
CB1 2DG

Telephone: 01223 578078
Fax: 01223 578079
Email: mail@a-m-a.co.uk

Design Paul Vater at Sugar Free Design, London 020 7243 2100
Printed in the UK by Piggott Printers, Cambridge

ISBN 1 903315 02 6

FIRST AND SECOND EDITIONS

JUDITH MEDDICK

Judith Meddick studied business and international marketing at Bristol Polytechnic. She has worked for numerous performing arts organisations on both the small and middle scale. Since 1988 she has run her own business as a freelance arts marketing consultant. Her clients have included the Arts Council of Great Britain, South East Arts, Dance Quorum, Nahid Siddiqui and the David Glass Ensemble.

ALASTAIR JAMES

Alastair James worked for various festivals and as Assistant House Manager at York Theatre Royal before becoming an Arts Council Touring Marketing Bursary holder. He recently became Alumni Officer at Campaign for Oxford.

STEERING GROUP

The Marketing Manual was originally compiled under the guidance of a steering group whose members were: Karin Gartzke (Drama Department, Arts Council of Great Britain), Vicky Harbord (Arts Administrator, mime), Sue Hoyle (Dance Department, Arts Council of Great Britain), Shobana Jeyasingh (Indian Dance soloist), Vivienne Moore (Touring Department, Arts Council of Great Britain), Robert Petty (Director, Midlands Arts Centre), Carol Stone (Arts Administrator, dance), Nick Sweeting (Arts Administrator, theatre) and Peter Verwey (Marketing & Resources Department, Arts Council of Great Britain).

ACKNOWLEDGEMENTS

We would like to thank Iain Lanyon for his contributions to and advice on Chapter 4, 'How to Produce Print'. Thanks to all the graphic designers whose advice is quoted in section 5.4, 'Briefing your designer'.

THIRD EDITION

HEATHER MAITLAND

Heather Maitland has worked for a wide range of arts organisations: from the smallest of touring theatre companies to running the London end of the Royal Shakespeare Company's marketing operation and including both classical and contemporary dance. She worked on audience and art form development with around 40 small scale venues and companies in the East of England while at Eastern Touring Agency. She spent over two years at of Midlands Arts Marketing working with 60 arts organisations of all scales on audience development, market research, business planning and marketing projects.

Heather has written *A Guide to Audience Development*, *The Golden Guide: Marketing for Touring*, *The Silver Guide: Marketing for touring companies with few resources*, all for the Arts Council of England and, most recently, *Is It Time for Plan B?* for the Arts Marketing Association.

She now works as a freelance arts consultant and is a part-time lecturer on the MA in European Cultural Policy and Administration at the University of Warwick.

STEERING GROUP

The Marketing Manual was entirely revised and updated in 2000 with guidance from Pam Henderson (Arts Marketing Association), Deirdre McGonagle (Independent Theatre Council), Dan Pinchbeck (Hull Time-based Arts, previously Colchester Arts Centre) and Ivan Wadeson (Royal Exchange, Manchester).

FOREWORD

CHRIS SMITH
SECRETARY OF STATE FOR CULTURE, MEDIA AND SPORT

I am delighted to have been asked to write a foreword to *The Marketing Manual*, published by the Arts Marketing Association in partnership with the Arts Councils of England, Scotland and Wales.

A fundamental purpose of Government art policy must be to ensure the widest possible access to the arts across the country. That is why I launched the Arts Council's New Audiences Fund in 1998. Providing grants totalling more than £5 million per annum, the fund allows arts organisations to discover how best to encourage new existing audiences to engage with both innovative and more traditional art forms. Importantly, it also allows organisations to find out what does not work, to learn from experience (their own and others'), to modify their approach in the light of research and evaluation, and to discover the 'missing link' that will make success more likely.

It makes sense to share experiences, and the AMA Marketing Manual is an excellent way of doing so. Aimed at both experienced marketing professionals and those who are new to the profession, it poses the questions which must be asked as part of any marketing strategy: what are we trying to achieve? How should we go about achieving it? How will we know when we've achieved it? And how will we measure our success? These are questions which must be posed if resources are to be used to best effect – a key factor in large and small organisations.

With technology moving so swiftly there are many new ways of presentation, new opportunities for participation and new ways of promoting access to the best that our cultural heritage has to offer. It is shocking that 50% is missing of any kind of arts event. I believe it is a duty for all of us who love the arts to ensure that necessary barriers to engaging with the arts, whether as a participant or a member of an audience, are removed. The educational and social benefits of the arts need not be at odds with a rigorous commercial and business strategy. A challenging, innovative and vigorous arts sector is an indicator of a strong and healthy society.

CONTENTS

PREFACE

In 1989, Vivienne Moore of the Touring Department at the Arts Council of Great Britain commissioned Judith, Alastair and me to update Jane Attenborough's 1985 Arts Council Publicity Primer. That's what we set out to do, but once started, there was no stopping us. We felt there was a need for a comprehensive guide to help anyone responsible for marketing on the small scale with their everyday work, so comprehensive was what we tried to be. Looking back, *The Marketing Manual* certainly reflected our personal experiences of touring on the small and middle scale. I remember being rather keen on creating cheap but highly elaborate displays and Judith had just been working on the corporate identity of one of her client companies.

Eleven years later, so much has changed. It is no longer necessary to justify the validity of marketing for small-scale organisations because marketers are doing so much well-planned and creative work throughout the sector. I do not need to explain laboriously what word processing is – instead we are all talking about e-mailing lists, on-line ticketing and websites. Back then, marketers (or publicity officers as we were known), along with wardrobe staff, were the people that performers shouted at when things were not going well. Now we are seen as marketing professionals: marketing plays a key role in most organisations' senior management teams and the annual Arts Marketing Association conference attracts more than 300 delegates. Arts marketing has certainly come of age.

Heather Maitland

INTRODUCTION

HOW TO USE THIS MANUAL

I have rewritten this edition of *The Marketing Manual* so that it is relevant to anyone responsible for marketing any performing arts event on any scale. I have aimed it particularly at newcomers to arts marketing, administrators who have to undertake marketing as part of a wide range of responsibilities and more experienced marketers who appreciate a reminder once in a while about what it is they are supposed to be doing.

The Marketing Manual is meant to be inclusive. The steering group and I believe that the old art form pigeonholes no longer apply so we hope that it will help you whatever you are marketing – comedy, gigs, DJs, live art, multi-media, clubs, outdoor events, community work and site-specific installations as well as dance, opera, drama and music.

The guidelines in the manual are based on my contact with performing arts organisations throughout the UK as well as my own practical experience. Do not feel constrained by them, however. Adapt the ideas to fit with your organisation's needs. The quotations, examples and case studies reflect a spectrum of approaches to arts marketing and not all of them follow the advice given in the text. They are there so that you can choose what is right for your organisation's particular circumstances.

Everyone should begin by reading the chapter at the beginning of the manual, 'Getting Started'. This gives a framework for everything else that follows. The rest of *The Marketing Manual* is divided into two main parts. Part I tells you how to do everyday marketing tasks. If you need to write a press release today, turn to Chapter 11 on 'How to get Press and Media Coverage'. Part II is about the bigger decisions that marketers need to make. It shows you how to think beyond your daily 'to do' list and decide which of all the marketing tasks in Part I, the 'How to ...' section, will best help you achieve your goals.

I hope that *The Marketing Manual* will help you make a difference in your organisation.

TELL US WHAT YOU THINK

Share your experiences of what works and what doesn't with other marketers. Tell us where you think *The Marketing Manual* has gone wrong – or right. If you are a member of the Arts Marketing Association, you can now visit the website on www.a-m-a.co.uk and share your views.

SOURCES OF MORE INFORMATION

The Arts Marketing Association website has an extensive and up-to-date list of marketing publications that other AMA members have found useful, with details of how to get hold of them.

1

GETTING STARTED

1 WHAT IS MARKETING?

Marketing can benefit every solo performer, promoter, venue and company – whatever their resources. The word 'marketing' is often used to imply a whole set of values, some of which seem to have little to do with the world of the performing arts. But marketing is simply a particularly effective way of approaching the work that your organisation wants to do.

Marketing involves standing back, taking a hard look at your organisation and working out exactly what it needs to do to achieve its objectives. This planned approach to your work means that you can concentrate your limited resources of time and money on the things that will get you where you want to be.

The starting point of publicity is a set of tasks such as producing leaflets or writing press releases. The starting point of marketing is thinking and planning. This thinking process will make sure that you spend your time and money on the publicity tasks that work and will achieve your objectives.

> We have just undertaken a review of our marketing. It wasn't working. We weren't getting the audiences. Basically what we do is press and publicity. We don't do much marketing and we must change that. **General manager, national touring theatre company, England**

1.1 WHY IS MARKETING IMPORTANT?

MARKETING HELPS YOU TO FORM A RELATIONSHIP WITH AN AUDIENCE

All performing arts events need an audience. Without one, the performance is meaningless and your organisation would find it very difficult to continue working. Marketing enables you to pinpoint audiences that are appropriate for your organisation and to find the best ways of communicating with them.

> We're booking a five-week tour and we've had enough response to fill ten weeks. They know us so well by now that they respond really quickly.
>
> I think we have such a positive response because we usually have a particular teacher who is our contact point in the school. You need that because secondary schools are so big that you can't rely on the head teacher as we do in primary schools. Our Schools Liaison Officer goes out to schools and talks to teachers about what we do. Teachers really like the big work pack she puts together for each tour as each one covers such a

large area of the national curriculum. We also ask them what subjects they would like us to tackle – recent suggestions have been sex education, eating disorders, bullying and drugs education – and we respond to what they say.

It has taken a long time to establish our good relationship with schools. But now, when teachers leave, our reputation seems to ensure that they pass information on to their successors. **Medwen Edwards, Cwmni'r Fran Wen, a Welsh-language theatre-in-education company**

MARKETING REDUCES RISKS

Even if you are involved in an area of the arts where you do not sell tickets for performances, you are still likely to have to show funding bodies that people want to come and join in or see your work. If you rely on ticket sales for part or all of your income, you will be faced with bankruptcy if you do not attract the audiences planned for. Even if you tend to be paid fees by promoters, you will find it extremely difficult to get repeat bookings if you do not get big enough attendances.

Marketing reduces the risks involved in this process. It means that you are more likely to get the audiences you need for all your productions, not just the occasional one.

MARKETING HELPS YOU
TO USE YOUR RESOURCES EFFECTIVELY

Pressure is placed on all arts organisations to increase the size of audiences they attract. This is very difficult as most of us have very limited resources of money and staff. In this situation marketing is extremely helpful because it enables you to increase the likelihood of getting the most from the resources that you do have. There are many different methods that could be used to sell a company, a venue or an event. It is a way of ensuring that you and your colleagues are not crushed under an impossible burden of work by helping you prioritise tasks and discard those that do not give a good return.

MARKETING HELPS YOU TAKE A COMMON-SENSE APPROACH

Marketing is mostly common sense. It involves taking a series of logical steps to decide on what your aims are and how you are going to carry them out. Do not be put off by the jargon used by some marketing specialists from outside the arts.

MARKETING IS GOOD FOR AUDIENCES

The general public benefits when arts organisations market themselves efficiently. Unless they know about the events on offer, they cannot decide whether they want to attend. By communicating effectively (and honestly) you will be enabling people to make a choice.

2 WHAT DOES MARKETING INVOLVE?

We've recently doubled the size of the venue, and we've taken the opportunity to have a complete survey of our marketing done ... looking at how it's been done up until now and how we should go into the future ... and we are putting the recommendations into operation now.

Publicist, alternative arts venue, England

Marketing involves thinking through the relationship between your arts organisation and its activities and the people around you, whether they are audiences, participants, funders or sponsors. Then you need to talk to the right people:

- about the right things
- in the right way
- at the right time.

3 HOW TO GET STARTED

STEP 1: DECIDE WHAT YOU WANT TO ACHIEVE

Use the information you have about your organisation's artistic, financial and social objectives to decide what you want your marketing idea to achieve. You may want, for example, to get existing audiences to attend more often, increase audience numbers for a particular type of event, increase your income or launch a new activity. Write down what you have decided.

STEP 2: TALK TO THE RIGHT PEOPLE

- Your organisation cannot possibly communicate with every single person in your community, so first decide which groups of people you are going to target.
- Find groups of people who have something in common. They might be interested in the same things or have a common experience of the arts, for example. Each of these groups is known variously as a target market, target audience or target group. The factor they have in common means that if you talk to them about the same things in the same way you are likely to get results.
- Start with the people most likely to respond: your 'best bets'. Usually these are:
  - your existing audiences
  - people who are already involved in arts activities similar to yours.
- You now need to identify your 'next best bets' as your best bets alone are unlikely to get you enough people to meet your objectives. Your next best bets could be people with a particular interest in the subject matter of your particular arts activity.

You need to know and understand your existing audiences to be able to identify your target markets. What sort of people are they? What do they like about your organisation and what it does? How often do they see your events? Who do they bring with them?

DEVELOPING NEW AUDIENCES

Although it is more cost-effective to market your activities to existing customers, many arts organisations want to develop new audiences. This means persuading people who are already involved in the arts in some way to try something new or persuading people who have never attended an arts event at all to give your particular activity a try for the first time. Then you need to build a sense of connection between the attender and your organisation, which you can develop into a sense of belonging. As before, there are non-attenders who are more likely to attend than others. You will need to invest significant amounts of time and money to persuade people who do not think the arts are for them to try your activity.

There are two sorts of new audiences. If arts organisations know what their existing audiences are like, they can find more of the same sort of people. They can also look at their audiences, compare them to the local community and see if there are any groups of people who are underrepresented. The first type of new audience will need fewer resources than the second, as these potential audiences are more likely to feel positive about the arts and arts organisations have more information to help find them. You need to understand what stops these new audiences trying out your events at the moment.

Hall for Cornwall in Truro needs to attract audiences from right across this rural county. Box office staff carried out telephone research to find out about the experiences of 100 people who had attended the Hall for Cornwall only once. They discovered that what stopped people in rural areas (district population less than 10,000) attending was:

- no public transport for evening performances
- problems with getting there by car (e.g. parking)
- little public transport for daytime performances
- limited experience of going to the theatre
- lack of information on events.

They tackled these barriers to attendance by:

- setting up a coach service for groups which they could pay for through the box office
- more direct mail campaigns targeted at these rural areas
- distributing leaflets to more places outside Truro
- getting volunteers to distribute information in rural districts
- putting information about transport on all leaflets and brochures
- promoting the box office as an information service as well as somewhere to buy tickets.

After six months, they had a 13% increase in the audience from rural areas and over 20% of the population in these areas have now been to an event at the Hall for Cornwall.

CASE STUDY

STEP 3: TALK ABOUT THE RIGHT THINGS

- Different target groups will be interested in different things about your organisation and its events.

- Imagine that you are talking face to face with someone from a particular target audience to persuade them to attend your arts activity. You are more likely to succeed if you see things from their point of view.

- Talk about the aspect of the experience you are offering that is most important to *them*.

- Now back this up with three or four other points.

- The facts about your arts activity are known as features. You need to turn these features into benefits – reasons that someone will want to attend. Do not say: 'experimental multi-media performance'. Do say: 'You've never seen theatre like this before. Your senses tingle in anticipation as the action builds in intensity ... people around you are gasping and laughing in wonder' (LIFT brochure, 1997).

- Now decide exactly what action you want your target audience to take. You may want them to telephone a box office to book tickets or simply to turn up at an event. Tell them clearly what you want them to do. Check that they have enough information to take that action.

- These rules also apply when arts organisations communicate with promoters, sponsors, venue managers and funders.

STEP 4: TALK TO PEOPLE IN THE RIGHT WAY

- The fewer resources your organisation has, the more important it is to concentrate on the communication methods that actually work and talk to people in the right way.

- You need to look at what you have decided to say to each target audience and choose the most effective way of getting that message across to that group of people. You will probably have to use different communications methods with different target audiences.

- Choose from: season brochures, posters, advertising in newspapers and magazines, posting leaflets or postcards to a mailing list, letters, invitations, articles and photographs in magazines, advertising on radio, listings magazines, simply talking to people, distributing leaflets to libraries and shops, items in community newsletters such as parish magazines, delivering information door to door, news features on radio or television, displays in shop windows and many more.

- The more personal the method of communication, the more effective it is. Talking face to face with people is the best method of persuading them to get involved in your arts activity. You cannot possibly talk to every single person in your target market, so you will have to concentrate on the key people who might persuade others and consider using letters or the telephone to communicate with the rest.

- Research tells us that, for most events, advertising in local and national newspapers, putting up posters or advertising on the radio only attracts a tiny proportion of the audience.[1]

- Newspaper and radio advertisements seem to reach lots of people but they are bad at persuading. All they can do is give basic information.

- Posters are not good at persuading your target market to attend either, because they do not give them anything concrete to take away with them. If they want to know where the performance is or how much tickets are, they have to find a pen and paper and write down the contact telephone number or the address. They are good at attracting people's attention, however.

- This does not just apply to audiences. Concentrate on the one or two methods that really work when communicating with sponsors, funders and promoters, etc.

[1] Peter Walshe, of Millward Brown International, *Research Digests for the Arts* (Arts Council of Great Britain, 1992)

STEP 5: TALK TO PEOPLE AT THE RIGHT TIME

- Find out when each of your target audiences is likely to make the decision to attend or not. Do this by looking at information from the box office computer system if you have one, talking to audiences, or handing out a questionnaire.

- Talk to them at the right time so that they take action and book their tickets or at least make a note in their diary. Too early, and a potential audience member may decide that they would quite like to attend and then forget all about it. Too late, and they will be doing something else or be unable to get organised in time.

STEP 6: SET GOALS

- In Step 1 you decided what you wanted to achieve. In Steps 2–5 you decided how you were going to achieve it. Now you need to set yourself goals. These will help you focus your work during the project and after it is over will tell you whether your marketing idea worked.

- Look at the target groups you have chosen and set a goal for the total number of people you want to get involved in your event or activity.

- Now set goals for the number of people you want from each of the target markets you identified as your 'best bets' and your 'next best bets'. Probably the most useful way of putting this is as a percentage of the total audience for each event. Setting goals is not always easy because you may find your target markets overlap. You may have to use your judgement.

STEP 7: SEE IF IT WORKED

- Your arts event or activity is not over until you have decided how well your marketing worked. You will want to see whether you achieved your goals and whether you got good value from your investment of time and money. This is particularly important if you have few resources.

- You need to decide in advance *how* you are going to tell if you have reached your goals. This will probably involve collecting a sensible amount of information about your audience. This is not an impossible task – many of the smallest of voluntary arts organisations carry out audience research.

- You might want to ask your audience members questions that will enable you to tell whether they come from any of the target markets you identified.

- You will also want to ask how they found out about the event.

- You will get more people to answer your questions if you keep them to the essential minimum.

REMEMBER ✳

MARKETING STEP BY STEP

STEP 1: DECIDE WHAT YOU WANT TO ACHIEVE

STEP 2: TALK TO THE RIGHT PEOPLE

STEP 3: TALK ABOUT THE RIGHT THINGS

STEP 4: TALK TO PEOPLE IN THE RIGHT WAY

STEP 5: TALK TO PEOPLE AT THE RIGHT TIME

STEP 6: SET GOALS

STEP 7: SEE IF IT WORKED

PART I

HOW TO ...

2

HOW TO PLAN YOUR CAMPAIGN

SEE ALSO CHAPTERS
1.   GETTING STARTED
30.   MARKETING TASKS FOR TOURING COMPANIES

The starting point of marketing is thinking and planning. Before you write a press release, produce a leaflet or do any of the promotional tasks described in this 'How to...' section, you must decide who you are talking to, what you should say, how you should say it, when you should say it and how you will see if it worked.

This means creating a campaign plan just like the one described in Chapter 1, 'Getting Started'. Opposite is a worksheet to help you.

CASE STUDY

PLANNING A MARKETING CAMPAIGN FOR ROUGH CROSSING

Before we discussed the campaign we read the script to gain knowledge of the product we were going to be marketing. We then talked to the director to find out what direction they were going to take with the piece: when it was to be set, casting ideas and if they had any strong preferences to the way the show was to be marketed.

We then looked at financial targets, budgets and what our objectives were – in this case to extend awareness of the Playhouse and its new season by increasing ticket sales to this, the first show of the season. In order to achieve this we picked out who we were targeting by pinpointing key selling points – with Rough Crossing these were the comical script and the 1930s setting and costumes combined with an established cast and creative team.

After discussing this we drew up a schedule of deadlines for the print, press release, direct mail (which at the Playhouse is one of our most effective marketing tools, in this case bringing an 11% response rate), distributions/displays and promotions as well as emergency measures.

At this point it was revealed that Matthew Kelly had been cast which had an effect on our campaign. It was a great opportunity to gain new attenders but we were aware that we also had to be careful not to alienate our present audience. The most effective way to do this was to gain as much press coverage by way of interviews with Matthew. This had the effect of reassuring our current audience by highlighting his background in theatre and acting experience whilst gaining increased awareness of the Playhouse to non-attenders through his TV profile.

Although we plan campaigns in advance, we find that it is essential to be flexible and constant evaluation is needed to know when to put emergency measures in place. **Rachel Hunnybun, Marketing Officer, Salisbury Playhouse**

Area of activity _____

YOUR TARGET GROUPS

Target group 1   **Target group 2**

_____   _____
_____   _____

What are they like?

_____   _____
_____   _____
_____   _____

Where are they based?

_____   _____
_____   _____

What is their experience of the arts?

_____   _____
_____   _____

What is their experience of your organisation?

_____   _____
_____   _____
_____   _____

What do you want your target groups to do?

_____   _____
_____   _____

What might stop them?

_____   _____
_____   _____

Objectives: how many people from each target group do
you want to book the activity?

_____   _____

How will you tell if you have reached your objective?

_____   _____
_____   _____
_____   _____

Target group 1   **Target group 2**

Area of activity _____

Main benefit

_____   _____

_____   _____

Other key benefits

1 _____   1 _____

2 _____   2 _____

3 _____   3 _____

Communicating with your target groups

Your message

_____   _____

_____   _____

_____   _____

_____   _____

Tone of voice

_____   _____

Most effective communication methods

1 _____   1 _____

2 _____   2 _____

3 _____   3 _____

Choose from:

- printed material posted to the mailing list
- printed material distributed to important places in the community
- posters
- advertising in newspapers and magazines
- writing letters
- sending invitations
- articles and photographs in newspapers

- advertising on radio
- listings in What's On magazines
- talking to people face to face
- telephoning people
- articles in community newsletters
- news features on radio or television
- displays
- and many more ...

Will you produce any printed material?

Type:

Size

❑ A4	❑ A5	❑ other
❑ A4	❑ A5	❑ other
❑ A4	❑ A5	❑ other

No. of colours

❑ one	❑ two	❑ full colour
❑ one	❑ two	❑ full colour
❑ one	❑ two	❑ full colour

Quantity

Direct mail

Who to?	What?	Mailed by?	When?	How many?

Advertising

In what?	Size of ad?	When?	Deadline?	Cost?

Press editorial (including newsletters, etc.)

In what?   Message?   When?   Deadline?

_____

_____

_____

_____

_____

_____

_____

Other activity

_____

_____

_____

_____

_____

After the event

Did you achieve your objectives?

_____

_____

_____

_____

Did you achieve anything unexpected?

_____

_____

_____

_____

Is there anything you would repeat next time?

_____

_____

Is there anything you would do differently next time?

_____

_____

1 MARKETING TIMETABLE

Chapters 4 and 12 on 'How to Produce Print' and 'How to get Press and Media Coverage' include more detailed schedules for those activities.

This section gives a general guide to the sorts of things that companies and promoters could do to market their events. Many of the activities happen simultaneously but have been grouped together in columns, in the two charts below, for clarity. On the left of each chart are activities that cover the whole tour or season. On the right are activities that need to be repeated for each venue or company visit.

The charts give ideal time-scales for activities. It will be impossible to keep to them exactly. You will not be able to do all the activities, either. Choose the ones that are likely to bring you the best results with the resources you have available. You will do more for some events or venues than others, although the dialogue between company and promoter should continue regardless.

The numbers in the charts refer to the steps in the description on the following page.

1.1 TIMETABLE FOR VENUES AND PROMOTERS

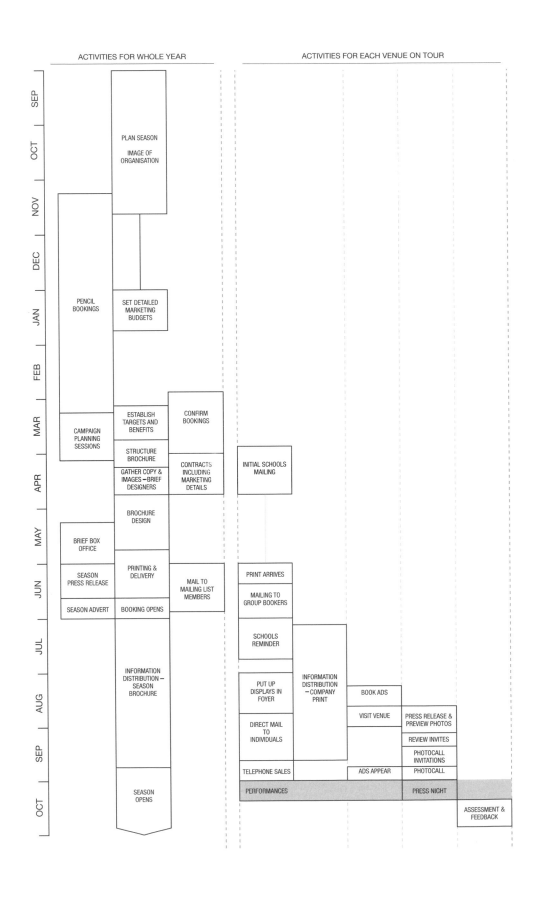

1.2 TIMETABLE FOR COMPANIES

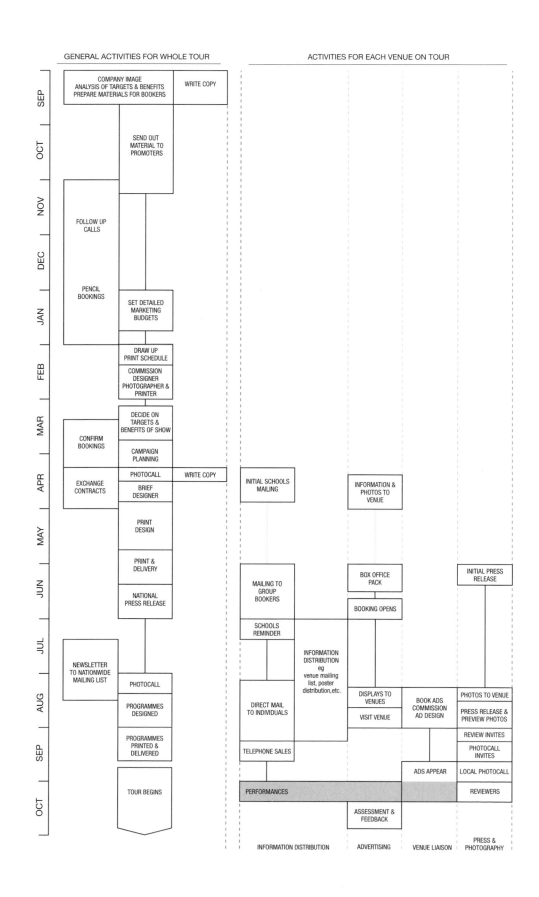

1.3 WORKING TOGETHER: A TIMETABLE FOR MARKETING TOURING EVENTS

Touring companies and promoters should maintain frequent contact with each other. At certain times, you will need to communicate especially closely. This schedule shows when you need to communicate about particular activities. It is based on an ideal situation so adapt it to fit your organisation's circumstances. Where the schedule states that you should begin an activity, assume that the activity should continue from this point on.

1. Company: about six months to a year in advance of your projected visit, send out the promotional information about your company and production. This will be your first point of contact with the promoter. If, however, you have already visited the venue in question, you should have mentioned this tour at the monitoring stage of your last visit.

    If at this stage you are planning a tour, but you know little or nothing about the show because it is, for example, devised work, send some information to promoters about your organisation. Tell them anything you do know such as the director's name and specify a date when you can provide more information.

2. Company: make a follow-up telephone call a week to ten days later.

3. Company and promoter: pencil in the booking. Companies may need to make additional follow-up telephone calls to reach the pencilling-in stage.

4. Company and promoter: agree the booking 3–6 months before the visit.

5. Company and promoter: exchange contracts.

6. Company and promoter: negotiate your campaign plan (face to face if possible). This will be the first point of contact between the people with responsibility for marketing. After this point both the company and the promoter should be clear about the levels of marketing activity needed to achieve the target attendance figures. Discuss pricing. Find out when the promoter needs copy, images and print.

7. Promoter: work out how this event fits into your subscription package, if appropriate. This is your sales promotion method for targeting your enthusiasts.

8. Company: work out the schedule for your printed information. Calculate when you will first need your print and work backwards from that date. Start the process of producing leaflets, posters and programmes, etc.

9. Company or promoter: about six months in advance of the event or at the latest, the end of the preceding school term, one of you should make contact with schools, if appropriate.

10. Company: if you are using photographs on print, commission a graphic designer now. Otherwise, do this after you have sent out your first press release.

11. Company: commission a photographer.

12. Company: about four to five months in advance of your first tour date, hold your first photo call. You need to do this now so that you have colour transparencies to offer colour publications. If you are using photographs on your print you will need them now. You also need to send photographs to promoters to meet their brochure deadlines which may be four or five months before your performance.

13. Company or promoter: contact any group bookers – those with monthly meetings need early advance notice.

14. Company: immediately after the photo call, send out your first press release to all press and media with long lead times.

15. Promoter: collect copy and photographs for brochure.

16. Company: send out your box office pack, i.e. an information pack to help box office staff sell tickets for your performance.

17. Promoter: brief the box office about the company and performance.

18. Promoter: produce brochure.

19. Company: produce leaflets and posters.

20. Promoter: distribute brochure.

21. Company: produce programmes.

22. Company: begin to distribute leaflets and posters to venues.

23. Company and/or promoter: begin to distribute leaflets and posters to target groups.

24. Company: create displays and send to venue.

25. Company: send out your second press release to herald the start of your tour. Send this to key press and media contacts only.

26. Company: send a few programmes to each promoter for further information.

27. Company or promoter: begin your direct mail campaign.

28. Company or promoter: book any advertising space. Get advertisements designed.

29. Company or promoter: begin to send out invitations to your press night.

30. Company: begin your face-to-face marketing visits to promoters.

31. Company or promoter: organise any press photo calls.

32. Tour begins.

33. Promoter: after the performance, send the company any reviews or other press cuttings.

34. Company or promoter: send out your third press release about performances at individual venues.

35. Company: send copies of press cuttings to promoters as they appear.

36. Company and promoter: one to four weeks after the performance, when it is still relatively fresh in your minds, monitor the effectiveness of your marketing activity. Did you reach your target attendance figures? Companies should also begin selling their next tour at this point.

3 **HOW TO WRITE COPY**

SEE ALSO CHAPTERS
20. TALKING TO THE RIGHT PEOPLE
21. TALKING ABOUT THE RIGHT THINGS

Copy is the term for any written information used in marketing: print, press releases, advertisements, direct mail letters and so on. Nearly everything you write is designed to do the following:

- make the reader want to see your show or visit your venue
- make the reader take action to satisfy that want.

You will achieve these aims by communicating the right things to the right people.

This is how V-Tol Dance Company (see the following two pages) described their production: '... and nothing but the truth ...', first to people who have attended dance before and then to people who have attended fringe-style theatre but not dance.

1 PREPARING TO WRITE

In order to write successful copy you need to consider the following points before putting pen to paper.

1.1 WHO ARE YOU TALKING TO?

You need to know with which target groups you want to communicate. Sometimes the copy you are writing will have to communicate with several or all of your target groups. List the appropriate group(s) and write down their characteristics, such as age, gender, the language they prefer to speak, etc. Use the benefits they have in common.

1.2 WHAT DO YOU WANT TO SAY?

You need to identify which benefits are appropriate for each target group. Add the other things you need to say to the list of benefits, including:

- what makes your organisation/show different from all the others
- any special offers you need to explain
- the dates and times of the show
- the address and box office telephone number
- how the reader can respond to your message.

Put all these points including the benefits into order of importance.

for previous dance attenders

V-TOL Dance Company
...and nothing but the truth...
a murder mystery

Artistic Director, **Mark Murphy**, and **V-TOL DANCE COMPANY** launch dance into the realm of the murder mystery genre with violent, challenging, and exciting results. The combination of highly physical choreography, intriguing storyline, original soundtrack, film and live theatre make *...and nothing but the truth...* an extraordinary fusion of cinema, theatre and dance.

> *"The danger is in the dance: they hurtle through the air, crash land, surge up again. The dancers are marvelously deft as they bargain with physical dance at its most accomplished."* Evening Standard

This is a high energy, high impact, physical experience. The dancers throw themselves into the air and each other, defying gravity. The company of four dancers includes **James Hewison**, **Christine Devaney** and **Marcia Pook**, all of whom have danced with V-TOL in previous productions. They are joined by newcomer **Karl Sullivan**, along with actor **Kieron Jecchinis**.

> *"Despite the dancers' silence, the depth of character they develop becomes more complex than most text-based theatre would dare to suggest; duplicitous, perverse, wilful, desperate."* The Times

This new production explores the intricate strands of guilt and innocence woven into a web of deceit and lies surrounding a murder. The actor plays as narrator, detective and prosecutor leading each character back through a seemingly straightforward reconstruction to the crime as seen through their eyes. Each reconstruction adds to the story and we see desires and motives gradually exposed. *The more we know the less sure we become of who is ultimately guilty.*

Join us and judge for yourself. See the enclosed leaflet for details.

8

V-TOL Dance Company 92-94 Judd Street London WC1H 9NT *tel* 0171 278 2432 *fax* 0171 278 0883 *e-mail* info@vtol.demon.co.uk

direct mail to fringe/theatre attenders

THIS IS NO ORDINARY MURDER MYSTERY...
THIS IS NO ORDINARY DANCE PERFORMANCE...

V-TOL Dance Company takes dance to dangerous extremes in its new production ***...and nothing but the truth...*** at (your venue) on (date).

This new production explores the intricate strands of guilt and innocence woven into a web of deceit and lies surrounding a murder. The actor plays as narrator, detective and prosecutor leading each character back through a seemingly straightforward reconstruction to the crime as seen through their eyes. Each reconstruction adds to the story and we see desires and motives gradually exposed. The more we know the less sure we become of who is ultimately guilty.

"[Murphy's] cleverest production yet: a sophisticated, superbly staged commentary...
virtuosic design by Miranda Melville, brilliantly lit by Jon Linstrum."
The Daily Telegraph

The clever, sharp-witted script from Gary Young, performed live by an actor, takes the audience on a journey through the action, revealing the double-edged dark humour of the plot. Choreographer and film maker, Mark Murphy extends the scope, scale and intensity of his film work using advanced technology. Through multiple film projections integrated into the set, a dynamic interplay between filmed and live action is explored. The unique physical language of film brings a cinematic dimension into the context of live theatre.

"Despite the dancers' silence, the depth of character they develop becomes more complex than
most text-based theatre would dare to suggest; duplicitous, perverse, wilful, desperate."
The Times

The combination of highly physical choreography, intriguing storyline, original soundtrack, film and live theatre make ***...and nothing but the truth...*** an extraordinary fusion of cinema, theatre and dance. This is contemporary dance at its most accessible.

Join us and judge for yourself. See the enclosed leaflet for details.

9

CASE STUDY

This is how **DanceXchange** from Birmingham describe the style of the dance classes they offer. Notice how they tell the reader what it will feel like to take part in a class as well as what they will get out of it.

African-Caribbean

This open class includes live percussion accompaniment and delves into exuberant traditional dances and vibrant musical rhythms.

Ballet

To live piano, these classes are non syllabus. They are an enjoyable way of working on alignment and posture through dance.

Contemporary

These exhilarating sessions provide a great way to develop both strength and flexibility, focusing on alignment, breath and weight.

Flamenco

Enjoy the flamboyance of Spanish folk dancing in colourful sessions. Build confidence and pride through dynamic dance rhythm.

Jazz

An exhilarating range of Jazz styles will work your body.

Club Jazz Aerobic exercise with dance moves for a serious night out.

Jazz Hype requires energy and skill at speed.

Jazz Fusion is an upbeat contemporary style of urban dance.

Salsa

Red hot urban dance from Cuba will seduce you with its infectious rhythms. Everyone welcome, no need to bring a partner.

Tap

Feet infectious show tunes will help you master the steps, putting you on the road to being a Tap Dog.

We all work together on copy, usually by using the old leaflet as a starting point. We look at how the dance styles have changed and see how we can put that into words. We always try to write in a voice that's like your friend telling you about a class. We write to professional dancers in a completely different way. All our copy goes through the mill at least five times. We ask ourselves is there any dancey jargon? Is this going to make sense to *everyone?* **Sally Francis, DanceXchange, Birmingham**

2 STYLE

In our personal lives we adopt different styles of talking and writing to suit the people we are communicating with. You do not use the same tone and vocabulary to talk to your bank manager and a friend. Choose an appropriate style for the target group you are communicating with.

You probably find it relatively easy to communicate using words but remember that your audience may include people who do not. Do not exclude potential audience members by making your copy unnecessarily difficult to understand. For instance, most tabloid newspapers have a reading age of around 10–12 years. Generally you should:

- Use simple, familiar words. Say 'new', not 'innovative'.

- Use short words. Say 'strong', not 'muscular'.

- Use active tenses. Say 'Book now', not 'Tickets can be booked now'.

- Make things personal. Say 'Have a good night out', not 'Everyone has a good night out here'.

- Use short sentences. Only 4% of the population can read sentences of 27 words, 75% can read sentences of 17 words and 95% sentences of 8 words.

- Avoid sub-clauses such as 'Acknowledged as one of the most challenging and acclaimed theatre companies in Britain, our work is a fusion of the best in drama and music.' Split it into two sentences instead.

- Keep to one idea per sentence.

- Use short paragraphs.

- A conversational style is usually more appropriate than a formal one.

- Avoid jargon like 'Restoration comedy' as few people will understand what that means.

- Use design and layout to make your copy easier to read. Make sure that people glancing at your copy know where to start reading and which is the most important information.

A Fog Index ia a rough guide for checking the readability of your copy. There are several – this is a simplified version of the one developed by Robert Gunning known as the Gunning Readability Formula.[1]

1. Select a sample of at least 100 words.

2. Divide the number of words by the number of complete sentences in your sample to find out the average number of words per sentence.

3. Count the number of words with three or more syllables – do not include proper nouns, verbs with suffixes like -ing or -es, or portmanteau words which combine shorter words, e.g. 'ratcatcher' 'another'.

[1] Gunning, Robert, *The Technique of Clear Writing* (New York: McGraw-Hill, 1968)

4. Add the average number of words per sentence to number of difficult words.

5. Multiply this by 0.4 to get your Fog Index.

6. This will tell you the level of readability of your copy:

Below 10	= easy reading
11–12	= readable by the top 20% of 12 year olds and above
13	= readable by the top 20% of 16 year olds and above
14–16	= first year university student level
17	= university graduate level

3 CONTENT

Your copy should concentrate on the benefits you have identified. Your potential audience members are very unlikely to be interested in long lists of (to them) unknown performers. They will want to know what the whole experience will be like and why they should spend money on it rather than stay at home with a take-away and watch television.

Communicate the benefits in order of priority. Avoid extravagant claims such as 'a tremendous event' unless you can back them up with facts. Avoid empty adjectives as in 'a unique company'. All companies are unique. You must say *why* yours is unique.

Use a framework. The following are both good examples:

1.1 MAKE A PROMISE

1. Get the attention of the reader: use a headline.

2. Make a promise: incorporate the benefit you want to emphasise.

3. Show that you can deliver your promise. Back it up with facts such as 'This year the company has performed to capacity audiences at international festivals in Europe and the US.'

4. Push for action: tell the reader what they should do to benefit from your promise, i.e. how they can buy a ticket.

CASE STUDY

DanceXchange have calls for action all through their leaflet about dance classes, inviting readers to:

• take a leap

• go for it!

• make that move

1.2 AIDA

1. ATTENTION – grab attention using a headline and images.
2. INTEREST – explain the headline and amplify it. Add any other essential information.
3. DESIRE – follow up the initial interest and persuade the reader that they want your offer.
4. ACTION – enable the reader to obtain what you are offering. Make responding as easy as possible.

4 GENERAL ADVICE

When writing copy do not use the first ideas that spring to mind. Leave your first draft overnight or for a few days if possible. It will look quite different when you see it again with a fresh eye. Test the effectiveness of your copy on others. If possible, show it to people who are members of the target group(s) at whom you are aiming it. Make sure that it tells them clearly what your event is about, what it is like and how they will feel when they watch it.

Remember you have just a few seconds to get your main message across to persuade people to keep reading. You should keep to the essentials although, once they are hooked, there is no harm in repeating yourself to emphasise your message.

5 OTHER LANGUAGES

If you are targeting communities that feel most comfortable communicating in languages other than your own, you need to consider more than simply the language itself. Different cultures have different conventions about the written language involving tone of voice, structure, formalities for the 'Dear ...' and 'Yours sincerely' bits and so on.

Rather than asking a fluent speaker to translate your copy, it is much better to brief them on what you are trying to achieve, give them lots of information about your event and the target group which includes, but is not restricted to, your own copy, and then leave them to create their own version. Test the result on a member of your target group before you use it.

An example of promotional material from the Brighton Festival follows.

Brighton FESTIVAL
6-28 May 2000

布莱顿
□文化艺术节
2000年5月6日 - 2000年5月28日

三家精彩绝伦的中国艺术团体将于5月
现艺布莱顿

广 东 现 代 舞 蹈 团
（广州）

广东现代舞蹈团是当今中国大陆最具活力的舞蹈团。

美国纽约时报评:" 动感的音域,惊人的动作美感与沉着文雅的表演的完美结合使广东现代舞蹈团成为一支独具特色的舞蹈团。"

由布莱顿文化节安排,此舞蹈团将首次现艺英国。舞蹈家将以一系列的表演来展示他们高超的演技。

由本地舞蹈作家CHARLIE MORRISSEY , BEC KY.EDMUNDS和申伟联合创作的一台新舞将于此次晚会上同观众见面。

CORN EXCHANGE THEATRE
5月10日（周三）~5月13日（周六）晚8：00
票价：£11（或£9）
演后免费剧组会谈
5月11日（周四）

屋 囚
金星与EDWIN LUNG的联袂之作
（北京）

金星是中国舞蹈奖金奖获得者，也是北京最炅火的一家夜总会的老板。

她原来是中国人民解放军一名男陆军上校，后来由于接受了了中国历史上首次性移植手术，所以在短期之内便名声鹊起了......

"屋囚"是金星与香港诞生的EDWIN LUNG的首之合作。EDWIN.LUNG是一名有发明天才的舞蹈作家，他的作品能将舞蹈同影像和多媒体技术有机得结合在一起。

"屋囚"探索的是人们生活中一种在文化，个性与政治上的隔离。

他们采用的舞台背景是一种特制的竹布置和金属布置及道具，他们演奏能使观众享受到独具中国传统韵味的游览。

CORN EXCHANGE THEATRE
5月15日（周一）- 5月16日（周二）晚8:00
票价：£11（或£9）

PARAVENT
汪建伟
（北京）

中国唐代的间谍活动是四川电影制作艺术家汪建伟创作剧本的无限源泉。

中国古代有这样一个故事：宫廷画师顾闳中接到皇上的密令，要他在晚间趁一朝廷大臣寻欢作乐之时进行窥刺。顾闳中将这位高级大臣的所有审露生活以一幅画的形式记录了下来---"韩西载的晚宴"。这幅画现收藏于北京故宫博物馆。

汪建伟融合当今高科技手段---录像，摄影，录音及对白，以一种现代方式讲诉一个古老传说。

此剧目曾以英文字幕汉语对白的方式上演过。

CORN EXCHANGE THEATRE
5月18日（周四）-5月20日（周六）晚8：00
票价：£11（或£9）
演后免费剧组会谈
5月18日（周四）

Coventry University赞助

中国国家杂技团：中国来技演员曾以钻圈和走钢丝而闻名于世，这次他们带来的精彩的杂技表演会令你更加心动魄。
PRESTON PARK 5月9日（周二）- 5月28日（周七）票价：£6 - £20
DOME 购票处 01273 709 709   WWW.BRIGHTON-FESTIVAL.ORG.UK 欲知详情,请拨01273 700747

由 Davis Landon, Everest, Hartley Fowler Chartered Accounts,
Kvaerner,Construction, RHWL, Whitby Bird & Partners赞助

Brighton FESTIVAL
6-28 May 2000

THREE FANTASTIC, MODERN CHINESE COMPANIES PERFORM AT BRIGHTON FESTIVAL IN MAY

Sponsored by Davis Langdon Everest, Hartley Fowler Chartered Accountants, Kvaerner Construction, RHWL, Whitby Bird & Partners

GUANGDONG MODERN DANCE COMPANY
(Guangzhou)

The Guangdong is mainland China's most dynamic contemporary dance company.

"A troupe with a difference. The dynamic range, balanced between an amazing athletic thrust and contained elegance, will not be seen elsewhere".
New York Times

On their first UK tour, produced by Brighton Festival, the dancers perform a range of work that illustrates their adventurous approach.

The evening features a new dance made in China with the company by Brighton based choreographers Charlie Morrissey & Becky Edmunds, and Shen Wei's dramatic new dance **Folding**.

Corn Exchange Theatre
Wed 10 - Sat 13 May
8pm £11 (£9)

Post-show talk
Thurs 11 May, free

JIN XING & EDWIN LUNG HOUSE ARREST
(Beijing)

Jin Xing is a prize-winning dancer and owner of Beijing's hottest nightclub.

But it is as China's first high-profile trans-sexual (she was formerly a male colonel in the People's Liberation Army) that she has really achieved fame.

House Arrest is a collaboration with Hong Kong born Edwin Lung, an ingenious choreographer whose work synthesises dance, text, image and multi-media.

As the title implies, the piece explores issues of cultural, personal and political isolation.

It is set in a specially created bamboo and metal installation, evoking the bamboo theatre of traditional Chinese touring players.

Corn Exchange Theatre
Mon 15 & Tue 16 May
8pm £11 (£9)

WANG JIANWEI PARAVENT
(Beijing)

Espionage in the Tang Dynasty is the origin of a fascinating play by Sichuan artist and film-maker Wang Jianwei.

The court artist Gu Honzhong was ordered by his emperor to spy on the night-time revelries of a high ranking minister. The artist recorded the illicit activities in a beautiful painting **The Night Feast of Han Xizai** which now hangs in the Forbidden City Museum in Beijing.

Wang Jianwei uses contemporary techniques - video, projections, recorded sounds - along with dialogue to tell an ancient story in a modern way.

Performed in Mandarin with English surtitles

Corn Exchange Theatre
Thur 18 - Sat 20 May
8pm £11 (£9)

Post-show talk
Thurs 18 May, free

Sponsored by Coventry University

CHINESE STATE CIRCUS The hoop-diving, pole-balancing Chinese acrobats return with a spectacular new extravaganza. Gasp as they defy *"the laws of physics and human anatomy"* Time Out
PRESTON PARK TUESDAY 9 - SUNDAY 28 MAY £6 - £20

tickets: **DOME BOX OFFICE 01273 709 709**
www.brighton-festival.org.uk
For more information about Chinese events or the full Brighton Festival programme
please call 01273 700747

4

HOW TO PRODUCE PRINT

Most arts organisations produce some sort of print: photocopied handbills, leaflets, brochures, posters, programmes and so on. Sometimes, however, they forget that it is a marketing tool.

The main advantage of having print is that it is an effective, tangible, targetable way of communicating with potential audiences. A useful by-product is that print is clear evidence of marketing activity to those not directly involved in marketing your organisation: performers, stage managers, funding bodies and sponsors.

Because of its high visibility factor, too much emphasis is often placed on the actual production of print. There may be other ways of communicating with your target groups which are better value for money, especially if your resources are particularly limited. Far too many resources may be channelled into creating an attractive poster, without due consideration to alternative uses of these resources, such as improving press and media coverage, or creating more effective mailing lists. This is especially the case if you do not have enough money to produce quality print. For example, it may be better to have direct mail letters printed rather than single-colour leaflets.

REMEMBER ✳

It is pointless to produce print that you cannot then afford to distribute to your target groups.

You need to assess the resources you have in terms of time as well as money, as print production requires a great deal of liaison with designers and printers.

1 HOW TO DECIDE WHETHER OR NOT YOU NEED PRINT

1. Look at any research on print effectiveness for your organisation or for similar organisations to your own. How do audiences like yours say they have heard about events? Companies can also ask venues about any research they have available.

2. Think about your target groups and decide what is the most effective way of communicating with them.

3. Consider the message you want to get across. Can you communicate this effectively on paper?

4. Assess your marketing budget.

5. Work out how much time you have in which to produce print.

6. Assess the amount of experience you have in producing print. The less knowledge you have, the more complex and time-consuming the process is going to be.

7. Think about whether you have access to appropriate systems for distributing print to your chosen target groups.

In light of all of this, decide which communication method will be most cost-effective in persuading your target groups to buy tickets.

An arts marketing consultant comments that South Asian dance companies or soloists should not produce lots of glossy leaflets but:

> Save that money and produce a small amount of specifically targeted print that could go to your particular community and/or allocate what little money you've got to specialist adverts in a particular region ... or radio advertising which is the best way to get to the Asian community

REMEMBER ✳

Establish what your proposed print is really for – you should not be making decisions about print to satisfy egos or please an incoming artist or performer. Equally, do not keep on producing a particular piece of print because that is the way it has always been done.

1.1 PRINT OPTIONS

Direct mail letters are an appropriate alternative to leaflets and can be a more personal form of communication. There follows an example of a letter from a voluntary promoter putting on regular concerts in his village.

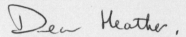

Dear Heather,

As mentioned at our last concert in March, I am now writing to tell you about a very special "one-off" series of concerts to take place in June in the Bingham Festival. Having secured funding from the Millennium Commission's *Awards for All* scheme, we are presenting four concerts around the theme of British Chamber music of the last 120 years. This period produced some of the finest composers in the history of British music, such as Elgar, Delius, Tippett, Ireland, Britten and Vaughan Williams, and we have put together as representative a sample as possible, producing programmes suitable for sunny(!) Summer's afternoons and evenings.

Sunday 11ᵗʰ June at 3 pm in St. Mary's Parish Church, Bingham
ST. MARY'S (NOTTINGHAM) CHOIR
Director: John Keys

A 60-minute concert of part-songs by Pearsall, Vaughan Williams, Elgar and others. The English Choral tradition is one of the glories of Western music and this programme mixes the religious with the secular, the light-hearted with the sad.

Sunday 11ᵗʰ June at 7.30 pm in Bingham Infants Concert Hall
MUSIC GROUP OF BINGHAM
Chris Franks, Liz Dobson, Anne-Marie Owen, Steven Halls
with Mervyn Cooke (piano) and Richard Roddis (Tenor)

Vaughan Williams *On Wenlock Edge*
Elgar *Piano Quintet*

This early Vaughan Williams setting of some poems by A E Housman captures the humour and the misery of the poet's rural world, producing a colourful series of effects from the accompanying piano quintet. The Elgar, on the other hand, is a product of the composer's final artistic flowering and contains a wealth of melody from the noble to almost café music.

Friday 16ᵗʰ June at 6.30 pm at 28, Nottingham Road, Bingham
BEAUFORT WIND QUINTET

A "promenade" concert of lighter works by Grainger, Arnold, Elgar, Jacob, Hallam & Drummond by the wind players who have featured in the series before. For your comfort, please bring along your own seat and please note that the capacity is limited to 50 people. Depending on the weather, the event will take place either outside or inside. Please note there is little parking nearby but plenty 300 yards away in the centre of Bingham.

Sunday 25th June at 7.30 pm in Bingham Infants Concert Hall

MUSIC GROUP OF BINGHAM

Chris Franks, Steven Halls and string ensemble conducted by Neville Ward

Warlock *Capriol Suite*
Elgar *Serenade*
Tippett *Little Music for Strings*
Delius *Air & Dance*
Ireland *Minuet & Elegy*
Holst *St Paul's Suite*
A series of short and tuneful works brings the series to a lively and exciting conclusion.

Because of the Millennium funding, admission to all these concerts is FREE (although you may wish to make a donation towards any refreshments). As all of you on the mailing list have supported us so well over the last three years, I am giving you priority by offering the opportunity to obtain tickets before their general release.

If you would like to order tickets, please complete the slip at the end of this letter with the requested information and send it to me at the address at the head of this letter. (Alternatively, you can also telephone me in the evening on ████████████ with the same information, if you prefer.) I shall send you your tickets within a week of receipt of your order, and this offer closes on Friday 18th May, after which the tickets will be available from the library (Tel. ████████████) or from Classical CD in the Lace Market (Tel. ████ ████████). Please note that there is a maximum of <u>four</u> tickets per concert per order except for the Wind Quintet concert, when there is a maximum of <u>two,</u> because of the limited capacity of the venue.

I do hope you enjoy the series and I look forward to hearing from you.

Yours sincerely,

Please send tickets for the following concerts:	
Sunday 11th June *St. Mary's Choir*	No of tickets (max. 4):
Sunday 11th June *Elgar Piano Quintet etc*	No of tickets (max. 4):
Friday 16th June *Beaufort Wind Quintet*	No of tickets (max. 2):
Sunday 25th June *String Ensemble*	No of tickets (max. 4):

Tickets to be sent to:	
Name:	
Address:	
	Post code:

new perspectives
theatre company

The first series of workshops and events staged under the banner of New Perspectives in Northamptonshire has attracted interest from across age ranges and across the county. Teens and bus-pass holders have stood side by side in workshops which have aimed to be instructive, informative, creative, taxing and enjoyable.

One common theme which has emerged in talking to people is that participants always feel that they will be the one who knows the least, is the worst actor, gets it wrong, whilst everybody else is brilliant and perfect.
Only by attending a session will you realise that the workshops aim to bolster up your confidence levels, not destroy them. You don't need to have any previous experience, just a desire to explore ideas creatively with other people (other people who are just as nervous as you are). A tip from a participant on one session is to come with a friend, that way you will know someone right from the start.

Another similar concern surrounds what a 'workshop' actually is. A workshop is distinct from either a master class or a seminar in that you will be expected to take an active, if guided, part. It is also different from a rehearsal or an adult education type of class in that it is more exploratory and more rooted in the creative process than the product. A week of workshops might have no product at all at the end. The learning, the enjoyment and the new ideas you take to your next project are the point of being there.
If you're still unsure if all of this is really for you, take a peek inside at what's on offer and see what other people have to say. Don't take my word for it, take theirs.

Inside you will see that there is lots of activity for younger people over the summer, please pass on the information to anyone young enough to avail of it. They are the amateur drama enthusiasts of tomorrow.

Richard Conlon.

PRINT OPTIONS

Print for general distribution

- Car sticker
- Flyer
- Insert for slipping into other publications
- Leaflet
- Magazine
- Newspaper
- Poster
- Sticker

Print for mailing

- Birthday card
- Booklet
- Christmas card
- Invitation
- Leaflet
- Letter
- Newsletter
- Photograph
- Postcard
- Private view card

Dual-purpose print

- Badge
- Balloon
- Beer mat
- Book mark
- Carrier bag
- CD or tape
- Diary
- Keyring
- Menu
- Mug
- Pen
- Sachet, e.g. of sugar
- Sticker
- T-shirt

Extract from
New Perspectives newsletter

2 STEP-BY-STEP PRINT PRODUCTION

It is important to understand the way print is produced. This is a step-by-step guide to the standard process so adapt it to your circumstances. You could design the print yourself or use a photocopier to reproduce your own original artwork, both of which would reduce your costs.

The individual steps outlined here are examined in detail further on.

1. Are there any non-print options that might get your message across to your target groups more effectively?
2. If not, consider all the different types of print that might fulfil your needs.
3. Calculate when you need each item. Work out your time-scale.
4. Calculate the quantities you need of each item.
5. Decide whether overprinting is necessary. Companies should gather overprinting copy from promoters if appropriate.
6. If you are using a graphic designer, choose, contract and brief them. You could ask them to take care of many of the following steps for you.
   - Get printing quotes and compare them.
   - Select and contract a printer.
   - If appropriate, get photographs taken.
7. Collect all essential funding and/or sponsorship credits and logos, etc.
8. Write the copy.
9. Brief the designer fully.
10. Approve the rough visual.
11. Proofread the copy.
12. Approve the final artwork.
13. Send the artwork to the printers.
14. Approve page proofs if appropriate or, if you are particularly concerned about a complex print job, go to the printers to check the ink colour(s) on the machine and the first copy off the machine.
15. Receive the finished print.
16. Distribute the print to your target groups.

REMEMBER ✳

Approval

How will you consult and liaise with those colleagues also involved in decisions about print (e.g. your artistic director) while ensuring that the piece of print communicates effectively with the target audience?

What is their input into the design brief?

What is an appropriate approval process?

2.1 PRINTING METHODS

There are different methods of printing information:

OFFSET LITHOGRAPHIC PRINTING (OFFSET LITHO)

This is the printing method most often used to produce posters and leaflets. You can produce large quantities of high quality print very quickly using this method. In lithographic printing, a separate metal plate is produced for each colour. This is done by taking the computer file provided by the designer and separating the areas of the artwork to be printed in each colour and etching the resulting information onto plates.

Two-colour printing presses have two drums around which the plates are fixed. Each drum is fed a different coloured ink. Large sheets of paper are fed into the printing press and each colour of ink is transferred from the plate onto a big roller and then onto the paper. Two-colour print is very cheap to produce on a two-colour press. If you want more than two colours, then when all your leaflets or posters have been printed with the first two colours, the printing press is stopped, washed down, the plates changed and the paper fed through once more to print the next two colours. This is why printing in four colours is hardly any more expensive than printing in three colours.

All of the big printing companies, and many small ones, have four-colour presses. It can be more expensive to print in two colours on a four-colour machine than two colours on a two-colour machine. This is why it is worth getting price quotations from different kinds of printers.

SCREEN PRINTING

This method of printing is often used for posters but is not suitable for anything smaller than A4 as it is difficult to reproduce detail accurately. It involves squeezing thick ink through a screen that, in the areas to be left blank, has had the fine mesh blocked up with gelatine so that the ink cannot get through. It is cheaper to use this method if you want small quantities of colourful print. Small organisations can sometimes get access to the necessary equipment in colleges or community workshops to produce their own posters.

FOUR-COLOUR PROCESS PRINTING

Full-colour print is produced by process printing. This is the only method of reproducing colour photographs on posters and leaflets. It involves a computerised scanning process which analyses the colours and reduces them to tiny dots made up of the four process colours: cyan, magenta, black and yellow. When printed on top of each other, these colours can make any other colour. Each colour of dots are transferred onto offset litho plates. Many printers have four-colour printing presses which print full-colour work very quickly. Some even have five-colour machines on which the fifth drum is used to print 'special' colours such as specific colours that cannot be reproduced accurately by process printing, metallic or fluorescent inks or for putting a layer of varnish over the leaflet or poster to make it more shiny and stop the inks from rubbing off.

WEB OFFSET PRINTING

This method is most often used for printing large quantities of full-colour magazines and brochures cost-effectively. It uses four-colour process printing at high speed onto a continuous roll of paper.

FINISHING

Printers use this term to refer to everything that happens to your leaflets after the paper has been printed and includes processes such as folding, saddle-stitching and gluing.

For a clear and entertaining explanation of printing methods try David Macaulay's *How Things Work.*[1]

[1] David Macaulay, *How Things Work* (London: Dorling Kindersley, 1988)

2.2   PRINT STYLE

You need to consider carefully the style of the print you produce. The style of your print is dictated by its size and shape, type of paper and colours. If you are using a graphic designer, it is their job to choose the size, paper and colours that will help communicate your message as they have an expert knowledge of what is available and how it can be used. This is why it is so important to brief your designer properly.

PAPER

Paper sizes are calculated according to an international system of paper sizes:

Al: 841 x 594mm across	A2: 594 x 420mm across
A3: 420 x 297mm across	A4: 297 x 210mm across
A5: 210 x 148mm across	A6: 148 x l05mm across

'A' SIZES

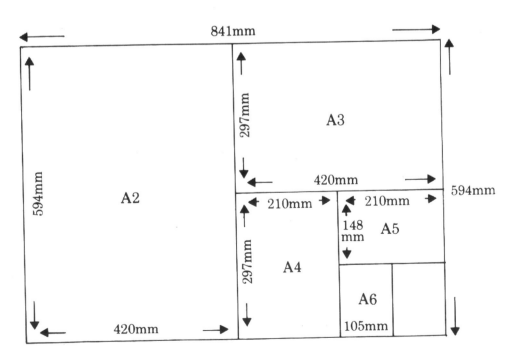

The more paper you use, the more it will cost you. The weight of the paper is measured in gsm (grammes per square metre). The higher the gsm, the denser and thicker the paper. Paper can be coated or uncoated. Coated papers have an ultra-smooth surface and absorb ink less readily. They come in matt or gloss finishes. Gloss-coated papers give depth to colours and are particularly suited to full-colour printing, especially with designs that include full-colour photographs. Many designers prefer the finish given by matt-coated paper. Both matt- and gloss-coated papers tend to retain fingermarks and some inks can rub off, in which case they will need to be coated with varnish after they have been printed. Designers often use uncoated paper effectively to give a particular style to your print. The surface of the paper is more absorbent so images and fine typefaces tend to lose definition and your print might be slightly less readable.

Paper comes in hundreds of shades of white as well as in tints and colours. Textured paper can look and feel interesting and does not mark as readily as coated paper but photographs do not reproduce at all well, and small or fine typefaces can become illegible. Recycled paper used to be comparatively expensive, but is now being competitively priced. There is a wide range of textured, recycled papers. Tinted and textured papers are slightly more expensive than the white equivalent.

Do not underestimate the importance of paper for getting your message across. It is usually much cheaper to upgrade your paper to give an impression of high quality than to add an extra ink colour.

COLOUR

You will need to work out how many ink colours you can afford. Consult your graphic designer, if you are using one, and/or your printer about the different costs of ink colours.

In lithographic printing, each colour that you use needs a separate printing plate and so extra colours add to the cost. In screen printing, a separate screen is needed for each main colour but colours can be mixed within each screen and small areas of additional colour added at little extra cost.

Standard colours such as black, royal blue, red and yellow are cheaper than non-standard ones because they come straight out of a tin. Black is even cheaper because it is often already on the machine which means that the printing press will not need to be washed down. Metallic and fluorescent inks are the most expensive.

Colours are sometimes referred to by an international system called Pantone. This tells the printer the proportions for mixing standard colours to create the exact shade you have chosen. You, or your graphic designer, should give the Pantone number that corresponds to the exact shade you require. Most graphic designers have a book of Pantone swatches which contains examples of all the different Pantone colours. The colours used in four-colour process printing are standard – cyan, magenta, yellow and black – so you do not need to specify them.

If you or your designer are working on computer, you can see the exact colours on screen. You should be aware that colours always look more vivid on screen than on paper. You or the designer will provide the printer with the design on disk and the colours will automatically be separated by the printer's software ready to be put onto plates. Sometimes problems can occur so it is always a good idea for you and your designer, if you have one, to check a colour proof before the printer starts printing your leaflet or poster.

Colours

Are they in keeping with your corporate identity?

Are they in keeping with the mood and emotional message of the print?

Ensure high legibility and contrast, e.g. reversed-out type needs good colour registration, lighting and eyesight before your potential audience member can read it.

Black is not the only single colour you can use.

HALF-TONE

Black and white photographs are formed from continuous shades of grey which cannot be printed. They need to be screened to convert the continuous shades into variable sizes of dots of solid colour. The screened photograph is known as a half-tone. The darker the grey on the photograph, the closer together the dots; the lighter the grey, the more space between them. You can easily see how this works by looking closely at a photograph in a newspaper where the dots are much coarser than in the printing methods you are likely to use for your leaflets and posters.

REVERSING OUT

You can print your text and images in any colour you like. You can also print the text or image in negative form. Instead of printing dark type on a light background, you can have a solid area of dark-coloured ink with the light image or type showing through. On the left is a particularly effective leaflet for Rushes' festival of short films using reversing out to turn the two colours they paid for into three.

2.3   WHEN TO START WORKING ON YOUR PRINT

Calculate the time you need for producing print by working backwards from the date you want it delivered. Use your diary. This is important because you will have to allow for any holiday periods, e.g. Christmas or bank holidays.

Count back two to three working days for delivery by the printer, parcel delivery or courier service and at least ten working days for the actual printing (check this with your printers). This should tell you the date when the artwork needs to arrive at the printers.

Now count back up to four working days for checking the final artwork, depending on how many people have to approve it. Ask the designer how much time they will need for producing the final artwork once they have received the corrected proofs back from you – they will probably require about one week. Allow two to three working days for you to correct the proofs. This is the date on which you should receive the proofs from your designer.

Count back ten working days and you will come to the date when your designer should give you a rough visual for approval.

Before this, you need to have: briefed the designer; written your copy; collected all essential logos; booked a printer; got printing quotes; contracted the designer; collected and typed up any information for overprinting; and calculated your quantities. These steps may take from four to twelve weeks.

See list on right.

This schedule is approximate and the time needed for each stage will change according to the complexity of the design and printing and level of skill and experience of those involved in the print production. The time-scale clearly indicates, however, that print production is usually a matter of weeks, not days, and in some cases it may take months.

Give the schedule to the designer and printer but always build in a margin for error. Tell them both that you need things earlier than you actually do. Many marketers find that their colleagues who have to approve copy and design are not aware of the importance of keeping to print schedules and so also tell them that you need the corrected proofs back a few days earlier than the actual deadline.

It is essential that you keep to your own schedule and deliver copy, photographs, logos, etc., by the agreed date.

Print delivery date
2-3 days
↑
Print despatched by printer
10 days
↑
Artwork to printer
4 days
↑
Check final artwork
1 week
↑
Proofs corrected
3 days
↑
Receive proofs for correction
1-2 weeks
↑
Receive rough visual
4-12 weeks
↑
Calculate quantities required.
Word process any overprinting.
Contract a designer if using.
Obtain printing quotes.
Book the printer.
Collect all logos.
Write your copy.
Collect information for the overprinting.
Brief your designer if you are using one.

2.4   CALCULATING QUANTITIES

Calculate print quantities item by item including leaflets or brochures, posters and programmes. Look at the targets you have set. Go through each of your methods of getting your print to your target groups and count how many of each type of print you need. If you have a mailing list of 1,500, a list of shops and libraries in your area that needs another 11,400 leaflets, and want to display the leaflets in your venue for eight weeks where your audience picks up around 200 leaflets per week, you will need to print 15,000 copies. Allow extra for sending to the media, circulating to your colleagues, using in displays and for your archives.

Touring companies should always consult with promoters about their requirements for print. Generally, you should supply the quantities they request, but if these seem unreasonable, ask for details of how they intend to distribute them. Add up all the amounts requested by the promoters. Add any distribution you will be doing yourself to this total, e.g. to your mailing list, plus the quantities needed for press and media and displays. Round this figure upwards to the nearest 500 for simplicity.

When calculating programme quantities estimate that about 30% of your target attendance will buy a programme. You will need to allow one per person if you are giving them away. You will need extra programmes for the press and media and for displays.

Storing or throwing away unused print costs money.

2.5   GETTING PRINTING QUOTES

Either you or your designer can obtain quotes from the printer. Consider who has the greater negotiating power and knowledge of print techniques. If the designer negotiates with the printer and then liaises with them throughout the print production process, they will charge you for this by adding a percentage onto the printing costs. This is usually around 15% or 20% but can be as much as 40%. This service is known as print buying.

You must obtain print quotes in writing for them to be binding. Ask for a quote for supplying the design on disk or for camera-ready artwork (this is artwork that requires little or no extra work by the printer before making plates). You will need to give the printer the following information:

- the name of your organisation
- the number of items needed (leaflets, posters, programmes)
- the quantity of each item
- the sort of paper (weight and finish)
- the size of each item in millimetres or standard A sizes (if you want a folded leaflet, give the size both when it is opened out flat and folded up)
- the number of pages (each panel of a folded leaflet counts as a page)

- the number of colours
- the number of half-tones
- any overprinting
- any folding and stapling or gluing
- delivery requirements.

Ask for a run-on price for each item: this is the cost of printing more copies while your job is still on the machine.

When you ask for a quote, give the printer a rough idea of the time-scale to which you are working. If the estimated completion date is a long way ahead, ask the printer about any impending paper price increases. You can also ask for samples of previous work by the printer if you have not yet seen any. If you want the printer to do the typesetting, find out in what format disk they need the copy supplied.

Make sure that each quote you get is for exactly the same set of specifications so that you can compare prices.

When you budget for print, you need to take VAT into account if your organisation cannot reclaim it. In June 2000, VAT was charged on posters, but not leaflets or brochures unless the booking form was more than 20% of its surface area. It was not charged on programmes.

Compare the total price of any printing quotes you obtain. Choose the printer that offers the best quality for the lowest cost and can meet your schedule. Once you have chosen a printer, write to them to confirm all the details. This is absolutely essential in case of any problems later (see an example overleaf).

> An awful lot of people don't know what they want. We probably have to do ten or fifteen permutations of some quotes because they don't know how many pages they want or whether they will be using two or four colours. Each permutation takes about an hour to work out. We could help them so much better if they thought through what they wanted before they got in touch. **Mike Rayment, APL, tel. 01273 566177**

2.6 OVERPRINTING

Overprinting is the process of printing additional information onto a piece of print. Any information that remains constant such as the name of the company, the main image and funding logos should be printed in one go. However, information that changes, like the name of each venue on your tour, may be added after the initial print run. It is not possible to overprint in a light colour onto a dark background because the inks used in offset litho and web offset are transparent. It is also expensive to add information onto more than one area of each piece of print. The design of your leaflets or posters must allow for a single appropriately sized space with a white or pale-coloured background.

As a touring company, if you are doing a tour playing one or two performances in each venue, it may not be cost effective (in terms of money or time) for you to

Aldrington Press Limited

Unit A4, Enterprise Estate, Crowhurst Road, Hollingbury, Brighton, East Sussex BN1 8AF

Tel: (01273) 566177 - 509756   Fax: (01273) 500283

```
For: Connaught Theatre,                      Estimate No:   9578
     Union Place,                            Job Ref:
     Worthing,                               Your Ref:
     West Sussex,
     BN11 1LG                                Date:        17/ 6/2000

   Tel:01903 239770        0903 215337

For the attention of David Smith

                         ESTIMATE
```

```
     Thank you for your enquiry.  We have pleasure in submitting
     our estimate as follows:

     Description:   50,000 32pp A5 THEATRE BROCHURE Printed 2 colours
                    throughout. Material 115gsm Art PLUS 4pp coming events
                    section printed on 80gsm White bond.


     Artwork:       Typeset and design as copy and scan 80 pictures
                    Laser proofs only. Extra for chromalin proofs.
     Finishing:     Fold, stitch, trim.

     Delivery:      Worthing



     Total:                   7648.12    Run-on per1000      105.27
```

```
     All prices exclude V.A.T.

     We hope the above will prove to be of interest and look forward to
     receiving your further instructions. Please contact us if there
     are any queries on the above specification as any changes may incur
     additional costs.

     Yours sincerely,
```

Registered Office: 63, Portland Road, Hove, East Sussex BN3 5DQ   Registered Number 1846050 England
Directors: M.K.W. Pountain, B.W. Lomax, M.L. Rayment.

supply promoters with overprinted leaflets and posters. Promoters, however, find it difficult and expensive to overprint leaflets and posters themselves and the results are often unattractive. If you really cannot afford to overprint the information for them, leave a space on your leaflets and posters that is at least 20% of the surface area of the leaflet and poster. Indicate where the overprinting should go on the poster and, if possible, send an overprinted example for the promoter's reference.

> We seem to be doing the overprinting on nearly all of the print we are sent. This is a recent development. It's a real bind! **Administrator, arts centre, England**

Promoters will need the print much earlier if they have to overprint it. Send the print in flat packages as it may have to pass through another printing machine. In this case supply the leaflets and posters untrimmed. Alternatively, the promoter may use a photocopier or felt pen to add the information. They won't be able to do this if the paper you have used is too thin or gloss coated.

> We have the relevant performance details typeset and provide each venue with artwork. The venue then uses this to photocopy the information onto the posters and often the front of the leaflets. It ensures that the overall effect of the leaflet and poster is not ruined. It also saves us money as we don't have to overprint lots of small quantities of print. **Administrator, regional touring theatre company**

You can put all your venue details on one piece of print to save money by listing them on the back of your leaflet. You can highlight individual venues using a fluorescent pen. This method is especially useful if you are touring to lots of venues that are close together. This means, however, that audiences have to search through the information to find out when your show will be visiting their local venue and the venues charging higher ticket prices may find that their audience travels to see you at the cheaper venues.

You can add individual venue details while your leaflets and posters are being printed. This also ensures that the print looks as good as possible. This is because the sheets of paper fed through a printing press are very big and several copies of your poster or leaflet are printed onto the sheet at the same time. When they are all printed, your printer will use a guillotine to cut the individual posters and leaflets out of the big sheet. This means that you can print the details for a different venue on each of the copies of your print on the big sheet. You must talk to your printer about this when you get your print quote. Tell them how many different versions you need and the likely quantities of each. They will work out the most economical way of doing it. It might mean adjusting the quantities for each venue slightly.

Overprinting centrally like this is cost effective because the printing machine will be up and running. It will increase the company's total print costs as you will have to have the overprinting details typeset as well as printed. You can ask venues to contribute towards the cost of overprinting centrally. Printers can usually itemise overprinting costs for you, so you can work out the exact price of each overprint. If the venue is intending to have their details printed onto your leaflets rather than using their photocopier or a felt pen, it is often cheaper for them to pay you do it.

It is usually very cheap to overprint just one venue's details at the same time as your main print run. This is useful if a promoter either requires their print very early (which means they will not have time to overprint themselves) and/or requires a very large amount of print.

> We produce leaflets that advertise the whole tour because we find that an effective way. Most Scottish touring theatre companies have the whole tour on the reverse of the leaflet ... This is very effective for getting into the community networks. Someone might go to see the show and then get in touch with friends and tell them where it's going to. **General manager, touring theatre company, Scotland**

COLLECTING OVERPRINTING DETAILS

See the form opposite and following page for an example of how to collect the relevant information you are going to need for any overprinting needed. Many companies use forms like this one to obtain accurate overprinting information.

ESSENTIAL INFORMATION SHEET

Please fill in all the relevant information and return to:

                                    TO ARRIVE NO LATER THAN:

                            ┌──────────────────────────┐
                            │   │
                            │   │
                            └──────────────────────────┘

OVERPRINTING: Please word as you would wish details to
                                appear on all print.

■VENUE: _____
Is theatre logo required?   YES ☐   NO ☐
If yes, please enclose good quality copy.
ADDRESS: _____

_____

_____ POSTCODE _____

■PERFORMANCE DATES: _____
PERFORMANCE TIMES: _____

■TICKET PRICES: _____
CONCESSIONS: _____

■BOX OFFICE TELEPHONE (including STD code): _____
CREDIT CARDS ACCEPTED: _____
CREDIT CARD TELEPHONE BOOKINGS: _____
CHEQUES PAYABLE TO: _____

■CREDITS FOR FUNDING BODIES: _____
LOGOS REQUIRED   YES ☐   NO ☐
If yes, please enclose good quality copies.

■ADDITIONAL INFORMATION: _____

_____

■PROPOSED PRINT REQUISITION: This can be amended at advance
                                        planning meeting.
Leaflets: ┌──────────────────┐   ☐
          └──────────────────┘
Posters: A3 (16½" x 12" approx) ☐
          A2 (23½" x 16½" approx)
                                  ☐

(cont/...)

110

■Please give details of wheelchair access, facilities for the disabled, hearing loops etc:

Please give details of childcare facilities available:

Signed _____ Date _____

PLEASE DON'T FORGET TO KEEP A COPY FOR YOUR RECORD!

2.7 LOGOS

Use your logo on any print you produce. In addition, you will need to collect copies of the funding and/or sponsorship logos you need to put on your print. If you are a company, you may need to obtain logos from venues for overprinting.

2.8 COPY

The content of print is discussed under the individual print items (see pp. 35–36).

Give the copy to your designer on disk and on paper. Keep a copy for yourself. Proofread your copy before sending it to the designer and get approval from all of your colleagues who have a say in the print production process. Any changes that you make after this point will mean that your designer might have to rework whole sections of the design. They will regard these changes as 'author's corrections' and charge you for the time it takes to deal with them.

Proofreading is best done by more than one person. Print out your copy onto paper and give it to somebody else who, ideally, should be seeing the copy for the first time. Then proofread the copy for yourself.

Does your copy get your message across to your target audience effectively?

Give it to members of your target audience to read.

2.9 ROUGH VISUALS

A designer should always show you a rough visual. This is the first impression of the design concept. It should tell you what goes where on each piece of print: it should give you an impression of the finished version. Sometimes a designer will present two or three rough visuals.

If you have to present the design to others for approval you may need to ask for a finished visual as well. This can be more expensive as it involves more work for the designer, but it is useful to help people without good visualisation skills understand the design concept.

2.10 TYPESETTING

Typesetting is the process of converting your word-processed copy into different typefaces.

There are hundreds of different typefaces. Different typefaces convey different impressions to the reader. They are the visual equivalent of your tone of voice. Typefaces can shout or they can be matter-of-fact or even elegant and refined. They all have names. Common ones are Helvetica, Arial and Times Roman – if you have access to word-processing software, compare their effects. You can also alter the appearance of type by changing its size and thickness (known as weight). Some typefaces are more legible than others and you need to make sure that your designer chooses one that is easy to read.

Your copy can be set in many different ways. Some of the most popular options are:

Ranged left
You can range the copy on the left
which means that the left edge is straight
and the right edge is ragged.

Ranged right
You can range the copy to the right so
that the right edge is straight
and the left edge is ragged.

Centred
You can centre the copy so that it is placed
in the centre of the page
with both edges ragged.

Justified
You can justify copy so that both sides are straight and neither are ragged. Justified copy normally means that the gaps between each word are slightly uneven so that each entire line is filled with copy, as in the example you are reading.

2.11 PROOFREADING

All sorts of mistakes can creep in while your designer is turning your word-processed copy into typeset text and then manipulating it to fit the design. You must therefore proofread every word both at visual and final artwork stages.

Always proofread on paper unless you are very experienced at it. First of all, make two photocopies of the visual or finished artwork. Give one to somebody else for proofreading. This person should be seeing the copy for the first time. Keep the second photocopy for your records.

Check the typesetting against the copy you sent to the designer. Errors include things that have been missed out or accidentally added. If you are familiar with them, use the standard proofreading symbols. Now return the corrected proofs to the designer. Shown left are some of the most common proofreading symbols.

Most printers have a comprehensive list of proofreading symbols if you want to use them.

Instruction	Textual mark		Marginal mark
Insert matter indicated in margin	λ		New matter followed by λ
Delete and leave space	—	through characters, etc., to be deleted	♂
Change to capital letters	≡	under characters to be altered	(U.C.)
Change to lower case		Encircle characters to be altered	(l.c.)
Substitute or insert comma	λ	through character or where required	λ,
Substitute or insert full-stop	λ	through character or where required	λ.

Many typesetters and printers have a comprehensive list of proofreading symbols.

Check the artwork before it goes to the printers.

Get someone not directly involved in the project to check the last stages for mistakes or anomalies.

2.12   FINAL ARTWORK

When the design is ready to be sent to the printers, it is known as final artwork. Ask for a printout, also known as a laser proof, and proofread it carefully, checking the position of the images and copy. Make certain that the colours specified will improve the appearance and legibility of the finished print. If you are unclear about anything on the final artwork consult your designer at this point. Keep a printout of the artwork for reference in case there are any queries from the printer. The artwork can be sent to the printer on disk or by e-mail – 'down the line' – using an ISDN line which is a high-speed telephone line that eliminates electrical interference which can corrupt the file.

2.13   PRINTING AND DELIVERY

If you, rather than the designer, are liaising with the printers, telephone them to check the artwork has arrived intact and to answer any queries they may have. If they have any questions, contact your designer, who can then speak to the printers directly.

It is a very good idea for you or your designer to make a final check. You can ask to see a printed version of your leaflet taken from the actual plates the printer will use. These are called *machine proofs* and are printed on a special printing press known as a proofing press.

Cromalins are photographic proofs taken from the colour separations which are used to make the plates. They enable you to check the colour separation and whether the colours chosen work effectively. It will be expensive for you to make any changes at this stage, but if the printer has made any errors, you will not have to pay for them.

When your finished print arrives, examine it carefully for quality and consistency. Send copies to your designer for their opinion. If it is of a good standard, telephone the printer and thank them for their work. Also thank the designer.

Occasionally, you may find that your print is substandard or the printer has made a major error. You will need to negotiate for a discount or reprint. Most printers will prefer to correct any errors rather than get a bad reputation. Keep a few copies of your print for reference. It may be useful for attracting funders and/or sponsors.

3 EVALUATING YOUR PRINT

Talk to your designer after your production is over. If you answer the following questions, you will produce even better print next time:

- Did you achieve your objectives?
- Was the print of an appropriate quality?
- Were the quantities right?
- If this is a piece of print you produce regularly, is the frequency appropriate?
- Was the print's distribution appropriate and effective?
- In terms of your target for the project as a whole, was the response good or bad?
- Was it cost effective?
- How much money did the campaign cost? How much income resulted in the short term? How much income will it generate in the long term? What else has it achieved?
- Were lead times and deadlines appropriate?
- What are the views and comment of work colleagues?
- What did audiences think?
- What monitoring methods did you use?
- What lessons did you learn from this project?
- Which elements would you be sure to repeat?
- Which elements would you like to throw out?

4 TYPES OF PRINT

4.1   LEAFLETS

SIZE

You may need to produce leaflets for individual events. The most popular sizes are one-third A4 (99 x 210mm across), A5 or two-thirds A4 (198 x 210mm across) folded in half to one-third A4. One-third A4 sizes are easy to mail. They fit exactly in standard letter envelopes (DL size). However, you need to adapt the proportions of your design to fit onto one-third A4 if you aim to use it for your leaflet as well as your A3 or A2 poster. This means increased design costs. A5 allows you a bigger surface area. A5 has the same proportions as A3 and A2 sizes so reduction of any poster image is simpler. However, you will need to use larger, more expensive envelopes (C5) for mailing your A5 leaflet unless you fold it. Folding is likely to make it look unappealing.

The fold down a two-thirds A4 leaflet means that it is less likely to flop over in a leaflet rack. You still need to adapt the proportions of your design if you want it on the front of your leaflet and your posters.

PAPER

Do not choose paper that is below 135gsm for leaflets, and unfolded leaflets may need to be on paper that is heavier still. Thin paper curls up and looks tatty quickly. The colour on one side of the paper may also show through to the other side. Remember that your leaflet must still look attractive after it has gone through the postal system and been displayed in a rack for several weeks.
If you are using lots of photographs and copy, then textured and uncoated papers will make your leaflet much more difficult to read.

CONTENT

It is generally accepted that leaflets and brochures are the most important items of print for generating ticket sales. All the information included in them should be aimed at making these sales. Any irrelevant information will make the print less effective.

Essential information for leaflets

- box office telephone number
- name and address of venue
- title of the show
- name of company
- dates of performances
- times of performances
- ticket prices
- funding and/or sponsorship logos
- by-line or headline that summarises the show in six or seven words
- information about how to get to the venue
- information about how to buy tickets
- information about access for disabled people
- information about the performance(s) – you may only need to use one or two phrases here to communicate the most important benefits of the event.

Optional information for leaflets

- photographs (especially important for productions that are hard to describe in words)
- any other images, e.g. illustrations
- quotations from the press and media or members of past audiences
- sales promotions, e.g. discounts
- credits (only include these if your target groups will regard them as benefits)

- map of how to get to the venue
- running time
- details of future shows
- details of future venues
- mailing list details
- booking form.

For venue brochures all the booking information should normally be contained in one place for easy reference.

GENERAL COMMENTS

It is always a good idea to make a dummy of your leaflet or brochure to understand how it will be folded and to help you visualise the relationship of images to text. Think about how your potential audience will open and read the brochure. Make sure that at each stage, your brochure or leaflet looks interesting. Put something interesting on the back as well, so that whichever way your leaflet is put into a rack or onto a table it will be communicating your message.

Will you be using positive images to reflect a wide cross-section of your community?

Will you be using positive images of your target audience?

Is it worth thinking about co-commissioning images or buying in photographs or illustrations from an agency or picture library?

Do your images show benefits, not features?

4.2   SEASON BROCHURES

SIZE

If your organisation promotes a series of events, you will probably need to produce a regular season brochure, usually on a monthly, bi-monthly or seasonal basis. These can be in a booklet format, or a sheet of A3 or A2 folded down to a pocket size. Audiences seem to prefer booklets as they find them easier to use, and complain that they find it difficult to refold the folded versions. Either of these formats can be mailed in DL or C5 envelopes depending on the shape you choose.

Designers sometimes make mistakes when working out how to fold your brochure, so you need to check that all the images and text are easy to follow because they are organised in a sensible way, and that they end up the right way up. Make a plain paper copy of the brochure at the rough stage for reference. This is known as a dummy.

Booklet format brochures are stapled through the middle to keep the pages together. Printers call this *saddle-stitching.*

PAPER

As with leaflets, you need to use a paper that is opaque so that the printing on one side does not show through to the other. You can use a heavier weight paper for the cover and a thinner paper inside, but this means that your cover will have to be printed separately, adding to the cost. Some organisations make use of this and print a full-colour cover with one- or two-colour pages inside. Unless you have a season brochure with a lot of pages, however, it will be cheaper to use the same paper for the cover (known as a self cover) so that the whole brochure can be printed on one sheet of paper at the same time.

CONTENT

The challenge of a season brochure is to maintain a strong corporate identity for the organisation while allowing the unique nature of each event to shine through. In many season brochures, all the events look the same at first glance and audiences find it difficult to choose between them or to find the kind of event they enjoy.

Another challenge is the decision whether to give all the events the same space and visual emphasis or to highlight some by giving them more space and additional illustrations and copy. This is particularly an issue for venues that hire out the auditorium to outside promoters, for producing companies that also present touring work and for venues with a strong amateur programme.

Essential information for season brochures

General:

- box office telephone number
- name and address of venue
- venue funding and/or sponsorship logos
- information about how to get to the venue
- information about how to buy tickets
- information about access for disabled people
- map of how to get to the venue
- easy-to-find diary-style summary of events (e.g. centre, inside front or outside back page).

For each event:

- title
- name of company
- date of performances
- time of performances
- photograph or illustration
- by-line or headline that summarises the show in six or seven words
- funding and/or sponsorship logos
- description of the event including key benefits.

Optional information for season brochures

General:

- introduction from the director or programmer with photograph
- general information about the organisation's aims
- sales promotions
- details of forthcoming shows
- how to join the mailing list
- how to join the Friends' scheme
- information about the education programme
- booking form
- staff list.

For each event:

- quotations from the press and media or members of past audiences
- running time
- guidance about suitability.

All the booking information in venue brochures should normally be contained in one place for easy reference. Ticket prices can either be set out with each event or summarised with the information about how to book. In a mixed programme venue with variable pricing, it is more usual to keep ticket prices with the event, although they can also appear on the diary-style summary of events.

4.3   POSTERS

We'd love to have a new poster for the new show, but because we've got this basic design and no money, we have to use it the whole time ... It's general enough to apply to any tour and in those terms it's cost effective.

Administrator, project-funded dance company

The poster's primary role is to catch people's attention and to remind them about your event. Posters are particularly useful for reinforcing any press and media coverage you may have obtained.

SIZE

Posters are usually produced in A3 and A2 sizes. A2 posters are bigger and may therefore be more eye-catching, but many shops and cafés refuse to display them as they take up too much wall or window space. For companies it is not always cost-effective to produce A2 posters if only a few of your promoters require them. Some organisations produce A4 posters as they find it easier to get people to display them.

   You may want to use unconventional poster shapes and sizes, e.g. one-third A1 or A3 landscape style to make your print stand out, but you must consider whether distribution outlets will be able to display these.

PAPER

Paper for posters can be lighter than that for leaflets and brochures: 115gsm is a good weight. You can print posters straight onto card for display purposes.

COLOURS

If you are producing a poster to accompany your leaflet or brochure, use similar designs and colours. If you do not maintain a consistent design, you will weaken the overall effectiveness of your campaign as your target groups may not connect your different print items with the same event.

CONTENT

Posters should reinforce the message of your leaflet. People usually see posters when they are travelling rather than stationary, which means that they see them at a time when it is impractical to book a ticket. They are not in a position to consult their diaries or their friends to arrange a convenient date, nor are they likely to be near a telephone. Also you cannot take a poster away with you. You need to write down any information you need to take action, such as the box office number.

Essential information for posters

- an image to catch people's attention
- box office telephone number
- name of venue
- name of show
- name of company
- date
- time
- funding and/or sponsorship logos
- by-line or headline conveying main benefit.

Optional information for posters

- repeat of the image(s) from leaflet
- quotes from the press and media or previous attenders
- sales promotions, e.g. discounts
- ticket prices.

GENERAL COMMENTS

When mailing your posters, roll them up and put them in special poster tubes. Creased and folded posters look shabby.

Lamination puts a gloss on the paper and removes creases. For a potential sponsor a laminated poster always looks much better. **Freelance graphic designer**

4.4   PROGRAMMES

Programmes should tell the attending audience more about the performance they are watching. They should help the audience understand and appreciate the performance and can often help people feel more confident about experiencing something unfamiliar. For some audience members attending particular art forms such as classical music and opera, they are an essential part of the performance. People may also see them as a permanent reminder of the event.

Programmes can be a useful source of additional income, but as a company you may need to help your promoter sell them to maximise sales. It is usual for small-scale companies rather than venues or promoters to produce programmes, unless that venue presents its own productions. Programmes are rarely overprinted with the details of each venue and so the quantity needed for the whole tour can be printed at once.

You can produce your programme in any number of ways: using a designer, typesetter and printer; using a desktop publisher; using a word processor and a photocopier, etc. Choose a method that fits in with your resources but do not forget that it needs to reflect the quality and style of your show and your organisation's corporate identity.

SIZE

Programmes can be any size or shape, a single sheet, a folded sheet or a booklet. Popular formats for organisations with few resources are A3 folded to A4, or A4 folded to A5. More than one sheet of paper should be stapled together. Generally, the bigger your programme, the more impressive it will look and the more you will be able to charge for it.

PAPER

The heavier your paper, the more impressive your programme will be. If you are having your programme printed, choose a weight between that of your leaflet and your poster to balance cost and quality. It is best to use paper with a matt finish that does not mark, as programmes inevitably get handled a lot. You can, of course, photocopy your programme. This will be much cheaper to produce, but you will probably not be able to charge much for it.

COLOURS

Use similar colours to your leaflet and poster to present a consistent image.

CONTENT

Essential information for programmes:

- name of company
- title of show
- address of company
- cast list
- credits
- biographies of performers – make sure these mean something to your audience

- funding and/or sponsorship logos
- information about the performance to help the audience understand and appreciate it
- information about the next show and tour.

Optional information for programmes:

- image from poster and/or leaflet
- information about company
- background information to performance
- thanks to sponsors in kind
- photographs
- date of first performance
- dates of future performances
- how to join the mailing list
- advertisements.

GENERAL COMMENTS

Send your programmes to promoters as soon as they are available to tell them more about the show. Give complimentary programmes to the press and media and VIPs.

You can offer your programmes to the public for free or you can sell them. If you decide to sell them, you will need to fix a price. Work out the production costs (including any design fee, typesetting, printing and delivery costs). Divide this figure by the estimated number of sales, which will probably be approximately 30% of your target attendance figure. The result should give you a rough idea what you need to charge, although you must also consider what other organisations charge and the price that you think people will pay. It is vital to charge a round figure, e.g. £1.50 not £1.25, as ushers will need to supply change.

You can sell advertising space in your programmes to subsidise the production costs. This can, however, be very time-consuming. You will need to select advertisers who fit in with your corporate identity.

You must liaise with the venue about programme sales. Most venues take a small percentage of sales (10–15%). It is a good idea to make one member of your company responsible for co-ordinating programme sales with tour venues. You can give them a form to help monitor sales and income.

Bundle the programmes into groups of 20 or 25 to make it easier to count them. Try not to give venues more programmes than they need as there is always a chance of damage or loss.

4.5 POSTCARDS

When you need small quantities of print, e.g. for a single event, it may be cost effective to produce postcards instead of leaflets. Postcards are quick and simple to produce as only very simple artwork is needed.

You will need to supply a black and white photograph or a colour transparency for the front image. You can set your copy on the whole of the back of the postcard or only on the left-hand side, which will allow you to mail the postcard without using an envelope.

Postcards are also useful for targeting your enthusiasts.

CASE STUDY

A solo mime performer produced 500 postcards for a single night at a small London venue. The performer sent 250 out to personal contacts and the rest were more generally distributed. The only other form of publicity was 30 posters and the venue brochure. The performance sold out.

4.6   ALTERNATIVE FORMATS

The Disability Discrimination Act (DDA) makes it unlawful for an organisation providing services, and this includes arts events, to treat disabled people less favourably for a reason related to their disability. It means that all arts organisations must consider making reasonable adjustments to the way that they deliver their services where disabled people find these impossible or unreasonably difficult to access. This includes 'access to and use of information services'.

Arts organisations need to provide their communications material in alternative formats on request. These might include:

- large print (a simple font in 16 point on yellow paper is best)
- a version on audiotape
- a Braille transcription
- a videotape of a British Sign Language version
- someone to read the information out loud
- a version in simple English.

What is considered reasonable for your organisation to provide will depend on its size and level of resources.

An introductory booklet on the implications of the DDA for small and medium enterprises with some examples of what might be considered reasonable for a wide range of organisations is available to download from **www.disability.gov.uk/dda**.

4.5   GLOSSARY

A sizes	Paper sizes are calculated according to an international system of paper sizes: A1: 841 x 594mm across A4: 297 x 210mm across A2: 594 x 420mm across A5: 210 x 148mm across A3: 420 x 297mm across A6: 148 x 105mm across
Art paper	A glossy coated paper.
Author's corrections	Corrections to the copy where you change your mind after the copy has been typeset. You will be charged for author's corrections.
Bleed	On the artwork, images that are supposed to go right to the edge of the paper with no margins are extended beyond the trim line where the printer will guillotine the edge of your piece of print.
Body copy	The main block of copy excluding any titles and headings.
Bromide	A photographic copy of artwork on special paper which is so accurately reproduced that it can be used in other artwork.
By-line	A phrase that expands a title or headline. It should convey the main benefit of the event to the reader, e.g. 'The latest smash hit from Jamaica'.
Camera-ready artwork	Artwork that needs little or no work by the printer before making the plates.
Centre spread	The middle two pages of a saddle-stitched booklet or programme.
Cromalin	A full-colour proof which shows you how the finished print will look and enables you to check the accuracy of colours.
Coated paper	Paper that has been coated with starch and china clay to give an ultra-smooth surface that takes ink well.
Colour separation	In lithographic printing, a separate plate is produced for each colour. This is done by computer software which analyses the artwork file produced by the designer and transfers the results onto a metal plate. Colour separation can also be done by the printer, using a photographic process. The phrase 'colour separation' is also used for the scanning process that separates a full-colour image into the four process colours (see *process printing*).
Crop marks	Tiny lines at the edge of your artwork to show the printer where to trim your print.

Die	Print that has edges that are not straight lines (e.g. a folder) cannot be trimmed with a guillotine and has to be stamped out using a die.
Double crown	This is the standard imperial paper size that is nearest to A2 but is slightly narrower and a couple of inches longer at 30″ by 20″. A few theatres still print double-crown posters because they have display cases this size.
Dummy	A plain paper version of your leaflet, folder, brochure or programme which indicates how a leaflet will fold out or what will go on each page in a programme.
Duotone	A half-tone that uses dots in two colours to give depth to a screened photograph.
Final artwork	Artwork ready to be sent to the printers.
Finish	The surface of the paper.
Finishing	Everything that happens to your print after the paper has been printed including folding, saddle-stitching or gluing.
Flat colour	Solid areas of colour.
Folio	The standard imperial paper size 10″ by 15″ that is nearest to A3 and is still occasionally used by some to mean A3 posters.
Four-colour process	The printing method used to produce full-colour print. This is the only method of reproducing colour photographs on posters and leaflets. It involves a computerised scanning process which analyses the colours and reduces them to variable sizes of dots made up of the four process colours: cyan, magenta, yellow and black. When printed on top of each other, these colours give the optical illusion of any other colour.
Four sheet	The standard imperial size for posters 60″ by 40″ still occasionally used to mean the metric equivalent.
gsm	The thickness and density of paper is measured in grammes per square metre by literally weighing a square metre. Leaflets, posters and programmes are usually between 100gsm and 170gsm. Card starts at about 250gsm.
Half-tone	A photograph that has been screened to convert the continuous tones of grey into black dots of varying sizes.
Hanging card	This refers to the practice of putting a loop of string through a poster printed on thin card and which lists the season's productions. Some people still use the term to refer to an A3 season poster although the last theatre to produce hanging cards stopped doing so about ten years ago.

Job	This is how printers refer to each set of prints they have been asked to produce: 'Your job is on the machine' means that your leaflets are being printed now.
Laminated	Sealed with a very fine gloss or matt plastic coating – can be used on the covers of high quality season brochures.
Landscape	A horizontal image, poster or brochure:
Laser proof	A final print-out of your artwork from the computer file.
Literal	Typesetting mistakes by the person doing the typesetting rather than by you. You should not be charged for these.
Lower case	Characters that are not capitals (see *upper case*).
Machine proof	A printed version of your piece of print taken from the actual plates the printer will use and made on a special proofing press.
Moiré	A chequered pattern that spoils a half-tone when it has been screened from an image that is already a half-tone itself.
Offset lithographic printing (offset litho)	The most popular printing method for producing posters and leaflets. You can produce large quantities of high quality print very quickly using this method.
Overprinting	The process of printing additional information in a single colour onto a piece of print. This might involve details of each of the venues on a tour.
Pantone	An international system for telling the printer the proportions for mixing standard colours to create the exact colour you have chosen. Designers specify a colour by giving its Pantone number. Most have swatches which contain examples of all the different Pantone colours.
Plates	Plates are usually thin metal sheets onto which the design is 'etched' photographically. Ink is applied to the plate to transfer the etching to paper via a big roller known as the blanket. Each colour has a separate plate.
Portrait	A vertical image, poster or brochure.
Printing two up	Each sheet of paper fed through the printing press has two copies of your piece of print printed on it. A leaflet printed eight up would have eight copies on each sheet. Once all the leaflets or posters are printed, the printer will cut out each one from the sheets using an electronic guillotine.

Registration	Making sure that each colour is printed precisely on top of the others.
Reversing out	The text or image is printed in negative form, e.g. instead of printing black type on white paper, you could create a solid black area with white letters showing through.
Run-on cost	The cost of an extra quantity of print while your job is still on the machine, usually a round figure like 1,000 leaflets or 100 posters.
Saddle-stitching	A process very similar to stapling.
Scan	A computerised process that turns a colour photograph into a series of dots made up of the four process colours (see *colour separation*).
Screen printing	This printing method involves squeezing thick ink through a screen that has had the fine mesh blocked up with gelatine in the areas to be left blank so that the ink cannot get through. It is a cheap way of printing relatively small numbers of posters but does not reproduce fine detail well.
Self cover	A cover on a brochure that is printed on the same paper as the insides.
Show through	When paper is used that is too thin or transparent, one side of the page shows through to the other.
Specials	An ink colour used in addition to the four process colours, e.g. a metallic or fluorescent ink.
Standard colours	These are usually cheaper than other colours because they come straight out of a tin.
Stock	The material on which a piece of print is printed.
Turn around	The amount of time a printer will take to print your leaflet or poster, etc.
Upper case	Capital letters.
Web offset	A printing method that is most often used for large quantities of full-colour magazines. It prints four-colour process at high speed onto a continuous roll of paper.

5 HOW TO WORK WITH YOUR GRAPHIC DESIGNER

1 DO YOU NEED A GRAPHIC DESIGNER?

It is not strictly necessary to use a professional graphic designer for producing print. With a great deal of practice, you may be able to produce reasonable results by using computer design software and a photocopier inventively. However, graphic design is skilled work and you will always benefit from contracting a professional person to do this for you.

Do not assume that you will save money by not using a graphic designer. You may sell more tickets by using a professional-looking piece of print that reflects the quality of your show, festival or venue. An experienced graphic designer will be able to use paper and colour imaginatively to save you money and may be able to get a better deal with a printer.

Season brochures present complex design problems because of the difficulties of organising the information and the sheer quantity of images and copy. Some organisations trying to do the design work themselves produce distressingly unattractive print that is often illegible because they do not know enough about the way that typefaces, half-tones, colours and paper behave. It is difficult to understand why they persevere as there is no point in producing print that does not sell tickets. It would be better not to use print at all.

Some organisations pay a professional graphic designer to produce a basic design template for posters or season brochures and then for each tour or season they themselves drop the images and the copy into the spaces provided. This can be a false economy as it is time-consuming for all but the simplest piece of print. Marketers often find that the process takes up a disproportionate amount of their time that might be better spent communicating with potential audiences.

2 CHOOSING A GRAPHIC DESIGNER

Look at other organisations' print. Start collecting leaflets and posters that you think do their job particularly well. Most designers credit themselves on anything they design – look on the back at the bottom or up the side. If a particular piece of print has no credit on it, telephone the organisation and ask for contact details. You can also ask around for recommendations.

You do not need to limit yourself to arts organisations – most graphic designers take on a wide variety of work, e.g. book covers, record sleeves. However, it usually helps if the designer has a clear understanding of your type of organisation and knows what marketing is about.

Identify a shortlist of graphic designers and find out what they tend to charge. Choose two or three whose work you think is appropriate for your needs and is effective in conveying a marketing message to an audience. Meet them and ask to see more examples of their work. Find out what they might be like to work with. Their job is to communicate your message effectively to your target audience. It is not to produce a great piece of art. This means that they need to be willing and able to translate your written and verbal brief into visuals. They need to understand the importance of well-structured, legible information that leads the reader through your piece of print.

Choose the designer who you think is most appropriate to your needs and will be easy to work with.

3 PAYING GRAPHIC DESIGNERS

Graphic designers usually charge a basic fee plus expenses. They need to know how you will use your design before they can work out the fee they will charge you. If you are asking them to create a design template which you will use to produce print in-house in the future, their basic fee will be higher than if you want them to design subsequent versions of that template themselves.

Expenses can include typesetting, photocopying, fees for using images, materials and any courier services. Expenses can be hard to estimate as they may change during the design process. Ask your designer to keep you informed of any overspend on the agreed expenses.

It is not appropriate to ask graphic designers to 'pitch' for a job without paying them. Pitching involves asking two or three designers to respond to a brief and produce ideas. You then choose the idea you like best. This is the same as insisting that designers work for free. It usually indicates that you and your colleagues have not developed an effective design brief and do not really know what you want to communicate. Your decision on which designer to work with is highly likely to be based on personal preferences and not on whether the designer has effectively communicated your message to the target groups you have chosen.

Effective design is not about producing visuals that appeal to you or your colleagues. You are not your audience. You may not even personally like it but it is good design if it appeals to your target groups.

REMEMBER ✳

Getting the best from designers

1.   Do not ask them to work speculatively for free.
2.   Judge their record from their portfolio and in discussions.
3.   Ensure they can work sympathetically with your organisation.
4.   Be very clear about the size of your budget.
5.   Get them on your side so that they know your needs.
6.   Help them to feel part of the arts environment.

4 BRIEFING YOUR DESIGNER

Once you have found a designer suited to your needs you must brief them thoroughly. You need to tell them who you want to talk to, what you want to say to them and then how you will use the print to get that message to the right people.

For the sake of consistency and clarity, it is usually best if only one person briefs and liaises with the designer, even if several people are involved in producing the print. You will need to involve your organisation's creative team including the director or choreographer in creating the brief.

> I don't like to end up dealing with half a dozen different people who all feel they have something to say.

> Working with a collective can be murder. It is almost impossible to work with a collective of eight. One will hate pink, another will hate serif typefaces. In any case only one or two will be visually aware and have noticed how print works.

> It can be useful to meet with the director, choreographer or artistic director early on but after that I prefer to deal with the person responsible for marketing. Print is the responsibility of the marketing person, who should be the one who knows about it. Artistic directors usually don't know much about it so it is the marketer's job to filter any useful information they may have through to me.

Explain the purpose of the print to the designer. Tell them what your message is and outline the particular benefits that need to be communicated and your target groups.

Supply any copy you have at this stage, including the box office telephone number, etc. Discuss all the different aspects of print production:

- the types of print you want and their respective sizes
- the sort of paper
- the number of colours
- which colours
- the use of photographs or other images
- the amount of copy
- any overprinting
- logos
- which printers might be appropriate.

The form on page 68 is a good way of summarising what you want to achieve. Give them any background information about your organisation: your promotional material; your letterhead; any merchandise; and examples of previous print as appropriate. Give them a script if you have one.

It can be really useful to have information that, on the face of it, seems irrelevant. I like to see in advance the script and copies of any previous print the company has produced so I have an idea of what we are dealing with and I know the names of the characters so we have something in common to talk about when we meet.

Graphic designers usually think visually, so if you have any ideas you want to suggest for the print, try to use images as well as words to convey these. Show images from books or magazines if you have any, but do not fall into the trap of becoming set on a particular image before the briefing.

It is very useful to have some visual back-up even if it is not something that will necessarily appear on the finished print. A video would be very helpful.

It is important that the marketing person is not too tied down with ideas in advance, for instance bringing along a specific photograph.

This graphic designer cites the example of a publicist who brought along a well-known photograph that the company wanted to use on the print. The copyright was unavailable so the company insisted on re-shooting it using a model. Even so, the result was very different to the original photograph and neither the company nor the designer was happy.

Ask the designer if any components of the design need itemising separately when you get the print quotes, e.g. large solid areas or half-tones. Agree which printers will be contacted for quotes. Agree who will contact the printers. Make absolutely sure that the designer gets in touch with the printer before they start work to find out in what format they need the artwork to be supplied. Not all graphic design software packages are compatible.

Give the designer a copy of your schedule for reference. After the briefing, confirm in writing all the arrangements you have made. This is very important as there are lots of small details involved in print production.

5 MANAGING YOUR DESIGNER

1. Match the designer to the job.
2. Make clear their relationship to you.
3. Prepare a clear design brief agreed by all your colleagues involved in the approval process.
4. Set realistic project deadlines and make sure that everyone understands and sticks to them.
5. Help them find out about your organisation and let them experience the work you do.
6. Communicate clearly and candidly.
7. Set and maintain high standards for the work.
8. Be flexible – think about unusual solutions too.

5.1 GIVING FEEDBACK

- Be objective. Ask yourself 'Does this design fulfil the brief?'
  Comments such as 'I don't like it' are unfair and unprofessional.

- Try to give constructive and specific comments.

- Be firm – you are the customer.

- No detail is too small for consideration.

5.2 EVALUATE YOUR PRINT

Talk to your designer about the print after your production is over.

- Did you achieve your objectives?

- In terms of your target for the project as a whole, was the response
  good or bad?

- Was it cost effective?

- Were lead times and deadlines appropriate?

- What are the views and comments of work colleagues?

- What did audiences think?

- What lessons did you learn from this project?

- Which elements would you be sure to repeat?

- Which elements would you like to throw out?

DESIGN BRIEF

PROJECT TITLE

What do you want this piece of print to achieve?

Describe the product.

Who is it aimed at (target audience)?

What is the message you want to communicate to the target audience?

Tone of voice?			
Format			
Usage			
Size		Colours	
Quality		Quantity	
Delivery deadline			
Key dates			
Design budget			
Print budget			
Funding credits			
Images			

Project team

Main contact

6 HOW TO USE PHOTOGRAPHS

SEE ALSO CHAPTERS
4. HOW TO PRODUCE PRINT
12. HOW TO GET PRESS AND MEDIA COVERAGE
16. HOW TO CREATE EFFECTIVE DISPLAYS
20. TALKING TO THE RIGHT PEOPLE
21. TALKING ABOUT THE RIGHT THINGS

1 WHAT ARE PHOTOGRAPHS FOR?

Photographs are a form of communication. They are fairly expensive to produce, but are essential for communicating in visual ways. They are used to market the arts in the following ways:

- in newspapers and magazines to accompany previews, listings, reviews and features, or on their own with a short caption – providing a good photograph increases the likelihood of getting coverage, especially in the local press on posters and in leaflets
- in season brochures
- on displays in venues or elsewhere.

Each of these uses requires a different sort of photograph.
All the photographs that you use have two purposes in common:

- to attract attention so that viewers read the accompanying written information
- to communicate something to the viewer to help make them want to see the show.

Therefore what the photos communicate to the viewer is extremely important.

2 PLANNING YOUR PHOTOGRAPHS

Different sections of your potential audience (target groups) are going to be interested in different things about your production (benefits). Photographs are one way of communicating benefits to target groups in order to make them want to see the show.

- Decide what you will use the photographs for.

- Decide which target groups will be reached by each use.

- Select which benefits will appeal to each of these target groups.

- Where you plan to reach more than one target group with a particular set of photographs, work out which benefits will appeal to all of the groups.

- Decide how those benefits are represented visually in the show. Discuss this with the director/choreographer and performer(s) as appropriate. You do not have to show exactly what will appear on stage, and indeed with devised work or dance you will not be able to. Your aim is to communicate the atmosphere of the show and you may use all sorts of visual ideas to do this.

- It is difficult to represent the benefits of a venue visually. Many organisations resort to images of empty auditoria which convey little or nothing to the viewer. The important factor to bear in mind is that a theatre building is very rarely a benefit in itself. What matters are the activities that go on inside, and the feelings that an audience member experiences when taking part in them.

Tag Theatre Company - Julius Caesar (photo: Renzo Mazzolini)

3 TYPES OF PHOTOGRAPH

3.1 PRESS PHOTOGRAPHS

The printing techniques used to produce newspapers are designed primarily for speed and cheapness. Photographs always reproduce badly, although recent technology has improved matters in newspapers like the *Guardian* and the *Independent*. As in lithographic printing, the photographs are 'screened', that is, reduced to a series of black dots. The dots in newspaper photographs, however, have to be comparatively coarse with fewer per square inch. This is because of the way in which they are printed and the poor quality of the paper and ink.

CONTRAST

Fine detail or subtle shades of grey are impossible to reproduce in newsprint so a photograph with a lot of contrast is needed. This means that a suitable photograph is one that has both very dark areas and white areas together with all the shades in between. An unsuitable photograph is one where only one end of the tonal range between black and white is used. This means that the shades of grey that make up the details of the image will be very similar. When screened, they will merge into one and the detail will be lost.

A rough test for suitability is to photocopy the photograph. If the faces become indistinct, or the figures merge into the background, the photo will probably not be suitable for press use. Large areas of black are difficult to print evenly, so keep these to a minimum. Newspapers prefer images with a light background, although if a particularly good photograph has a dark background, it may get used.

FORMAT

The shape of the photograph to be used is dictated by the layout of the page, so you are more likely to get your photo used if you provide both a landscape shot to be used across several columns and a portrait shot to be used down one or two columns.

A newspaper will not necessarily use the whole of the image you have sent. Often they will crop the photograph, cutting off strips at the top, bottom and sides. Sometimes they will just use a small section. A suitable size for press photographs is 10″ x 8″.

CONTENT

Newspaper photographs should be of not more than three people, preferably of one or two. This is because the photo will probably be reduced to a small size so a crowded photo will nearly always lose impact.

Local newspapers are more likely to use movement photographs, e.g. dance or mime, if they show faces clearly. This is because picture editors judge them as they would any other photograph.

COLOUR

It costs little more for your photographer to shoot colour photographs at the same time as black and white. This will involve them using two cameras, and repeating the material to be photographed to allow both to be used.

Good colour photographs are in demand for colour sections in listing magazines, colour supplements, glossy magazines and even as stills on television. Even black and white magazines almost always have colour covers.

Ask the photographer for transparencies, not prints. The quality of an image reproduced from a print is usually very poor. Do not send the original transparencies to the press, as they may get lost. Have duplicates made at a reprographic house. Some photographers provide colour transparencies in photographic mounts. If not, you will have to cut them out and mount them yourself. Ask the photographer how to do this.

Black and white photographs can be hand tinted with colour. The photographer paints semi-transparent colour by hand onto selected areas of the photographic emulsion. The finished photograph will have pastel shades of colour over part of the image. The effect can be used to convey an atmosphere of nostalgia.

CAPTIONS

Label press photographs on the reverse with:

- the name of everyone in the photo (listed from left to right or top to bottom)
- a very short sentence saying what thc photograph shows
- the name of the company
- the name of the photographer
- the name of the choreographer/playwright
- a request that the photo should be returned, with a return address.

Unfortunately it is rare to get more than a small proportion of photographs back from the press. Remember this when you estimate the quantities of prints you require.

Never write the caption directly on to the back of the photograph as this will make indentations on the front which will show when it is screened. The best way is to type onto sticky labels or to sellotape a piece of paper to the back. Never use glue as this will buckle the surface of the photograph.

3.2 POSTERS AND LEAFLETS

You need to consult with your graphic designer before you commission photographs to be used on posters, leaflets and programmes. It is worth arranging a meeting between you, the designer and the photographer. The designer could even attend part of the photo call. These factors must be considered:

- The image must be the right shape for the poster or leaflet and have areas in which to put the name of the organisation, the name of the show if appropriate, and any other information necessary. An image for a one-third A4 leaflet will have to be long and thin. A poster image will probably need to be squarer.
- The printing technique to be used will affect the sort of photograph you

need. Screen printing needs simple images that can be reduced to areas of solid colour.

- A completely white background may be necessary so that the image can be cut out or placed on a different background. The graphic designer may want a black background, or to have a busy background that shows the set and props.
- If the photo is to be specially treated, e.g. with a mezzo-tint or reversing out, this may affect the type of photograph needed.
- The designer may need prints of a particular size.

As with press photographs, an image that shows no more than three people has much more impact and is easier to work with.

It is particularly important that you look carefully at what you need to say about your organisation and the production. The image should be compatible with your corporate identity and convey the appropriate benefits. An unusual or striking photograph is most effective in attracting attention to posters and leaflets. This is particularly important with dance and mime productions which are hard to describe in words.

It is possible to use a computer scanning process to distort photographs, usually vertically or horizontally. The photographer can also distort the image as they are printing it up or can make a collage of various different images. These methods can result in particularly striking effects.

3.3 SEASON BROCHURES

Photographs in season brochures are usually reduced to a very small size because of the quantity of information that must be included alongside them. It is therefore very important to use a photograph with plenty of contrast and depicting just one or two people. Otherwise the image will be virtually unrecognisable.

The image needs plenty of impact to stand out from the crowd. No detail will be visible, so faces should have strong expressions.

3.4 DISPLAYS

Photographs for displays should be as eye-catching as possible. They need to arrest the attention of the casual passer-by. You can add visual interest by providing a range of sizes of photograph. It is not very expensive to enlarge images to 16″ x 20″, which is approximately A3. Additional interest can be provided by mixing landscape and portrait shots. Because they are not going to be reproduced, these photographs can contain atmospheric effects such as grain or light and shade.

Display photographs will survive longer if they are mounted onto card for strength. Photographs that will be particularly well used could be laminated (covered with plastic for protection).

If you cannot afford large colour prints, colour photocopies can be taken from transparencies. These can be very effective.

7 HOW TO WORK WITH YOUR PHOTOGRAPHER

1 COMMISSIONING A PHOTOGRAPHER

Before you commission a photographer, decide what benefits you need to communicate in the various photographs you need and what elements of the production might illustrate these. At the time of the photo session, the show may not even be in rehearsal and there may be no script, but do not feel restricted by this. It is not necessary to use sections from the actual show. If you have talked sufficiently with the director/choreographer and the performers, you should be able to set up some shots between you that reflect what the feel of the show might be. This is often more effective in conveying the benefits of the show than restricting yourself to what actually happens on stage.

1.1 CHOOSING A PHOTOGRAPHER

You now need to decide what photographic style is compatible with your needs and with the organisation's image. Choose a photographer who can produce this style of work.

Talk to other companies about the photographers they use. Ask to see their portfolios of work. It is also important to check that they can work well with different sorts of people.

If you cannot afford to work with a professional photographer, try talking to tutors of photography courses at colleges in your area. Some students produce extremely good work, but you risk things going wrong because of their inexperience. If a student or even a friend or a member of your organisation is going to take the photographs, still go through the process set out below. Indeed, this is even more important to avoid costly misunderstandings.

1.2 PAYING THE PHOTOGRAPHER

Tell the photographer briefly what you need. Discuss:

- what the photos will be used for
- what they need to convey
- the nature of your company (you may wish to send them background information)
- any decisions about shape, size, etc. that you made with the graphic designer
- how many photographs you want and how many copies of each
- when you want them by.

On the basis of this, draw up an agreement in writing with the photographer. This will prevent problems later and may even save money.

There are several ways to pay a photographer:

1. A session fee to cover the time spent taking the pictures.
2. The cost of rolls of film (state a maximum number) and contact sheets (these are tiny copies of the photographs taken straight from the strips of negatives).
3. A price for each print that you want from the contact sheet.
4. A copyright fee (also known as a usage fee) for each photograph that you decide you want to use. This means that you will be able to reproduce it as many times as you choose without paying the photographer any more.

PAY 1, 2 AND 3 ABOVE PLUS:

Agree to buy all your prints from the photographer. This will be more expensive than getting them reprinted commercially, but some photographers insist on this to maintain quality. Agree how much the prints will be, usually one price for single prints and then discounts for quantities (i.e. 11–20, 21–30, 31–50, over 50).

PAY 1, 2 AND 3 ABOVE PLUS:

Agree to buy all your prints from the photographer to an agreed maximum (e.g. 200). Beyond this limit have them reproduced commercially. This can be a much cheaper option.

PAY 2 AND 3 ABOVE PLUS:

A higher session fee than you would in the other three examples so the photographer can make up for not receiving any further income from the set of photographs.

Photographers automatically own the copyright of all their photographs rather  than the organisation that commissions them. This means that most reproduction houses will require you to show them written permission from the photographer before reproducing any photographs.

1.3 BRIEFING THE PHOTOGRAPHER

Once you have agreed a fee, tell the photographer in detail:

- what the photos will be used for

- what they need to convey

- the visual and other starting points for the production if appropriate

- any decisions about shape and size, etc., that you made with the graphic designer

- how many photographs you want, and how many copies of each

- when the photo call will be and when you want the contacts and prints by

- the nature of the photo call – will it be in a studio, on stage or on location?

You may want to send the photographer a script of further background information at this stage.

You must work out which sections of the production to photograph, or set up a series of shots to convey the atmosphere of the show with the director/choreographer, the photographer and the performers. Tell them what each photo must communicate, and any restrictions on size and shape. They will be able to tell you what is most appropriate.

Discuss lighting requirements, whether a backdrop will be required and what props and costumes will be necessary. Many photographers find it useful to see a rehearsal or to talk with the director/choreographer before the photo call.

1.4 THE PHOTO CALL STEP BY STEP

1. Agree with the photographer the amount of time they will need to produce the images you want. This will normally be between two and five hours. If the production is a devised work or dance, the photo call may be the first time that the company works together which will make the session very long.

2. Book the studio or make sure that everyone in the organisation knows that you will be using the stage. It is especially important to liaise with the technicians. Make sure that they know how long the photo call is likely to last so they can plan around it.

3. Talk to the stage management team, if any. Liaise with the people responsible for wardrobe, wigs, props and make-up and ensure that they have been fully briefed.

4. Tell the performers which sections will be photographed and when they will be required. If you are working with dancers, allow time for them to warm up.

5. Discuss the lighting needed. If the photo call is on stage, you will need a very bright lighting state and possibly some of the photographer's own lights to fill in awkward shadows. Ensure that the technicians are prepared for this. If your photo call is in a studio, the photographer will need to provide lighting.

6. Many photographers find it difficult to judge the lighting necessary to allow for black and white performers in the same photograph. This is because different types of skin need different lighting techniques. Ensure that your photographer is prepared for this, otherwise you may end up with photographs that you cannot use.

7. You need to control the photo call. Act as a go-between, telling the performers what the photographer wants them to do. Watch the session carefully to ensure that you are getting the photographs you need. Listen to the photographer and the performers as they will almost always contribute good ideas. You can also keep an eye open for such details as threads hanging from costumes.

8. Everyone is likely to be tense, but they will be more relaxed if they know precisely what is supposed to happen. Make sure that you have given a written schedule to everyone who might be at all involved in the photo call. Talk to them about your aims at the beginning of the session.

9. Relax everybody by providing refreshments and food. Make sure especially that the photographer has everything that they want and be prepared to run errands.

PRODUCTION PHOTO CALLS

Dress rehearsals do not usually produce good photographs unless the photographer is particularly experienced. They will only have one opportunity to catch each moment, and it is likely that the lighting will not be suitable or the performers will be facing the wrong way. Consider having a special session where short sections of the production can be run and repeated. The photographer can then make small changes in them so that they can produce a superb image that is still 'true' to the production. There is a danger that these 'staged' shots will look wooden.

HOW TO WORK WITH YOUR BOX OFFICE

SEE ALSO CHAPTER
26. MANAGING INFORMATION

The box office staff are a crucial part of the marketing process. They are the people in direct everyday contact with your potential audience. They are your organisation's sales force.

Almost all the customers at the box office will belong to one of your priority target groups. While they are purchasing their tickets or making their enquiry, the box office staff have their full attention. This is the perfect time to tell those customers about other events they will enjoy. In Southern Arts' publication *Marketing the Arts*, Hilary Burr says:

> We can spend an awful lot of time, money and ingenuity getting people through the front door and then blow any number of opportunities by not taking the greatest possible advantage of the fact that we have lured them onto *our* territory …
>
> Talking to people is by far the best way of selling tickets … I have been amazed at how easy it can be to persuade people to join our membership scheme, or to buy tickets then and there, instead of letting them 'go away and think about it'. That's why box office staff – the people who actually sell the tickets – are, or should be, the most important resource we've got.

It is essential to make sure that the box office staff have all the information they need to sell tickets to potential customers. If they are fully informed about the benefits of every event in the season, they will be able to make a judgement about which will be most appealing to each customer they meet. They can respond to what the customer buys:

> I know that you will enjoy Nahid Siddiqui's performance tomorrow – she's very good. Did you know that next month we have Priya Pawar and his company who also specialise in Kathak dance?

> You'd get to see Trestle free if you bought a ticket for Les Bubb's performance as well as the ones you've asked for – we're doing a special offer for the festivals.

Have you thought about joining in the beginner's workshop Phoenix are doing on stage the afternoon of the performance? I think it should be fun – people certainly enjoyed the one they did last year.

They can give information that will help a customer make up their mind:

The company have suggested that the play may not be suitable for children under 12 because there is some bad language. It is swearing rather than anything obscene so it really depends how you feel about that.

A 'piano tour' means that the music will be performed by a pianist rather than a full orchestra. But you'll still get the whole opera sung really well and the performers will all be in full costume.

They can also sell tickets by being helpful to the customer:

I'm very sorry but that performance is sold out. There are good tickets available for the next day, or if you wanted to go out on that particular night, we have another play on in the studio. It's not a comedy but it's very good.

The actual ticket buying process should be as pleasant as possible. If it is not, people are less likely to repeat the experience:

Do [your customers] have to elbow their way through a milling throng of your box office receptionist's friends? … Or do they have to crick their necks and raise their voices to communicate through a little grille and inch-thick glass to a frosty lady more interested in the persistently ringing telephone? **Hilary Burr, *Marketing the Arts***

Because we know our audiences so well, we can put together people who we think might want to sit next to each other. We can also keep apart people who don't like each other. We can put single people next to others who we think they might like to join. **Director, theatre in rural Scotland**

Some promoters operate very successful incentive schemes for their box office staff. They give them sales targets and offer pay incentives if these are reached. The schemes often make the staff feel more involved in the organisation and certainly add to their motivation.

If the box office staff are to function as a sales force, they need to be kept fully informed. Promoters should hold a briefing session as a matter of course before each season, paying particular attention to unfamiliar art forms. They should understand the way that each event is being marketed and the target groups on which to focus. If possible, box office staff should see rehearsals of in-house productions or attend performances by incoming companies at other venues in the region.

1 BOX OFFICE PACKS

Incoming companies need to provide the box office with all the necessary information about their performance(s). Staff need to have summaries of the information they need easily to hand. The best way of doing this is in the form of a box office pack. A pack usually consists of brief notes about each performance mounted on thick card for durability. You could include:

- a plot summary
- a list of benefits
- a list of target groups
- a guide to the pronunciation of difficult titles or names
- a very brief biography of any performers, etc., that the more knowledgeable customers may ask about
- a couple of sentences about the company
- brief notes about the art form if it is unfamiliar.

For easy reference, the box office staff sometimes like to stick your information to the back of the seating plans or input it into the information window of their box office computer system.

FEEDBACK

The box office staff are in a position to give you information. They have face-to-face contact with the public, so can give you feedback about the response to particular events, to any print you produce, to sales promotion schemes and so on.

NAME CAPTURING

Your most important target group is the people who attend your events already. They are the people most likely to want to see other, similar events. It is crucial to ensure that as many of this group as possible make repeat purchases.

The best way to communicate with this target group is to send them a direct mail package telling them that they are likely to enjoy a forthcoming event because it is similar to the one they have already seen and liked. To do this you need their names and addresses.

Box office computers record the names and addresses of attenders automatically. It is also possible to do this manually. Give the box office staff pads of printed slips and ask them to fill in the name and address of the customer and the name of the show they are attending as they make a sale. Explain why this is important. Clearly, if the box office is very busy, e.g. during the half hour leading up to a performance, they will not be able to do this. However, at all other times, they should ensure that the information is recorded. If this is not possible, it is likely that the box office is understaffed – a problem that must be remedied.

EARTHFALL BOX OFFICE BRIEFING SHEET

Rococo Blood running time is 1 hour 10 minutes with no interval

Rococo Blood is the latest production from Cardiff's internationally acclaimed dance theatre company earthfall. Rococo Blood is a combination of dance, drama, boxing, live music and visual images, in a fast-moving, exciting and accessible performance. With emotion and humour, poignant personal histories of love, hate, truth and lies are unmasked in cinematic fusion by powerful dance theatre to trip-hop, choice samples and cutting-edge live music.

The Production is accessible to everyone above 14.

Selling Points:

- Earthfall are an internationally renowned company, praised for their exciting, groundbreaking and intelligent work.

- Earthfall have just won the BAFTA Cymru Award for Best Short Film which will be broadcast on BBC1 in 2000.

- Risk-taking, exciting and powerful dance – this is new, exciting, different – more than dance.

- This is not orthodox contemporary dance – this is new, exciting, different – more than dance.

- Rococo Blood is 'total theatre" – drama, dance, live music and text – so there's something for everyone.

- Original live music from established musicians

- Rococo Blood is vital, energetic and skilful

- Strong narrative and thought-provoking drama

- Emotional depth and humour

Recommended for anyone from 14-80. The show contains some strong language.

There are 6 performers, including 2 musicians providing live music throughout the performance. The composers have worked with Travis, The Blue Aeroplanes, jazz-punk combo Blurt, Grand Drive, The Wood Children and most recently with Onalee from Reprazent. The Other performers have worked with many other renowned film, dance and physical theatre companies alongside earthfall.

Themes
- Bigotry and boxing
- Poetry and boxing
- Political Dance, humour and taboos
- Biographies of fact and fiction
- Hypocrisy
- Love, lust, hate and violence to your partner
- Psychology and tyranny within human relationships
- Personal Histories

THE PLACE THEATRE
FREEPOST WC3948
17 DUKES ROAD
LONDON
WC1 9BR

with

dance

FREE!

JOIN THE PLACE THEATRE MAILING LIST

the **place** theatre

17 Duke's Road
London WC1H 9AB
Box Office:
0171 387 0031

9 HOW TO DISTRIBUTE YOUR PRINT

There are many ways of distributing printed information. You will not be able to undertake all of them. Look carefully at your target groups and select the methods that reach them most effectively.

REMEMBER ✳

Do not waste too much of your valuable time doing unskilled tasks. It is often better value for money to employ casual staff to do leaflet drops, leaving you to carry out the tasks for which you have specialised knowledge.

Many regions have distribution systems run by the regional Arts Marketing Agency, by consortia of arts organisations or by independent companies. They are often good value for money as the costs are shared between a number of organisations.

A touring Black theatre company organises their marketing on a regional basis. The venues are grouped according to the Regional Arts Board and all those in each area are included on the same piece of print. This means that the company can pool the small amounts of money available for each venue and so afford bulk distribution. The marketing and press representative working for them part-time says:

> The advantages for distribution were obvious. Some of the venues were very close. They were sending their leaflets to the same places anyway. Some of them weren't sending their leaflets anywhere at all. Now we are able to cover a whole area with one leaflet.

1 AUDIENCES CAN COME TO YOU FOR INFORMATION

The following methods allow you to maintain communication with existing audiences and make contact with casual callers.

1.1 LEAFLETS & POSTERS AVAILABLE IN THE VENUE

You will be unable to keep track of the people who are interested enough in your events to pick up a leaflet or look at a poster. Consider making attractive mailing list application forms available alongside the other information.

1.2 INVITE PEOPLE TO PAY TO JOIN A MAILING LIST IF THEY WANT INFORMATION

This method allows you to contact only particularly enthusiastic existing audiences. This means that you can be sure that they are a priority target audience, but the number of contacts you can make is severely limited because it excludes all but the most committed. The income from the membership fees will help to cover the cost of postage.

In 1989 funding cuts meant that an Asian arts centre in London had to start charging for membership of their mailing list. Full membership costs £11.75 a year which includes membership of the centre and the benefits that involves. This is half-price to residents of the borough. A simple information service with no other benefits attached costs £3 a year.

1.3 INSERTIONS

Information can be slipped into programmes, handed out to audiences or inserted into ticket envelopes for appropriate shows at the relevant venue or similar shows at other venues nearby.

2 YOU CAN LEAVE INFORMATION OUT FOR PEOPLE TO PICK UP

These methods allow you to make information available to a wide range of people but because of this you can only communicate in a general way with all-purpose print. You will be unable to keep track of who has expressed interest by picking up information. These methods require relatively large quantities of print.

2.1 VENUE DISTRIBUTION SYSTEM

Most promoters have a system that distributes their print to libraries, Citizens Advice Bureaux, other venues, shops, restaurants, pubs, sports centres, doctors' waiting rooms. These lists are often patchy because of the lack of time to research and maintain them. There will inevitably be a lot of other information in these places which competes for the onlooker's attention. The material will reach a large number of people but a relatively large proportion of these will not be in your target groups. The systems normally cover the immediate neighbourhood of the venue comprehensively and become more selective further away. In adjacent towns, print may only be distributed to prime sites such as other arts venues, libraries, galleries, bookshops, etc.

2.2 OTHER CENTRALISED DISTRIBUTION SYSTEMS

Other organisations have centralised systems to distribute their own information and some may include your print in them. These systems include: county library internal mail; Local Education Authority internal mail to schools; internal mail to council employees; and 'desk drop' or pigeonhole distribution in large businesses.

2.3 SPECIALISED DISTRIBUTION

Distribution systems can be set up that focus on particular benefits of an event or series of events. These allow carefully targeted distribution, e.g. venues distributed information about Hull Truck's play about hairdressers, *Cut and Dried*, to hairdressing salons throughout their catchment area by using Yellow Pages. If you make the link with the performance clear, people will usually be willing to help by displaying or passing on the information.

Other specialised distribution includes reciprocal promotions, e.g. a fast-food chain made information about a children's show available to all their customers in return for the opportunity to promote a fizzy drink to audiences at the show. This specialisation allows information to be relatively well targeted. Instead of, or as well as, using all-purpose print it is possible to produce printed or photocopied material to communicate the appropriate benefits. It is not possible to follow up any interest shown.

2.4 TRANSPORT ADVERTISING

This includes placing specially produced advertisements on tube trains and buses and large posters at railway and underground stations. This method reaches large numbers of people, but in an indiscriminate manner. Most of the people who see the information will not be interested. The onlooker has to make an effort to record the information necessary for them to take action by buying a ticket. This method can be very effective for events with a wide appeal. It is relatively expensive.

2.5 FLYPOSTING

This entails putting posters up in unofficial sites such as hoardings, telephone cable boxes, lamp posts and trees. It provides an extremely effective blanket coverage of an area. It is, however, illegal. Your organisation, the staff member responsible and the person caught pasting up the posters could be arrested and fined for flyposting. Local authorities are now no longer allowed to turn a blind eye to flyposting. If you do choose to risk flyposting, you will need large numbers of posters – to cover a neighbourhood of London or Manchester you will need approximately 700 posters.

10 HOW TO CREATE A DIRECT MARKETING CAMPAIGN

SEE ALSO CHAPTERS
3. HOW TO WRITE COPY
11. HOW TO CREATE A SALES PROMOTION
24. MARKET RESEARCH
26. MANAGING INFORMATION

1 WHY DIRECT MARKETING WORKS

Most people are very bad at making decisions. They have to be persuaded to take action. Of course you will not be able to change their minds if they do not want what you are offering, but you *can* persuade the ones that are interested to do something about it.

When they look at a piece of printed information about an event or set of events, the potential audience member asks 'What's in it for me?' You must answer that question in order to persuade them to buy. Each target group will be interested in different things about the event so will be looking for different answers to the question. This is why the more personalised you can make your communication, the more likely you are to get a response – you can give the right people the right answer to 'What's in it for me?'

Direct marketing techniques involve writing to or telephoning carefully chosen people with targeted information. This usually means collecting information about individuals in your audience so you must stick to some simple rules in order to comply with the Data Protection Act.

Small organisations find direct marketing methods very useful. Far more of the people you contact will be actively interested in what you have to offer, because you have chosen them carefully. The more precisely you target, the fewer people you have to contact to reach your goal and the smaller the cost. This means excellent value for money.

Direct marketing does have a drawback. If you target too precisely, you are only ever getting in touch with people who are similar to the ones who already attend. This can prevent you broadening your audience. You need to find a balance between the two extremes based on the resources you have available. Each time you distribute information in this way, you could choose a small group of non-attenders to target, expanding your audience little by little.

1.1 DIRECT MAIL

It isn't terribly effective. I suppose people aren't used to receiving direct mail. It's quite a turn-off to get a selling tool for a small venue. I've come across a few letters from people complaining about the gimmicky nature of a mailshot brochure. **Director, mixed programme venue, rural Wales**

Some people look upon this sort of marketing as 'junk mail'. Junk mail is simply inappropriate mail that tells people about something irrelevant to them. Arts organisations have a head start because a good night out is something almost everyone wants to hear about.

Avoid sending junk mail by:

- targeting accurately so that you write relevantly

- taking note of what people say, e.g. removing them from your list if they request this

- spelling their name correctly and ensuring that you have the right address.

Subscription schemes are usually sold most effectively by direct mail. Target groups for subscription schemes consist of existing theatregoers at the venue and elsewhere. Lists of current and lapsed subscribers easily available through the box office can be mailed with personalised letters addressing them as 'special' customers.

For the geographical area we're covering, direct mail is really the only way … It's a matter of getting to people individually – putting print in the relevant people's hands. It's just about targeting really. **Marketing officer, theatre company touring to non-traditional venues in rural areas, England**

1.2 TELEPHONE SELLING

Mail is not the only way to get in touch directly with your target groups. Telephone selling is a highly effective form of communication because:

- you can find out about the person you are talking to and offer something relevant to them

- they can ask you questions

- you can answer their objections

- it can be an informal and friendly way to communicate.

Your box office staff are likely to have collected the telephone numbers of people who have bought tickets for your events so they can ring them if there is a problem with the booking or with the performance. This makes the telephone a potentially quick and cheap way of talking to them in the future.

You could use telephone selling to follow up a direct mail package. This should dramatically increase the number of responses by jogging people into action.

For small-scale arts organisations, telephone selling is only feasible if the list is very precisely targeted and fairly small. There are professional telephone sales people you can hire to call large target groups but you probably will not be able to afford this if you have a small budget.

1.3 E-MAIL

Some venues have set up direct marketing campaigns using e-mails. This is particularly successful in those towns and cities where there are a lot of businesses with staff who use computers, such as university towns. An e-mail campaign involves inviting people to join an e-mailing list and sending them direct marketing communications on-line. The most successful campaigns get people involved with the organisation, so that they feel they can have an on-line dialogue by commenting and giving feedback.

2 THE ESSENTIALS

You need to think about five things when you plan a direct marketing campaign:

1. What you want to achieve (your objectives).
2. Who you want to get in touch with (the list).
3. What you are offering them (the offer).
4. How you will tell them about it (the direct mail package or telephone sales script).
5. When you will say it (timing).

2.1 SETTING OBJECTIVES

Whether you choose to use direct mail or the telephone, you need to be clear about why you are doing it and what you want to achieve. Do not start thinking yet about what kind of direct marketing campaign you might run. Instead decide:

- **What is the issue or problem that you want to tackle?** e.g. people are increasingly buying their tickets just a couple of days before the performance.
- **What is your campaign for?** e.g. to persuade regular attenders to buy their tickets earlier.
- **What, exactly, do you want to achieve?** e.g. to increase the proportion of people buying tickets between four and eight weeks in advance from 12% to 20%.
- **When do you want to achieve it by?** e.g. for the four-week run of the musical in September/October.

Your objective could involve numbers of people who respond to your campaign, the number of tickets you sell as a result of your campaign or the amount of money that respondents spend on their tickets.

Now, decide how much you are willing to spend on your campaign. You could express this in two ways:

- For every £1 I spend on this direct marketing campaign, I want to bring in £7.

- I want to bring in £3,500 in ticket sales by spending £500, giving a net income of £3,000.

Helen Dunnett at Buxton Opera House ran a very successful telephone campaign with Arts About Manchester. She called the scheme TelePrompt and it was designed to persuade first-time attenders to reattend She wanted to test whether the telephone would be a successful way of doing this, so she set up a control group who would not be contacted and a test group who would. She could then compare how many tickets the two groups bought to see how effective the campaign had been. Her objective was 'to call 400 patrons, getting hold of 250 of them and recruiting 200 to the scheme.' The results were impressive even though the campaign did not take a 'hard sell' approach but aimed to develop a relationship with each first-time attender and give them the information they needed to choose what to see next.

	Control group	TelePrompt group
Number of people	200	200
Booked tickets during the test period	6%	27%
Income per ticket buyer	£1.25	£9.00

Collecting this information means that she can now set measurable objectives for income and attendance for the next stages of the campaign.

> We didn't offer any discounts on tickets or any added value offers like tours, talks or other events. All we did was talk about the shows and, if they were interested in any of them, the next day sent an information sheet headed 'The Facts About the Show'. People just needed detailed information to convince them this was something they wanted to see. **Helen Dunnett, Marketing Manager, Buxton Opera House**

2.2 THE OFFER

Who you get in touch with and what you offer them are the most important elements of a direct marketing campaign. Get these wrong and no amount of creative thinking about letters and telephone scripts can make your campaign work.

The term 'offer' here simply means how you talk about what you're offering the potential audience member and the incentive you give them to respond.

REMEMBER ✳

To make an effective offer, you need to know what it is about your event or venue that the people on your list think is most important. It does not have to involve money off – many existing and potential attenders simply do not think that ticket price is important and will not respond to discounts.

CASE STUDY

Chris McGuigan from Symphony Hall decided that the most important benefit for a children's concert was that it gave parents something to do with bored children over half-term. He made the offer 'We'll keep your kids entertained!' and went on to promise 'Boredom will be banished as kids are invited to explore the wonders of a symphony orchestra – 100 musicians on stage with no amplification necessary'. He did not overtly offer money off tickets but said 'Booking is child's play' and instead offered the convenience of a ticket for any group of four at £18 (although this is in fact cheaper than full-price tickets) – he does not think that his potential audience is particularly worried about price.

3 SETTING UP A DIRECT MAIL CAMPAIGN

3.1 THE LIST

FREE MAILING LISTS

Venue mailing lists

If you do not have a box office computer system, a highly important method of distribution is a free mailing list made up of audience members at previous events. When you collect people's names and addresses, you should ask about their interests so that you can divide up the list.

> We do three mailings, timed to arrive on Saturdays. We more or less sell all our seats through mailings. We have a list of 300 addresses in the area. We spend a lot of time researching that mailing list, keeping it up to date and adding to it. When new people move to the area, if they happen to visit the Arts Centre to see the exhibition, we try to get them on the mailing list which is free. **Director, arts centre operating part of the year, Scotland**

If you have computer facilities available, these categories can be very specific to help with precise targeting, e.g. opera lovers can be divided into romantic opera, contemporary opera and chamber opera. Use the results of any audience research to check what other art form interests attenders at particular types of event, e.g. attenders at visual theatre events are likely to enjoy dance performances. Unfortunately research, particularly by Roger Tomlinson when helping venues install new box office computer systems, shows that there can be a vast difference between people's stated interests and their actual attendance.

A much better way of targeting people is to discover what shows each person has attended. Most box office computers can do this. Even if you do not have one, your organisation should try to record the names and addresses of attenders at particular shows through the box office. These people are definitely interested in the particular product and are prime targets for similar events. A direct mail letter that says 'You enjoyed Frantic Assembly's performance so you will enjoy this show by Blast Theory' is likely to produce results. To help the box office staff, give them each a pad of pro-formas. If they are too busy to collect names and addresses, then your box office is probably understaffed.

You must keep your mailing list up to date because people move house on average every seven years and students only stay at the same address for twelve months at a time. Make sure that your organisation's address is on the envelope so that the Royal Mail can return undeliverable letters to you. If you cannot afford to have your envelopes printed then use a rubber stamp, a sticky label, or even print your address in tiny type along the top of the customer's address label.

Be creative about which art form sections to use – look at the results of your research and then think laterally. For a contemporary classical music event, Cambridge Corn Exchange targeted people with eclectic tastes. They mailed people who had been to at least three events in the past 18 months, including one traditional event like ballet or a Beethoven concert, one rock or comedy event plus something contemporary.

If you are working in areas where people prefer to communicate in a language other than the one most often used in your organisation, then give people the opportunity to opt to receive information in the language of their choice and record this in their customer record on your box office computer system.

The list should also include potential party bookers such as the social secretaries of local societies and groups. These are important target groups because there can be a high return on any effort to sell to them – instead of selling two or three tickets, you could sell 20 in one go. Only try to sell appropriate events to party bookers and, just as before, the more personalised the approach, the better the result, e.g. a tailored mailing to youth theatres for an adventurous drama company.

With this sort of mailing list, you can assume that fairly like-minded people live in the same areas. You can gain new audiences by looking at your existing list and mailing the immediate neighbours of everyone on it with an offer of regular information about your events. Where there are two people on the list from a particular street, mail each of their immediate neighbours plus one house on either side; where there are three people, mail the neighbours plus two houses on either side; where there are four or more, mail the whole street.

You must keep your mailing list up to date because people move house on average every seven years and students only stay at the same address for twelve months at a time. Make sure that your organisation's address is on the envelope so that the Royal Mail can return undeliverable letters to you. If you cannot afford to have your envelopes printed then use a rubber stamp, a sticky label, or even print your address in tiny type along the top of the customer's address label. Whatever you do, do not delete these people from your mailing list or you will never again have an accurate picture of your audience. Instead use your particular box office computer system's method for indicating 'Do not mail' and remember to take these people out of your selection each time you choose to whom you want to mail.

Company mailing lists

Companies should keep a record of attenders at their productions for mailing with information, perhaps including a newsletter as a way of maintaining interest until the company's next visit. Collect the names and addresses by including an attractive mailing list application form on your leaflets, programmes and questionnaire forms (if you have them), or by slipping a form into programmes.

Other mailing lists

Joint mailings

Promoters and companies can either swap appropriate sections of lists or insert material into each other's mailings. Arts organisations can also share mailings with commercial organisations, charging them to cover some or all of the postage costs.

Buying lists

You can purchase sections of other arts organisations' lists from, for example, regional marketing agencies, lists from outside the professional arts world such as an amateur dramatic society's membership list or the local Chamber of Commerce list. Commercial list brokers compile large lists of target groups for sale, but these are expensive.

Specialised lists

Specialised mailing lists may be available for some of your target groups: a list of local teachers for an appropriate curriculum area may be held by the Local Education Authority; many national dance agencies have lists of people involved in dance and most arts marketing agencies hold specialist lists. You could compile your own lists of particular businesses through Yellow Pages or business directories which you will find at your local library.

> For *Whale Nation* we targeted local wildlife groups … Greenpeace and things like that which seem to be in abundance round here. We filled it virtually, I should say, on the basis of writing to them. **Administrator, mixed programme venue, Wales**

INFORMATION NETWORKS

Many systems for distributing information already exist for other purposes. Find the key person in this information web and they will distribute information for you, if you can show that the members of the network will benefit. Examples of networks are: volunteer networks at some venues, teachers' support groups, trade union regional organisers, National Women's Register regional organisers, disability transport scheme volunteers, ethnic minority social centres, etc. The networks often have newsletters so you could ask to submit editorial or slip a leaflet into the mailing.

One touring black dance company uses an agency that specialises in marketing to black communities. They estimate that half their audience at their first visit to a large London venue was from those communities.

> We encourage the promoters to use networks. In any community there are networks … If you want to be successful you have to get into these … It varies from place to place who they are and how effective they are. Networking can work against you as well because it needs only a few folk to say 'It doesn't sound like something we really want to see, does it?' and it can just about clean you out! **General manager, theatre company touring to non-traditional and non-professional venues in Scotland**

DOOR-TO-DOOR DISTRIBUTION

This is a way of expanding or setting up your venue mailing list. It works on the principle that like-minded people are likely to live in the same neighbourhoods.

Look at your current mailing list or the results of audience research to see which villages or districts recur. You could also use ACORN (A Classification Of Residential Neighbourhoods) which is a commercial system devised using census returns which can tell you what sort of people live in each area, street by street. Look at the information from Target Group Index and the results from your research information to find out into what ACORN grouping current attenders fall. If you are funded by one of the arts councils or by a regional arts board, they can provide you with the Area Profile Report for the area you are interested in. Use it to search for other postal sectors in your region where there are lots of people from that ACORN group.

Map out a list of areas that look promising. You now need to mail every household in each area. You could do this through the Post Office's Household Delivery Service or through a commercial distribution firm but both of these methods are expensive. A number of small organisations could pool their resources to undertake this, perhaps under the guidance of their regional arts boards.

Most venues have volunteers or groups of casual staff front of house and back stage who could distribute effectively and cheaply. If your resources are very limited, this method would enable you to cover very small areas, perhaps even a single street, at little cost. You need to motivate your volunteers or casual staff and give incentives for good work or you could find that most of the material they should have distributed has ended up in the bin.

Distribute a direct mail package using a general salutation at the head of the letter rather than an individualised one. This can be a highly effective and very cheap form of direct mail.

3.2 THE DIRECT MAIL PACKAGE

If you produce a leaflet (see example on p. 96), it will inevitably take a general approach because it would be too expensive to print a different leaflet for each target group. But a general leaflet, even if it is well written and designed, only goes part of the way towards answering the question 'What's in it for me?' You therefore need to add something to give the specific information required. This will have to be cheap and easy to produce, so the best format is a letter. Roger McCann from marketing experts McCann, Matthews, Millman says that tests have shown that if you miss the letter out you can reduce your response by as much as 50%.

So, if your resources are particularly small it may well be best not to produce leaflets and posters at all. Concentrate your resources on direct marketing using a cheaply produced but effective letter.

The most effective direct mail uses all four of these elements to get its message across:

- **The envelope** – use this to get attention and persuade your potential customer to open it and read on.
- **The letter** – use this to be personal and talk about things that are relevant to that target group of potential customers.
- **The leaflet** – use this to give more information about your offer and to be even more persuasive.
- **Something to help them respond** (a telephone number, freepost address or reply envelope, etc.) – if it is hard to respond, they will not do so.

If you are writing to a target group that prefers to communicate in a language other than the one most often used in your organisation, then get a fluent speaker of that language to write your direct mail letter. Think about how you want your target group to respond. If they do not speak a language familiar to your box office staff, how will you deal with booking forms or telephone calls? It may be best to set up a ticket agent within the community instead.

4 HOW TO WRITE DIRECT MAIL LETTERS

Remember, the purpose of your communication with your target groups is to tell people about the elements of the event or set of events in which they are interested and to persuade them to take action.

Chapter 3, 'How to Write Copy' gives a series of guidelines for writing various types of copy but there are additional factors that you need to bear in mind when writing direct mail. You must comply with the Data Protection Act and only write to people who have given their active consent. You should also check your list with the Mailing Preference Service to make sure that you do not write to people who have said that they do not want to receive direct mail at all. Four letters are given as examples on pp. 97–9.

TAG THEATRE COMPANY
presents

JULIUS CAESAR
by William Shakespeare
in a unique, day-long combination of workshop and performance for primary 4 - 6
for an amazing £2.00 per child!
regular cost is £260 + VAT - Eden Court Theatre / Highland Region will be subsidising the cost for schools

**(For smaller schools it will be possible to include Primary 7's in the project
or you could share the residency with neighbouring schools.)**

In April and May 1999, TAG, Scotland's national theatre company for young people will tour an exciting and energetic 60 minute version of Shakespeare's **JULIUS CAESAR**. More than just a performance, TAG will spend a full day in every school encouraging children to address the issues in the play through a process of communal storytelling.

For the astonishing price of **£200 (+ vat)** TAG can offer you a full day residency in school which includes:

- **3 workshops with up to 100 children**
- **led by experienced, professional drama practitioners**
- **pupils engaged in 'active storytelling'**
- **a 60 minute performance of JULIUS CAESAR using audience participation**
- **also using the power of Shakespeare's language presented in an accessible and understandable form**

TAG's JULIUS CAESAR will feed into the programmes of study for Environmental Studies, in particular issues raised will directly link to *Understanding People in Society* and *Understanding People in the Past*. The main areas covered will be:

- **Studying people, events and societies of significance in the past**
- **Developing an understanding of change and continuity, cause and effect**
- **Developing an understanding of time and historical sequence**
- **Social rules, rights and responsibilities**
- **Conflict and participation in decision-making in society.**

In addition, the workshop programme will encourage pupils to work in groups exploring issues in a practical capacity and to develop the confidence to show initiative and imagination. *A high quality teachers resource pack will accompany the project and will be FREE of charge to all participating schools.*

Only 4 day-long, in-school residencies are available in your area
at a cost of £200 (+ vat) each for up to 100 primary 4 - 6/7 children.
The dates available are w/b 7/6/99.

For further information please contact:
CAROL HEALAS, EDUCATION DIRECTOR on 0141 552 4949.

■ TAG Theatre Company, 18 Albion Street, Glasgow G1 1LH tel: 0141 552 4949 fax: 0141 552 0666 e-mail: tag@glasgow.almac.co.uk ■

TAG Theatre Company is part of the Citizens Theatre Limited. Registered in Scotland No. SC22513 Registered Office: Wylie Frame 166 Buchanan Street, Glasgow G1 2LS Charity No. SC001337

STAMFORD
FOLK & BLUES
GUITAR FESTIVAL

Stamford Arts Centre
27 St Mary's Street, Stamford, Lincolnshire, PE9 2DL

Box Office: 01780 763203
Administration: 01780 480846 **Fax:** 01780 766690

Dear Friend

It's only a week away and bookings are going well but there's still time to make this year's festival a sellout!

This year the focus is much more towards lesser known or new and exciting talent. I feel strongly that the "traditional" exists to evolve whether it be blues or folk guitar. Players like **Woody Mann** and **Gordon Giltrap** (to name but two) are fine examples where their music transcends technique. It's not about how good they are (and they're really good), it's about music that comes from within. That takes a special talent.

You won't be surprised that **John Miller** also has such a pedigree, having featured alongside Woody, John Fahey, Larry Johnson and Jo Ann Kelly on the Blue Goose label in the early 1970's. But this is his first visit to the UK - so I can't overstate how rare an opportunity this is to hear and learn from one of the finest fingerstyle players. I have four of his albums and will be first in the queue for an autograph (sad but true).

I was given a prediction by a guitar playing colleague just yesterday as to the highlight of the weekend ahead (last year it was the late night session in the juke joint, they say): **Tommy Emmanuel**. I've only ever witnessed him action on video, but I can say that, at the very least, he'll leave you astounded. His schedule is so packed that he's playing in Nashville on the Monday evening, the start of an impressive US tour. I've met only one person who has heard of him. You could be the next person to discover him (and witness some brilliant boogie and Chet Atkins-style picking…).

And finally a word about **Michael Roach** who will be playing with wizard harp player Ian Briggs. He was at last weekend's Bishopstock Music Festival, the UK's biggest blues festival which was featured on BBC Music Live and reviewed the day after:
"…I reckon the best value on offer at Bishopstock was the Blues Workshop tent, where you could pick up tips on finger-picking, guitar tunings and harmonica technique from bluesman Michael Roach and friends. Maybe this was the breeding ground for next year's bill."
Adam Sweeting The Guardian Tuesday 30th May 2000

I'm looking forward to another stunning festival. You'll know what the special atmosphere is like - all those people talking and playing guitar for two days. Like last year, I'll be shattered and elated when it's all over. I've already got ideas for next year and I'm more than open to your ideas too - tell me about them.

There's a timetable enclosed of workshops with some indication as to content. Things always change and I apologise in advance if that happens and causes inconvenience. The concerts are firm though and are ideal for partners and families. They deserve to see what the fuss is about.

See you next weekend.

CWMNI'R FRÂN WEN

2 Medi 1998

I Sylw: Y Prifathro
  Cydgysylltwyr A, B a CH
  Cyd-Gysylltydd yr ysgol â'r Cwmni
  Pennaeth Adran Gymraeg
  Pennaeth Adran Ddrama

Annwyl Bennaeth

'Cyffordd'
Prosiect Theatr mewn Addysg ar gyfer Disgyblion Blwyddyn 9

Yn ystod y Tymor hwn bydd y Cwmni yn teithio Ysgolion Uwchradd Gwynedd, Ynys Môn a Chonwy gyda'u prosiect diweddaraf - 'Cyffordd'. Bydd y Cwmni yn cydweithio gyda'r Adran Hybu Iechyd wrth baratoi'r prosiect a'r pecyn gwaith. Bydd y perfformiad ynghyd â gweithdy dilynol, yn sbarduno'r disgyblion i ystyried y ffactorau sy'n dylanwadu ar bobl ifanc i gymryd cyffuriau anghyfreithlon. Llunnir y prosiect gogyfer â Blwyddyn 9.

Amgaeaf wybodaeth pellach ynglŷn â'r prosiect ynghyd â ffurflen archebu sydd i'w dychwelyd i'r cwmni erbyn **dydd Llun, 21 Medi 1998**.

Hoffwn eich atgoffa bod gwasanaeth y Cwmni yn parhau i gael ei gynnig i chwi yn rhad ac am ddim. Gobeithio felly y gwnewch sicrhau bod eich ysgol yn manteisio'n llawn ar ein gwasanaeth.

Diolch am eich cydweithrediad.

Yn gywir

Medwen Lloyd Edwards
Gweinyddwraig

Amg 2

Cyfeiriad/Swyddfa Gofrestredig:
Yr Hen Ysgol Gynradd, Ffordd Pentraeth, Porthaethwy, Ynys Môn, LL59 5HS
Rhif ffôn: 01248 715048   Rhif ffacs: 01248 715225
Gweithreda Cwmni'r Frân Wen sy'n gwmni Theatr mewn Addysg, gyda chymorth
Cyngor Gwynedd, Cyngor Sir Ynys Môn, Cyngor Bwrdeistref Sirol Conwy a Chyngor Celfyddydau Cymru.
Cwmni'r Frân Wen, cofrestredig yng Nghymru. Rhif cofrestredig 3079992
Mae'r Cwmni yn gwmni cyfyngedig dan warant a heb gyfalaf cyfrannau.
Elusen Gofrestredig wedi ei chofrestru gyda'r Gofrestrydd Elusennau. Rhif cofrestredig 1065046.

KEEP YOUR NOISY KIDS ENTERTAINED THIS HALF TERM!

symphony hall
birmingham

Symphony Hall

Broad Street
Birmingham
England B1 2EA

Registered Charity No. 1053937

Director: Andrew Jowett

Telephone +44 (0) 121 200 2000
Facsimile +44 (0) 121 212 1982

www.symphonyhall.co.uk/symphony

Dear Parent

Sunday 18 April   11.30am - 1.00pm
AT HOME AND AWAY with the RPO

Have you got **NOISY KIDS?** If the answer is 'YES' then we want them!

The Royal Philharmonic Orchestra visits Symphony Hall this April with 'At Home And Away', a lively, child-friendly concert which is guaranteed to entertain and excite kids and parents alike.

The concert features orchestral 'tasters' - short pieces of music to whet childrens' appetites - including film score favourites, stories and anecdotes plus the chance to learn about life as a musician. In addition the audience will be asked to help compose a piece of music from scratch, illustrating some of the amazing sound effects an orchestra can create.

No musical experience is necessary to participate in this lively, fun-packed event. It's ideal for children who can't sit still!

IT'S EASY TO BOOK
Simply call our Box Office on **0121 212 3333** and we'll confirm credit / charge card bookings straight away. Tickets are priced at £5.00 (children*) and £8.00 (adults). A family ticket for 4 people can be purchased at £18.00.
Children must be accompanied by an adult.
*Aged 14 and under.

There are still some seats available but tickets are selling fast. So call us now to take part in this fun family concert.

Yours faithfully

Chris McGuigan
PERFORMANCE/MARKETING ASSISTANT

**PS - Remember - the noisier your kids the better!!
Book now on 0121 780 3333**

Registered Charity No. 1053937. Registered in England (No. 3169600). Symphony Hall (Birmingham) Ltd is a subsidiary of The National Exhibition Centre Ltd. Registered office: The National Exhibition Centre, Birmingham B40 1NT.
Directors: Roger S. Burman CBE BSc LLD DL (Chairman) Anita Bhalla Professor George Caird MA FRAM ARCM FRSA Councillor Andrew C. Coulson PhD MA George S. Jonas James Moir Mervyn Pedelty
Councillor D.C. Roy DMS Dennis Scard Miss T. Slater Professor C. R. Timms Company Secretary: Nigel Dudley FCIS
No contract for the grant of a Licence by Symphony Hall (Birmingham) Ltd shall be created until execution of a formal Licence Agreement.

1. Think of your leaflet (if you are using one), your letter and the envelope that contains them as a package. The appearance of the package and the tone of voice you use are very important. Well-written material implies that the show is of high quality.

2. Use a style appropriate to the particular target group. Make your material attractive by adding images from your posters or photographs. Use different typefaces and bold text to emphasise important sections but do not overdo it and make the letter difficult to read.

3. Talk only about the positive aspects of your event or set of events. Pointing out the negative elements of other forms of entertainment or even other venues or productions will make the reader uncomfortable.

4. Use a good framework for your package.

The following framework is based on Christian Brann's book *Cost Effective Direct Marketing*:

GET THE READER'S ATTENTION. Use your envelope to do this. It is expensive to have envelopes printed but you could get your message put onto a large rubber stamp and use it until it wears out. The message tells the recipient that your package is not a gas bill but something exciting and intriguing.

KEEP THE READER'S ATTENTION. Expand on the message on your envelope with a headline at the top of your letter.

MAKE THE LETTER RELEVANT TO THE READER. You know what sort of person you are writing to because they belong to one of your target groups. Refer to this knowledge, e.g. their past visits to the venue or their interests.

SHOW THEM THAT THEY WANT WHAT YOU ARE OFFERING. Base this on the most important benefit of the event or set of events.

MAKE A PROMISE TO SATISFY THAT NEED.

MAKE THEM BELIEVE YOU CAN KEEP THAT PROMISE. They are going to be sceptical about that promise so make them believe you can deliver by using a comment by a past audience member, talking about your organisation's track record, etc.

SUMMARISE THE ESSENTIAL ELEMENTS OF YOUR LETTER SO FAR. This retains their attention and reminds them of why they are interested.

REPEAT THAT YOU CAN DELIVER – make them believe in you.

SUMMARISE THE WHOLE ARGUMENT AGAIN. People do not take things in the first time, so you need to repeat the essentials again and again.

FORCE THEM INTO ACTION. Put a closing date for orders or offer an incentive if they reply within a certain time.

MAKE IT AS SIMPLE AS POSSIBLE TO REPLY. Enclose a self-addressed envelope with a real stamp on (people hate to waste stamps), or use a Freepost address which means that they do not need to use a stamp. You can find out more about Freepost from your regional Royal Mail Business Services Manager.

MAKE SURE THAT YOUR ORDER FORM IS ATTRACTIVE AND SIMPLE TO USE. Use symbols on the form to simplify any complex information and do not expect them to do complex sums. Repeat the benefits on the form to remind them why they have decided to respond. It is better to use the more familiar phrase 'order form' rather than 'booking form' as the latter does not imply that they are making a purchase. Repeat the date of the events, the address of the venue and the box office telephone number.

MAKE A FINAL PUSH. Add a hand-written postscript making a final summary of the most important benefit at the foot of letter. This will make the letter seem more personal. Do not add new information at this stage; reinforce something you have already told the reader.

A long letter is more effective than a short one as long as you press for urgent and immediate action and do not allow your message to be lost in irrelevant waffle. Use simple words and simple sentence structures.

You can increase the number of responses you get by including an added extra to encourage the reader to reply. Consider adding an incentive to reply quickly as the longer they take to act the less likely they are to respond. Try getting a local store to sponsor you by offering a prize such as a crate of wine in a prize draw for all those who respond, plus discount vouchers for those who reply within 14 days.

The box office must be prepared to deal with the direct mail responses. Warn them how many responses you expect so that they can add extra staff to the rota if necessary. It is crucial that you give them information about any special offers that you have devised. Ensure that your mailing does not coincide with other marketing activities, for example the particularly busy time just after a season brochure goes out, to avoid overloading the box office. Customers will not keep on trying to get through if the telephones are engaged.

Measure the results from every distribution that you do. You can code the reply envelopes or the order form by running different colour felt pens down a stack. You will know by the colour of the marks which mailing the booker received.

Over a certain limit, the Royal Mail will offer a rebate on postage costs as long as most of the addresses on your mailing list or database have correct postcodes. Contact your local sorting office for information. Many have a Business Services Manager to answer just such queries.

5 SETTING UP A TELESALES CAMPAIGN

This communication method is highly cost effective because you will achieve a better success rate than you would with direct mail letters. Finding telephone numbers, however, is time-consuming, so it is usually best for small organisations to concentrate on using records from the box office computer system where staff have already collected the phone numbers of people who have bought tickets. You could also use telephone numbers from questionnaires or booking forms. It is essential, however, that you have complied with the Data Protection Act and got people's active consent that you can call them. You should also check your list with the Telephone Preference Service to make sure that you do not call people who have asked not to be.

Making calls is a skilled task so pick the people who are going to do it carefully. You could recruit your colleagues or people from your organisation's volunteer network, if you have one. A good communicator can make five or six calls an hour. To keep them motivated, some organisations offer the people making the calls incentives such as a commission or a prize for sales they make. If you are calling people at home, it is usually best to ring between 6pm and 9pm. Your callers will need to be able to take credit card bookings over the phone.

Write a script for the sales people that structures the call. Do not insist that they stick to it word for word – your potential ticket buyers should feel that they are having a conversation with people from your organisation. The structure of the call will depend on the objective of your campaign.

Here is a structure for a telesales campaign to follow up a mailing based on Keith Diggle's book *A Guide to Arts Marketing*:

- Say hello.
- Introduce yourself and your organisation.
- Explain why you are calling.
- Check that the timing of your call is convenient. Arrange to call back if it is not.
- If the person objects to being called, it is important to make a note against their name on your list or database to make sure that you never call them again.
- Ask if they have decided when they would like to attend.
- If their response is favourable, operate the sales procedure.
- If their response is unfavourable, use the call to verify their name and address and confirm that they still want information about your organisation.
- Say thank you and good evening.

Tara Arts used a telephone sales script to follow up a mailing that contained a letter and an application form for membership. Compare it with the script from Buxton Opera House's TelePrompt campaign (see p. 104) which aimed to build relationships rather than use hard sell techniques:

'Hello, this is Petra Bishai, Marketing Assistant at Tara Arts. I'm just ringing to find out if you've received our current membership letters.'

If NO – check address and full name.

If YES – 'Good, great, wonderful!'

(We've had an enthusiastic response to our plea.)

'Could I take this opportunity to ask you a few questions as we're doing a survey of our audience interests so we can serve your needs best. Have you visited Tara Arts Group recently?'

If NO – 'Which other theatres do you visit?'

If YES – 'Was it …'

☐ Alternative theatre

☐ Drama

☐ Community theatre

☐ International dance/drama

☐ Music

☐ Seminar/lecture

☐ Voluntary help

'We are in the middle of clearing out our mailing list as we have over 1,500 members on our list and this is costing us £4,000 to keep you all informed. We feel it's important to retain this contact, however we're simply unable to afford it. So we've started up a special membership scheme. This keeps you informed five times a year of all the events which are going on at Tara as well as the other exciting venues which use our list for only £3 for the year. However, if you wish to be more generous, we have an executive membership. Do you live in Wandsworth?'

If YES – 'For you we are able to offer a 50% discount on full membership.'
    (Follow on as for NO.)

If NO – 'Full membership entitles you to discounts of up to 50% on your tickets, priority booking and invitations to special events with the chance to meet the director and cast, as well as the mailings. This gives real value for money at just £11.50. We have members from all over the country on this list.

  'If we don't receive any response from you within the next two weeks, we will have to delete your name from the mailing list.

  'Thanks for your time and I'll wait to hear from you. I look forward to talking to you again.'

Script 2

CALL BACK CUSTOMERS FROM FIRST CAMPAIGN

STAGE 1: INTRODUCTION

Did they receive info requested last time?
Did they find it useful / inforr

Hello, can I speak to ...

[If named person is not available, check if the person who answers is an appropriate contact. If not, find out a good time to call back]

any improvem
changes

My name is ...

towards the end of last

I'm calling from Buxton Opera House. We called you ~~earlier~~ this year about a new information scheme we are trying out, and you said you were interested in being called again when our new brochure was out. Is this a convenient time to tell you about the ~~summer~~ and ~~autumn~~ events at the Opera House? The call should take no more than 5 minutes. _Spring o Summer_

Yes **PROCEED.**

[If no, arrange a date and time to call back]

Do you still wish to continue being part of this scheme?

No (probe gently for reasons why not).

If they don't - make a note on the call sheet.

EXIT.

Yes PROCEED.

STAGE 2: INFORMATION ON PRODUCTIONS

So can let me start by going through the types of productions you have already indicated an interested in ...

(see previous call sheet) - _are these correct? branch out_
list again to confirm
chosen AND rejected.

[If they are interested in plays]

STEP 1

May

If I run through a list of the plays we are presenting between now and the end of ~~September~~, please could you tell me if there are any plays you are interested in.

[List of plays in current season in date order. Information on each production to include: title; type e.g. comedy; cast i.e. any well known actors; playwright (if well known) and a couple of sentences of description e.g. From 10-15 March we have Shakespeare's 'Merchant of Venice' performed by English Touring Theatre. Starring John Thaw. It's a powerful and gripping drama which has recently won the xxx Award for Best Play. Also mention pre-show talk if appropriate]

STEP 2
[For their selected productions...]

Would you like me to send you information about xxxxxxxxxxxxxxxxxxx. **ACTION.**

[If they said that they were also interested in comedy, repeat STEPS 1 and 2 for all comedy, opera etc. You may need to limit this to 3 categories if the calls take too long]

CASE STUDY

5.1 BUXTON OPERA HOUSE TELEPROMPT

After the pilot TelePrompt scheme, **Buxton Opera House** extended the project in collaboration with Morris Hargreaves McIntyre and talked to 947 infrequent attenders. There were 663 who joined the scheme, although 20 of them subsequently dropped out. For every £1 Buxton Opera House invested in the scheme, they got back £3 additional income at the box office. This is how Helen describes the thinking behind the scheme:

> The classic model of the marketing communication process is AIDA: raise Awareness; arouse Interest; stimulate Desire; and call to Action (booking). Clearly, for the core group of frequent bookers, the theatre's publicity (particularly the season brochure) is fulfilling all of the AIDA steps. We know this because they book. However, for the majority of patrons, whilst the publicity is doing a good job in raising Awareness, its success diminishes rapidly in the IDA steps. In short, the publicity simply isn't persuasive enough.

> TelePrompt is a free telephone 'what's on' information service targeted at infrequent attenders (those attending once or twice per year) with the aim of 'activating' them – prompting a higher frequency of bookings. Using the records held on the theatre's PASS box office database, we identified patrons who booked infrequently and contacted them by telephone. We offered them the opportunity to be telephoned every three months with details of forthcoming events in their preferred choice of art form categories (dance, plays, opera, etc.).

> TelePrompt concentrates on the 'arouse Interest' and 'stimulate Desire' stages of the process, with the 'call to Action' being implicit, not explicit. This is a deliberate 'soft sell' approach. We have found that the most effective way of creating interest and desire is to build a relaxed and trusting relationship between the operator and the patron. Because we don't pressurise patrons to book tickets, they are more open to our message and willing to ask questions about the work.

> It has proved to be a successful way of getting more patrons to book more tickets, at higher prices, for more shows.

6 E-MAIL

> A couple of years ago, we instigated an e-mailing list and advertised it in the gig guides and listings bulletins saying 'if you want information then e-mail us at this address' and we slowly built up an e-mailing list. We get one or two new people joining every day even now. **Catherine Moore, Programme Development Co-ordinator, The Junction CDC**

This is a highly targetable form of on-line marketing. It is very similar to direct mail except that the actual communication is electronic.

Avoid spamming people (the on-line equivalent of junk mail) by:

- targeting accurately so that you write relevantly
- taking note of what people say, e.g. removing them from your list if they request this
- ensuring that you have the right e-mail address.

You need to think about the same five things as you would for any other direct marketing campaign:

1. What you want to achieve (your objectives).
2. With whom you want to get in touch with (the list).
3. What you are offering them (the offer).
4. How you will tell them about it (the e-mail itself).
5. When you will say it (timing).

Subscribe to as many e-mail bulletins as you can so that you get a feel for how other organisations are communicating.

Be sensitive. Before you send an e-mail to a net group or post information on a bulletin board, learn how the group operates, what they are interested in and in what style they communicate. Do not be pushy, or you may find yourself spammed in revenge.

An e-mail from CDC Junction in Cambridge

```
Dear

Still not sure what you're doing this weekend?.............

Well here's a suggestion........

I'm sure you're off to ooo and ahhhh  at the Fireworks on Midsummer Common,
but why rush off to the already overcrowded pubs afterwards? Cambridge
Drama Centre and The Junction are offering you a fabulous alternative. At
8.30pm Chris Green (creator of Eurotrash's Tina C) will be at the Drama
Centre for Pop Junkie, a whirlwind trip through the last 3 decades of
popular culture. Be prepared to 'almost end yourself with laughter' whilst
he portrays a whole range of Abba-obsessed characters. And if this isn't
enough you, The Junction will be just opening its doors for a night of
funky retro tunes, the infamous Boogie Wonderland.

All this fantastic evening's entertainment will cost you is ?8, yes that's
right ?8, (sparklers not included!) That's the same price as 4 pints of
beer, but without the hangover! Or alternatively a ticket just for Pop
Junkie will cost you ?5 (student) or ?7.50 full price.

Book your tickets now on 01223 322748 or 01223 577555. Or if you'd prefer
to be more spontaneous, we can sort out this offer on the door.

Pop Junkie, this Friday night at 8.30pm and Saturday at 8pm, Cambridge
Drama Centre.
We hope to see you there!

Rose Caudle
Marketing Assistant
```

11 HOW TO CREATE A SALES PROMOTION

SEE ALSO CHAPTER
22. TALKING IN THE RIGHT WAY

1 WHAT IS A SALES PROMOTION?

A sales promotion is an offer designed to persuade your potential audience to do one of the following:

- buy more tickets
- buy more often
- buy now rather than later
- buy for a particular event
- buy for the first time
- buy for the second time
- buy something different
- spend more money on their tickets.

A sales promotion promises added value that is only available for a limited time. If the added value is regularly on offer, the promise will be devalued and the potential ticket buyer will have little incentive to respond. A 'two tickets for the price of one' offer that is available every Monday evening is not a sales promotion, but part of your pricing structure. You could turn this idea into a sales promotion by, for example, making a 'buy one get one free' offer to persuade your existing dance attenders to bring someone who has not been before when they see a dance event this season.

Sales promotions are only effective when they are developed in response to a marketing challenge, otherwise they are just schemes without a purpose. Your challenge might be:

- a high proportion of people who attend once and do not come back
- a low proportion of under 25 year olds in the audience
- few existing attenders who are willing to take risks with new work
- people tending to buy their tickets just a couple of days before the performance
- hardly any attenders eating in the bistro when they see a show and so on.

There are three types of promise that a sales promotion can make to your potential audience member:

1. Free
   - free extra value: get more of the same for your money or get additional privileges such as a post-show discussion or free transport
   - free gift sent with your tickets
   - free gift when you collect a certain number of proofs of purchase
   - free sample, e.g. Test Drive the Arts[1]

2. Save
   - save money on this purchase
   - save money on your next purchase
   - save money on a special item such as a T-shirt by collecting proofs of purchase and paying cost price
   - save to help charities: we'll give a fixed donation to charity for each purchase you make

3. Win
   - competitions
   - free draws

[1] These audience development projects invite non-attenders to try out an arts event for free

2 CREATING A SALES PROMOTION

Please note that there are strict rules covering certain types of sales promotion in particular competitions and prize draws, which you must stick to in order to avoid breaking the law. The key issues are summarised below. Additional information about the law as it applies to sales promotion and direct marketing is available in the on-line Information Pack on Direct Marketing and Electronic Commerce in the United Kingdom at:

www.md-lab.com/fedma/infopack/Royaume-Uni/UK_English/RU_sales_promotion.htm

The Committee of Advertising Practice has also developed a series of rules about best practice which you can consult on the Advertising Standards Authority website at www.asa.org.uk.

2.1 A STEP-BY-STEP GUIDE

1. Quantify the marketing challenge to which you want to respond, e.g.:

   (a) analyse your box office database to find out how many people book once and then do not book again within 18 months

   (b) hand out a self-completion questionnaire at three performances to find out how many under 25 year olds attended

   (c) find out from the bistro manager how many people have eaten in the bistro after the show in the past three months.

2. Define your target group – to whom, exactly, do you want to talk.

3. Identify what the people in your target group think about what your organisation is offering. What are the barriers that might stop them taking the action you want?

4. Set an objective for your sales promotion, e.g.:

   (a) reactiviate 100 people who bought tickets for the first time last year and have not returned to buy tickets for an event so far this season

   (b) increase the proportion of under 25 year olds attending your events this season by 5%

   (c) increase the number of meals eaten in the bistro on a show night by 25%.

5. Think creatively about what added value you might promise to persuade your target group to take action. If price is not a barrier and your target group is not worried by how much tickets cost, then there is no point in offering a discount. You will need to take into account:

   (a) your budget

   (b how much time it will take you and your colleagues to manage the sales promotion

   (c) what impact the sales promotion will have on how people think about your organisation and what it has to offer

   (d) the legal requirements and guidelines covering particular types of sales promotion summarised below.

6. Identify the most effective way of telling your target group about your sales promotion.

7. Work out what percentage of your target group you expect to respond to your sales promotion. Now calculate how many people you need to communicate with in order to reach your objective, e.g. if you expect 5% of people who have only attended your venue once to reattend in response to your sales promotion then to reach your target of 100, you need to communicate with 2,000 people.

8. Think about how you want people to respond to your sales promotion – it must be easy for them to take action or they will not bother. Consult your colleagues at this stage, especially those in the box office.

9. Identify how you will monitor how many people respond to your sales promotion so that you can tell if you have reached your objective and if the sales promotion is worth doing again.

2.2 PRIZE DRAWS AND COMPETITIONS

These can be effective sales promotions because they are relatively easy to run and can be set up quickly. However, you need to design your competition or prize draw carefully because under the Lotteries and Amusements Act 1976 it is an offence to promote an unlawful lottery or prize competition.

PRIZE DRAWS

It is important to understand the difference between a prize draw and a lottery. All organisations are allowed to use prize draws as a sales promotion technique *as long as it does not cost anything to enter*. If the participant has to buy something, e.g. tickets, in order to enter then they are making a payment. This means that you are running a lottery, not a prize draw, and must stick to some important rules.

A lottery involves all or most of the participants making a payment in order to get a chance to win a prize. Only certain sorts of lottery are permitted. 'Society lotteries' are allowed. These are lotteries promoted for purposes other than commercial gain and include those run by charities or clubs for a good cause. To run a lottery like this with proceeds under £20,000, you need to apply for a licence well in advance from your local authority. For larger lotteries, apply to the Gaming Board for Great Britain.

The rules are as follows:

- no single prize may exceed £25,000 in value or 10% of the total value of tickets sold, whichever is the greater, even if the prize is donated
- not more than 55% of the proceeds of the lottery may be used for prizes
- at least 20% of the proceeds must go to the good cause
- not more than 35% may be taken in expenses.

COMPETITIONS

Competitions must involve the participants exercising a substantial degree of skill and judgement. Chance must not play a significant role in deciding who wins. You must not ask participants to forecast the outcome of a future event (this counts as betting and involves complying with a whole new set of regulations to avoid breaking the law).

Wherever possible, all the rules must be set out in the promotion for the competition. If this is not possible, then the most important rules should be stated along with details of how to get a full set of rules.

The British Codes of Advertising and Sales Promotion set out some additional guidelines to follow which are essential good practice:

Before making a purchase, participants should be informed of:

- the closing date for receipt of entries
- any geographical or personal restrictions such as location or age
- any requirements for proof of purchase
- the need to obtain permission to enter from an adult or employer
- the nature of any prizes.

Before or at the time of entry, participants should be informed:

- of any restrictions on the number of entries or prizes
- if a cash alternative can be substituted for any prize
- how and when winners will be notified of results
- how and when winners and results will be announced

- of the criteria for judging entries
- where appropriate, who owns the copyright of the entries
- whether and how entries will be returned by promoters
- of any intention to use winners in post-event publicity.

Promoters must either publish or make available on request details of the name and county of major prize-winners and their winning entries. Promotional material should make clear how this will be done.

Unless otherwise stated in advance, prize-winners should receive their prizes no more than six weeks after the promotion has ended.

2.3 FREE GIFTS AND SAMPLES

The British Codes of Advertising and Sales Promotion state that an offer should only be described as free if consumers pay no more than:

- the current public rates of postage
- the actual cost of freight or delivery
- the cost, including incidental expenses, of any travel involved if consumers collect the offer.

Promoters should make no additional charges for packing and handling. Promoters should provide a cash refund, postal order or personal cheque promptly to consumers participating in 'try me free' offers or those with a money-back guarantee.

3 NEW AND UNFAMILIAR WORK

There is a link between how confident people feel that they will enjoy an event and the amount of money they are willing to spend. Although they say that price does not affect their decision to attend something they really want to see, a substantial ticket price makes the risk of going to an unfamiliar event even greater. If they think that the event sounds interesting and they are available to see the performance, reducing the risk can be effective in persuading them to give it a go.

These are effective sales promotions which manage the financial risk of attending unfamiliar work:

- A money-back guarantee if they do not enjoy the event.
- Many people dislike seeing performances on their own. Some potential attenders decide not to come to an unfamiliar event because there is an increased risk that anyone they persuade to buy a ticket and go with them will not enjoy it. Bring a friend for free means that it does not matter so much if their friend or partner does not like the event.

- Money off for extra visits can encourage regular attenders to add an event they see as more risky to the list of shows they want to come and see in a season.

4 PACKAGES

Packaging an event with other events or services for one price can persuade people to attend more frequently or to spend more during their visit. These packages need not necessarily involve discounts as you are offering your audiences added value by creating an experience that goes beyond the particular event they originally intended to see. Examples of effective packages include:

- buy a ticket for a workshop and see the performance free or at a discount (particularly effective when the workshop and performance are in different places)
- see the show and have supper before or after (the Derngate's bistro offers themed post-show suppers, e.g. tapas after a performance of Northern Ballet Theatre's *Carmen*)
- come early and see foyer performances or exhibitions
- bring the kids to a fun day before seeing the performance
- buy a ticket for the performance and a party afterwards
- buy a ticket for two linked events in different venues.

5 SUBSCRIPTION SCHEMES

This form of sales promotion can come in all shapes and sizes. What subscription schemes have in common, however, is that a ticket buyer is asked to commit to paying in advance for a certain number of events. Subscription benefits arts organisations because it can:

- improve cash flow
- encourage regular attenders to commit to come to multiple events, thus potentially increasing the overall number of seats sold in the season
- provide a mechanism for occasional attenders to become loyal attenders
- guarantee a level of advance sales which means less last-minute marketing
- encourage audiences to attend unfamiliar work.

1 Vanessa Rawlings-Jackson, *Where Now? Theatre Subscription Selling in the '90s* (Arts Council of England, 1995)

Because of these advantages, many large-, middle- and small-scale venues and companies operate schemes and many are very successful, although the number of subscribers tends to be in the low hundreds. Opera companies and orchestras have the largest number of subscribers.[1] The Queen's Theatre, Hornchurch, however, is in its fifth season of a flexible subscription scheme which in spring 2000 attracted 5,000 subscribers paying a total of £19.50 to see three shows.

We've been carrying out market research and people really appreciate the value for money. They're getting quality entertainment for half the price. A huge percentage of the audience couldn't afford to come before. Now, they can come on any night and sit where they want to. They also don't have to book the actual performance they want to see until later. **Paul Griffiths, Press and Marketing Officer, Queen's Theatre, Hornchurch**

Although the benefits of subscription depend on the particular scheme, some of the reasons audiences buy subscriptions are that:

- they get priority booking
- it offers a way of committing themselves to being attenders, not intenders ('I always mean to come but never get round to booking in time')
- they get better value for money
- they feel as though they belong to a special group of people
- they can get the seats they prefer for every show
- they can plan their leisure time in advance so it is less hassle.

Subscription packages have traditionally offered substantial discounts to those who can pay up front and are willing to commit to a series of events, but individual organisations' research into their subscribers' views usually reveals that such benefits as priority booking and the sense of 'belonging' to the organisation are just as important as cheap tickets.

5.1 DISADVANTAGES

In the early 1990s, organisations reported trends of static or declining subscription sales. This seems to be because audiences:

- want more choice
- have less free time and so are reluctant to commit in advance
- are reluctant to commit to a whole season if they perceive artistic quality to be variable.[2]

2 Vanessa Rawlings-Jackson, *Where Now? Theatre Subscription Selling in the '90s* (Arts Council of England, 1995)

Managers and marketers worry that they are giving discounts to people who are able to pay full price and in doing so are creating an elite audience. Some feel that subscription does not encourage audiences to be adventurous and try unfamiliar work – their audiences, instead of committing to see all the shows in the season because they trust the organisation to produce quality work, will refuse to buy subscription packages where they perceive an element of risk. Producing theatres, in particular, can have difficulty in confirming their programme in time to sell their subscription scheme effectively.

Subscription schemes can be too successful. The staff at the Queen's Theatre,

Hornchurch, found that although they had increased attendances from 35% to 89% in just one year with the help of their flexible £5 per ticket scheme, they were turning away full-price ticket buyers on Fridays and Saturdays because they had sold out to subscribers. There was a danger that the scheme would not be financially viable because of the numbers of discounted tickets they were selling. They decided to increase the ticket price to £6.50 and at peak times to reserve an allocation of tickets for non-subscribers. In autumn 2000, they put ticket prices up by 50p to £13.50 and 'Jump the Q' prices correspondingly went up to £7.

5.2 TYPES OF SUBSCRIPTION SCHEME

There are a wide range of subscription schemes being operated by arts organisations in the UK.

THE SAME SEAT FOR THE SAME NIGHT IN THE RUN FOR EVERY SHOW

This guarantees audiences early in the week or early in the run and is easy for box office staff to manage. It is possible to design straightforward booking forms that are easy to fill in. Audiences can see it as too inflexible.

SEE EVERY SHOW BUT YOU CAN CHOOSE THE NIGHT YOU SEE IT WHEN YOU BOOK

Audiences can fit their theatre visits around the rest of their life. Booking is more complex for both customer and box office staff and forms become difficult to fill in.

SEE EVERY SHOW BUT THERE IS NO NEED TO CHOOSE THE NIGHT YOU SEE IT IN ADVANCE

The customer gets a book of vouchers which they exchange for tickets later. Several organisations give subscribers a plastic 'credit' card which they show to the box office to get their tickets. Audiences appreciate the flexibility and ease of booking but sometimes the performance they want is sold out by the time they exchange their vouchers.

BUY TICKETS IN ADVANCE FOR X NUMBER OF SHOWS FROM THE SEASON

This type of subscription is most frequently used by orchestras. Customers can choose from a series of different packages. These may be themed, e.g. concerts by a particular composer, or may be created for particular target groups, e.g. a series of concerts for children or for people who are unfamiliar with classical music. Mixed programme venues also use this scheme for series of particular types of event, e.g. dance seasons.

BUY TICKETS IN ADVANCE FOR X NUMBER OF SHOWS OF YOUR CHOICE FROM THE SEASON

Subscribers do not have to see every show in the season. They can, for example, choose which four productions out of five they want to see. They appreciate the flexibility and choice but they tend not to choose the unfamiliar shows which may therefore have smaller audiences. It is difficult to design a straightforward booking form for this type of subscription.

DISCOUNT CARD

Customers buy a discount card in advance and this entitles them to money off a ticket for each show. This means that the more they buy, the more they save but they only start saving once they have seen enough shows to get back their initial outlay. Again, they may not choose to attend the unfamiliar shows. Nottingham Playhouse have 790 members of their in-house discount card scheme.

MULTI-BUYS

The customer gets money off if they book a certain number of shows in advance. The more shows they book, the bigger the discount. This is used particularly in mixed programme venues. It can be very complicated for the box office staff to account for as there are several levels of discount which can be applicable to each of the shows in the season.

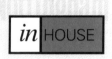

*in*HOUSE is Nottingham Playhouse's membership scheme.

If you like the theatre, *in*HOUSE offers an unbeatable range of benefits. The scheme was created in consultation with our customers, and is designed to help you enjoy your visits to Nottingham Playhouse more.

*in*HOUSE gives you greater flexibility and exclusive access, plus *in*HOUSE membership saves you money every time you come to the Playhouse - whether you normally buy full price or concessionary tickets.

*in*HOUSE is interactive, and from your suggestions we're constantly updating and improving the scheme. Following is a list of just some of the exclusive benefits you'll receive as an *in*HOUSE member...

Stay *in* ADVANCE... *in*HOUSE members are guaranteed priority booking for all Nottingham Playhouse shows

Keep *in* TOUCH... the *in*HOUSE newsletter has articles, special offers and the latest Playhouse news

Have *in*SIGHT... a sneak preview party at the start of each season

Get *in*VOLVED... *in*HOUSE organises behinds the scenes visits, chances to meet with actors and directors, visits to other theatres and volunteer schemes

Arrive just *in* TIME... you are guaranteed a seat for any Playhouse show (excluding pantomime) when you turn up 45 minutes before curtain-up

Collect *in* THINGS... exclusive, limited edition souvenirs and merchandise

Be *in* THE MONEY... *in*HOUSE members save money every time they come to the Playhouse:

The unique "ticket upgrade" scheme means that *in*HOUSE members save up to 40% on Playhouse tickets - you'll never have to pay top price for a ticket again - and you'll save money even if you normally pay concessionary prices

in ADDITION...
The benefits of *in*HOUSE membership go beyond the Playhouse - members also receive discounts at Broadway cinema and Dillons bookstore, and money off food in The Limelight restaurant and advance tickets at Nottingham Forest and Just the Tonic Comedy Club

Membership of *in*HOUSE costs just £10 for 12 months - or just £7.50 each for more than one person at the same address. To join fill out the attached application form, or call Nottingham Playhouse Box Office on **0115 941 9419**

5.3 SELLING SUBSCRIPTIONS

RENEWALS

The key strategy in running a subscription scheme is to maximise renewals. It is significantly cheaper in terms of marketing expenditure and staff time to persuade an existing subscriber to renew than it is to get a new one.

All organisations running schemes write to their existing subscribers either enclosing a special subscription brochure or the organisation's standard season brochure with an insert or supplement detailing the subscription offer. They almost always include a separate or tear-off booking form as this is the easiest way for box office staff to process complex bookings.

A number of larger organisations also use telesales to encourage those who are late in renewing to take action. The most successful present this as an additional information service to potential renewers, answering their questions about the programme and performers in order to help them make a decision. This kind of telesales campaign also gives the organisation an opportunity for a dialogue with their most loyal audience members, providing useful feedback on their perceptions of the programme, the organisation and the scheme itself.

The importance of these direct marketing techniques in maximising renewals means that the information kept about subscribers must be accurate, complete and up to date. The details of exactly what customers have bought in the past are essential if you want to offer particular types of subscription package to the target groups most likely to respond.

Many organisations work hard to maintain and develop their relationship with subscribers. They communicate regularly with them during the period of their subscription, usually through a newsletter giving additional information about the programme, behind-the-scenes insights and news and views. They believe that this kind of relationship building is a more effective strategy to maximise renewals than simply offering big discounts and expensive print.

Some organisations have run successful campaigns to win back people who used to subscribe but have not done so for some time. These campaigns have offered lapsed subscribers added value as an incentive to return, such as:

- a preview event at which performers and the creative teams involved in the forthcoming performances talk about the work and the box office is open to sell subscriptions

- mini-subscriptions involving fewer events as a stepping stone to committing once more to a full subscription

- an invitation to try out the first concert in a series free or at an additional discount after which the box office will be open so that the lapsed subscriber can buy their new subscription.

PRINT

Many organisations, particularly opera companies and orchestras, invest significant resources in their subscription brochure with high quality design and print. Often they see this as an excellent opportunity to reinforce their corporate

identity and to talk about their work as a whole rather than just talking about individual productions or events.

The most effective brochures start by making a clear promise to their readers which highlights the most important benefit of the scheme, e.g. the Queen's Theatre, Hornchurch, offers potential subscribers the opportunity to 'Jump the Q'.

Subscription print does not have to be expensive to produce:

> In the past the print has been plain text on a white background and it was very successful. Our research has told us that there are still people in the audience who haven't heard about Jump the Q. So this time we're going for colour and images to make Jump the Q more attractive and accessible in order to attract new subscribers. Images will help people visualise the show if they've not heard of it. **Paul Griffiths, Press and Marketing Officer, Queen's Theatre, Hornchurch**

The most challenging aspect of creating a subscription brochure is communicating what can be complex packages simply and clearly. This is easiest if you want to emphasise money-off as the key benefit and if the discount is straightforward:

- 'see five shows for the price of four'
- save £15
- 20% off.

Subscription schemes can, however, offer different discounts for different packages or a sliding scale depending on the number of events booked. This can confuse potential subscribers and stop people booking unless your copy and booking form present the information logically and with a visual layout that leads them through the process step by step.

Many marketers believe that to concentrate too much on discounts will devalue the shows. They focus on other benefits but do not always communicate them clearly. If you offer too many benefits, the customer can become confused.

You must design the booking form in collaboration with the box office staff who will process the subscriptions. It is also a good idea to test your draft copy and booking form on someone outside your organisation.

12 HOW TO GET PRESS AND MEDIA COVERAGE

SEE ALSO CHAPTERS
13. HOW TO SET UP AND RUN A PRESS PHOTO CALL
22. TALKING IN THE RIGHT WAY

Press and media coverage is one of the ways you can inform your target groups about your company and its work and so needs to be carefully planned. Press and media coverage is useful in different ways:

- It informs the public about your organisation or event. It often (but not always) increases ticket sales.

- It can help sustain your profile when your organisation is not active.

- You can use it as an endorsement of your organisation because comments by the press and media are generally perceived as objective.

- It provides material about your organisation which can be used on a long-term basis, perhaps to attract future funding or sponsorship, to provide research material for educational projects, to include on publicity or to secure new touring dates.

There is a wide variety of media to choose from: local radio news or magazine programmes, television programmes including magazine formats, youth, local news and arts programmes, national newspapers, local newspapers, colour supplements, monthly magazines, listings publications, arts publications, student publications and specialist magazines. Each medium will reach a different audience and will be interested in a different type of story and different subject matter. Each will need to be approached in a different way and at a different time.

Try to get coverage in the publications and programmes that interest your target markets. Think about what sort of coverage will get your message across most effectively:

- news: something important has happened (local and national media will have different definitions of what is important)

- feature: longer articles about an interesting aspect of your company or show, often involving interviews

- photo story: an interesting picture with just one or two sentences explaining it

- review: the opinion of a critic about your particular event

- listings: brief information about what's on where.

The main advantage of using this method of getting your message across to your target groups is that the actual space on the page or the programme slot is free. Compare the cost of advertising in the same medium to see how much coverage you are getting without paying for it. Persuading the press and media to cover your story is usually very time-consuming, however. Forward planning is essential to make sure that you use your time effectively.

Another disadvantage of press and media coverage is that you do not have control over the information published or broadcast. There is always the risk that you might get bad reviews or the newspaper could get something wrong, perhaps your box office telephone number. Not only will you lose the potential sales but people who ring that wrong number may blame your organisation for their frustration and wasted time even if it is not your fault.

You need to be determined, organised and thorough in your approaches to the press and media but if you follow some basic procedures, the press and media can be important allies in helping you get your message across.

1 HOW TO FIND OUT ABOUT THE PRESS AND MEDIA

The simplest way to find out about the press and media is to read newspapers and magazines, listen to the radio and watch television. It is important to remember that the press and media's primary consideration is to cover material suited to their publications and programmes. They are not concerned with improving your audience figures.

There are a range of publications that contain up-to-date information about press and media contacts such as *BRAD* and *PR Planner*. These are very expensive to subscribe to but you can consult them in larger public libraries with good reference or business sections, although they may be out of date.

There are three main types of coverage:

1. General coverage: feature and news.
2. Coverage before an event, often known as pre-publicity.
3. Coverage after an event, including reviews.

2 HOW THE PRESS AND MEDIA WORK

This sub-section outlines all the different sorts of general and pre-publicity coverage you may obtain. For easy reference each medium is covered individually. The advantages and disadvantages of the medium are explained under simple headings: possible sorts of coverage; where it might be printed or broadcast in the publication or programme; why a publication or programme might cover your organisation; who to send your information to; and when to send it.

Photographs are often essential for obtaining general or pre-publicity coverage. You will usually need to supply your own black and white prints or colour transparencies. You can also set up press photo calls.

2.1 NEWSPAPERS AND MAGAZINES

The main advantage of coverage in newspapers and other publications is that it is easy for the public to respond to information about your organisation – to book a ticket – as they have the information in front of them. Aim to get coverage in the newspapers or magazines read by your target groups.

You can also exploit coverage very easily. It is cheaper and simpler to photocopy an article in a newspaper than it is to copy a tape of a radio or TV item. Photocopies can be easily distributed to other people. In addition, there is a greater degree of flexibility in arranging an interview that will appear in print than one for radio or TV, both of which require recording equipment.

On the negative side, it can be difficult to describe dance, mime and physical or visual theatre in words – you cannot show what is happening as you can on television, although photographs help. Coverage in newspapers is usually restricted by the way a page is arranged, e.g. a display advert may necessitate pruning the last paragraph of an interview.

NATIONAL DAILY NEWSPAPERS

It is difficult for small-scale arts organisations to obtain coverage in the national press, but it is by no means impossible.

Types of coverage

Several of the broadsheet newspapers publish arts listings which can include brief articles, captioned photographs and critics' recommendations as well as the usual information about what's on where. The *Guardian* publishes regional versions of their listings section, 'The Guide', covering a wide range of events in every type of venue.

The paper's arts pages might contain short items, captioned photographs, longer articles and interviews. These focus on a specific event, an anniversary, new developments at an organisation, particular people involved with the arts or on specific issues affecting the arts in general. Occasionally, editors perceive an arts story as particularly important and of interest to the broad readership and so it is covered on the news pages. Other sections of the paper have strictly defined areas of interest.

Where you might get coverage

You are most likely to get coverage on the arts page. This is likely to reach readers who are already strongly interested in the arts. Other places you might get coverage are the women's page, social issues page, education page and young people's page. It is not worth approaching the news pages of national daily papers unless you have either a hard news story, a soft news story such as a royal visit or an excellent photograph (see Chapter 6, 'How to Use Photographs').

If you do approach journalists working on sections other than the arts page, make sure that you emphasise the most appropriate angle of your event or organisation so that they are clear why your story is relevant to their readers.

Why you might get coverage

The newspaper will be interested in your story if it is appropriate for its readership and is newsworthy.

Work by a well-known or fairly well-known choreographer is newsworthy. Alternatively, work by a choreographer in a very distinctive style. **Dance reviewer on a national newspaper**

Who to send your information to

Send a letter or press release to the individual section or page editor and to staff and freelance journalists who write for that section. Make sure that you address the press release to the right person – find out his or her name wherever possible. The section or page editor is likely to have excellent specialist knowledge about the subject. They will usually decide what is published in the section, but ideas for stories or features may also come from staff or freelance journalists. It is also very helpful to get to know the arts correspondent from each national broadsheet newspaper.

When to send your information

Timing is crucial. It is almost as bad to send information too early as too late. The volume of information that national newspapers deal with means that your press release is likely to get lost and/or forgotten about if it arrives too long before the event in question. For preview articles, send your press release about three to six weeks before the time you hope for publication. For listings, short items or captions, send it one or two weeks beforehand. Remember that, although national papers are published daily, many sections only appear weekly.

NATIONAL SUNDAY NEWSPAPERS

Obtaining coverage in the national Sunday newspapers requires a very similar approach to that for the national dailies.

Types of coverage

As well as the suggestions listed above, you may be able to obtain coverage in the colour supplements. The type and length of coverage is similar to that outlined below for general interest publications, except that the colour supplements carry articles about the performing arts more frequently.

When to send your information

Timing is as crucial as for national daily newspapers. For a preview article, send information six to eight weeks beforehand. For a short mention or photograph caption, send it two to four weeks in advance, and for coverage in the colour supplements, send it at least three months in advance.

REGIONAL AND LOCAL NEWSPAPERS

Types of coverage

You may obtain a listing, a short item, a photograph caption or an article, which will usually be based on an interview with someone involved with your organisation. At the regional and local level, specialist knowledge of the performing arts is likely to be limited, so your press release may be reproduced verbatim, rather than used as a starting point.

Where you might get coverage

Most regional and local newspapers have an arts or leisure section, which usually appears weekly, generally towards the weekend. Coverage in this section will most likely be read by arts enthusiasts. As with the national newspapers you can also approach the women's page, education page, social issues page and young people's page, but your story will nearly always have to have a local angle. If you have a very strong local angle there is usually a good chance of obtaining coverage on the news pages in this type of publication.

Why you might get coverage

As for national newspapers, the paper will be interested in your story if it is newsworthy.

> Anything with a tenuous local angle is the most important thing. **Local newspaper journalist**

Who to send your information to

Send your press release to the person who deals with the performing arts: this may range from an arts editor with good specialist knowledge to a news reporter with very little knowledge of or empathy with the arts. As with the national press, make sure that you address your information to the correct person.

When to send your information

Deadlines remain very important. For a listing or short item, send your information about one to two weeks in advance; for a preview article, about three to four weeks.

GENERAL INTEREST PUBLICATIONS

This section includes women's magazines, style magazines like *The Face*, lads' magazines like *Loaded* and specialist newspapers with a wide readership and broad content such as *The Times Educational Supplement*. Aim to obtain coverage in the publications likely to be read by your target groups.

The main advantages and disadvantages of coverage in these sorts of magazines are similar to those for newspapers. Coverage in publications is tangible: it is easy for readers to respond to information about your organisation as they have the information in front of them. Also, any colour coverage is particularly attractive for reproduction in displays.

Types of coverage

You may only get a mention, just a couple of lines of editorial or a short item. This will usually concentrate on a specific event or an interesting person involved in that event. Colour magazines almost always require colour photographic material: transparencies or hand-tinted prints.

Where you might get coverage

Most general interest publications have a 'what's on' section where you may get a mention or a short item. You are unlikely to get a big article or profile about anything other than a relatively well-known performer. It will be easier to place the story if they are recognisable from roles in films and television.

Why you might get coverage

Women's interest magazines will usually be interested in any events related to women's issues. Likewise style magazines will be keen to cover anything with a strong fashion element. Match the angle to the publication as appropriate.

Who to send your information to

Send your press release to the editor of the 'what's on' section and also to freelance journalists who write for it.

When to send your information

For monthly magazines you will need to send information as early as five months in advance. Some examples of lead times:

- monthly women's magazine: three to four months
- monthly style magazine: three months
- weekly newspaper: one month for an article, one week for a listing.

SPECIALIST ARTS PUBLICATIONS

Arts interest publications are magazines and newspapers like *Plays and Players*, *The Stage* and *Dance Theatre Journal*. They are likely to be read by committed enthusiasts only. Some of the less well-known arts publications have small circulations.

There are a handful of publications aimed at arts professionals which are effective ways of raising your organisation's profile among, for example, venue managers or officers working within the funding system. They may be produced by professional associations for their members, like the Theatrical Management Association's *Prompt*, or they may be independent publications like the fortnightly *Arts Business*.

Types of coverage

It is possible to obtain many different sorts of coverage in these publications: listings, short items, captioned photographs and full-length articles. These types of publication contain plenty of in-depth articles on all aspects of their particular specialist area.

What we want from arts organisations is news, particularly news that is of national interest to colleagues in the industry. This includes information about forthcoming conferences and seminars. We want them to tell us about their unique, groundbreaking projects so we can feature them in our themed issues. We are also interested in individuals with an interesting role within their organisation or an interesting career path or career plans. **Brian Whitehead, co-editor,** *Arts Business*, **tel. 01954 250600**

Where you might get coverage

You may obtain coverage anywhere in the publication.

Why you might get coverage

The only criterion for possible inclusion is that your story is relevant to the appropriate subject area of the publication, e.g. more traditional forms of drama for *Plays and Players*.

Who to send your information to

Arts interest publications are usually run by a tiny staff. Sometimes the editor and assistant editor produce the entire publication between them. Send information to all the editorial staff, plus any contributing freelancers.

When to send your information

Most of these publications are monthly or bi-monthly and need information three to four months in advance. Weekly publications like *The Stage* need press releases about six to eight weeks in advance for big articles. For short mentions, they require it two to four weeks beforehand.

LISTINGS MAGAZINES

Listings magazines are local publications. They publish information about entertainment and leisure which is used mainly by people who are intending to attend an event of some sort, so they are an important area of the press for arts organisations. They cover all the performing arts as well as film, television, politics and consumer information. The arts are hard news in these publications. On-line listings services are being developed. Currently those with the highest profile include Time Out on-line, Yahoo and lastminute.com.

Types of coverage

Usually the venue, date, time and title of your event will be listed along with a five- or six-word description. There are often opportunities for short items and captioned photographs, as well as longer feature articles about specific shows and performers, anniversary celebrations or new developments.

Where you might get coverage

There are usually separate sections for specific art forms and specialist interests such as events for children and gay and lesbian arts and entertainment. They often have their own editors.

Why you might get coverage

Listings magazines are interested in arts, entertainment and leisure events within a specific geographic area. In some cases you will find that there is intense competition for coverage in these publications, similar to that on the arts pages of national newspapers.

Who to send your information to

Send your information to the individual section editors and any freelance journalists who contribute to that section.

When to send your information

For weekly and fortnightly publications information is usually needed ten days in advance. If you are seeking coverage in the form of short items, then send your information about three weeks in advance and for longer articles about six to eight weeks.

STUDENT PUBLICATIONS

The students in many higher education institutions produce their own magazines and newspapers. These are written by the students for the students attending that college or university and are important communication tools if your target groups include young people over the age of 18.

   The main student newspaper or magazine may be funded by the college or university as well as the students' union and can aspire to high journalistic and graphic design standards. The editorial team will probably change every year. Other publications can be produced on an *ad hoc* basis so you may have difficulty getting hold of the right person at the right time.

Types of coverage

The amount of coverage you may obtain will vary enormously as the editorial policies of these publications can be very different. They generally have listings and short items about the performing arts. Some may devote feature space to the arts on a regular basis; others may only run occasional articles or interviews.

Where you might get coverage

Most large-scale student publications have specialist arts and entertainment sections. A newsworthy story or one with a human interest angle can appear anywhere in the paper.

Why you might get coverage

Student publications will only cover events aimed at student audiences and in stories that will interest their readers.

Who to send your information to

These publications are usually run by a small team of volunteers so the best way to find out who to send information to is to obtain a back copy from the students' union. Alternatively telephone the students' union and ask.

When to send your information

They are only published in term time, usually on a weekly or fortnightly basis. Send information about two to three weeks in advance.

ARTS NEWSLETTERS

Arts newsletters are publications produced by the arts profession. They can be free or might be on a subscription basis only. Examples include *Mailout* and the on-line publication *Dispatches*.

Types of coverage

All these publications include listings, short articles and photographs complete with captions.

Where you might get coverage

You may obtain coverage anywhere in the publication.

Why you might get coverage

These newsletters will publish any interesting arts information relevant to their readership –that is why they exist.

Who to send your information to

They are usually run by one or two people on a part-time basis. It is best to telephone the organisation concerned or find a back copy to identify who to send your information to.

When to send your information

Lead times can vary from two weeks to two months, depending on the individual publication.

> *Dispatches* is assembled on Sunday/Monday from e-mails, mailing list stuff, what's in the papers/on radio/TV and gossip. I find stories in *Arts Business* and *The Stage* (but it's reciprocal). **Bill Thompson, Editor,** *Dispatches*, **bill@andfinally.com**

OTHER NEWSLETTERS

Other newsletters may be published by community and special interest groups such as the Welsh language community newsletters *Papur Bro*. It is helpful to get coverage in this sort of publication if you are targeting a particular audience group. However, the quality of these publications varies a lot.

Types of coverage

You may get listings coverage, short mentions and captioned photographs. Occasionally the publication may want to cover your story in more depth.

Where you might get coverage

Newsletters tend to be small in size so you may obtain coverage anywhere within them.

Why you might get coverage

The newsletters will be interested in any information relevant to their specialised readership.

Who to send your information to

As with arts newsletters, these are usually run by one or two volunteers. Again, it is best to telephone the organisation concerned or obtain a back copy to identify who to send your information to.

When to send your information

Lead times can vary from two weeks to two months, depending on the individual publication.

2.2 RADIO

Radio is an ideal medium for telling people about performances that involve speech or music. Many speech-based local stations broadcast 'what's on' slots throughout the day (and night) which feature the equivalent of listings.

Radio may less suited to promoting more visual art forms, like physical theatre, mime and dance. It is still worth sending information to appropriate programmes as long as you write your press release with the medium of radio in mind.

A national radio programme wanted to profile a small-scale dance company. They tried to tape a rehearsal, but it did not come out well, so they settled for interviews with the dancers/choreographers:

> They were interested in the working structure of the company, things like that … and being on the scene to find out how we rehearsed and got things together. **Administrator, dance company**

You will need to provide the production team with full details of any music they wish to broadcast, so that they can complete the log they have to return to the Performing Rights Society on a regular basis.

NATIONAL RADIO

National radio is usually thought of as including BBC Radios 1, 2, 3, 4 and 5, Classic FM and the BBC World Service.

Types of coverage

It is possible to obtain short items on many different sorts of programmes. These will usually involve an interview with someone involved with your organisation. Programmes may be interested in specific events or performers, anniversary celebrations or new developments at your organisation. Radios 2, 3 and 4 and the BBC World Service schedule arts magazine programmes sometimes broadcast full-length programmes about a particular aspect of the arts, although each station has a distinctive overall style and content aimed at particular segments of the population. Classic FM gives classical music concerts a welcome high profile but many of the listings they broadcast arc paid for by thc arts organisation.

Where you might get coverage

Possible places for coverage are current affairs, general magazine, women's and arts programmes and news bulletins. Some hardy perennials are 'Front Row' and 'Woman's Hour' on Radio 4, Sheridan Morley's show on Radio 2 and 'Night Waves' on Radio 3. Radio 1 will occasionally run an arts story on its hourly news programme, 'Newsbeat', if it is of particular interest to under 25 year olds. Specialist magazine programmes such as 'In Touch' will run stories if they are of particular interest to their listenership, for example a feature on audio-described performances.

The *Radio Times* is essential research, and listening to at least one edition of the programmes is to be recommended.

Why you might get coverage

Programmes will be interested in stories that match the editorial policy of the specific programme and the station's overall output.

Who to send your information to

Send your press release or letter to a researcher or producer on the programme you are approaching. These are listed in the *Radio Times* or in the credits at the end of the programme. If you do not have a specific name, write to Forward Planning.

When to send your information

For magazine programmes send your information about three to six weeks in advance of the anticipated broadcast date. For news and current affairs programmes you will need to send it one to four weeks beforehand.

Local radio

Local radio stations are run by the BBC or ILR (Independent Local Radio). Stations that mix music and speech, notably BBC local radio, are often interested in covering the arts. Many music-only stations, however, have a policy of keeping speech to a minimum. Occasionally they will have a drive-time slot that gives information about entertainment and leisure events locally.

Types of coverage

Most local radio stations carry listings in the form of a regular 'what's on' slot in a particular programme. They may also broadcast short items on news programmes, magazine programmes and the arts programme, if they have one. These will usually involve an interview. Regional local stations may also accept a ready taped interview from your organisation, known as a syndicated tape, as long as it is of broadcast quality and not too obviously a 'plug'.

Where you might get coverage

As with national radio, you may obtain coverage on news, general magazine and arts programmes. Many local radio stations also broadcast magazine-style special interest programmes, for example those targeted at particular sectors of the local community. You will have a good chance of getting coverage on local radio news programmes if you have a hard news story with a strong local angle.

Why you might get coverage

The same criterion applies as for local newspaper coverage: local radio stations will be interested in stories with a local angle.

Who to send your information to

Send your press release to a researcher or producer on the programme you are approaching, to Forward Planning or to the station's programme controller. Also make sure that you send information to the 'what's on' slot.

When to send your information

For magazine programmes information is needed three to six weeks before the anticipated broadcast date. For news programmes it will be needed one to four weeks in advance.

COMMUNITY AND PIRATE RADIO

Although they often have small audiences, it may be worth contacting community radio stations if you have a story with a particularly strong local angle.

It is worth approaching illegal pirate radio stations if music plays a key part in your event. They can have strong audiences among particular sectors of the community, although many of the most successful stations of the 1980s and 1990s now have official licences to broadcast. Listen to the programmes to find out who to contact and how to get in touch.

2.3 TELEVISION

Television seems an ideal medium for arts coverage because it can show the combination of movement and sound and your two minutes of air time may reach several hundred thousand viewers. Venues report that this can have a significant impact on sales.

Getting television coverage and organising filming is complex and time-consuming so it is worth considering the drawbacks. Watching something on television is quite different from attending a live performance. Many viewers, particularly of regional news programmes, may prefer to stay at home and watch television rather than go out. An exciting, vibrant show can end up looking dull and this can decrease your potential audience rather than increase it. On the other hand, a less than marvellous event may be transformed into the spectacle of the year by a good producer, presenter and cameraman.

The trades union agreements covering filming for publicity purposes and the subsequent broadcasting rights are complex. Rates depend on the length of the performance and the type of programme. You will need to find out what the current Equity and Musicians' Union agreements are and ensure that your discussions with the television company cover who is going to pay the relevant fees. Also, many organisations charge a facility fee to television companies for shooting in their theatre, so you will need to agree who is going to pay this. If you work for a touring company you may be able to negotiate with the venue presenting the performances. You will need to supply details of music, if

appropriate, for the records that the broadcaster must submit to the Performing
Rights Society.

A television company was asked to film sections of a new play for use in a
documentary. What was it like for the company?

> Very, very hard. The actors had to do bits four or five times over. And they
> don't give you much money ... It should always be organised beforehand,
> very, very clearly, and written down in a contract. And the venue wanted a
> facility fee. Those kinds of things really have to be sorted out at the
> beginning. **Administrator, national touring theatre company**

NATIONAL TELEVISION

National television is usually thought of as BBC 1, BBC 2, Channel 4, Channel 5 and
the main satellite stations. Many ITV programmes are broadcast nationally, but most
of those that cover the arts are just seen within the particular ITV region.

Types of coverage

You may obtain a short item, which will usually involve an interview and will
nearly always be about a specific event. There are occasional full-length
programmes about a particular aspect of the arts, normally broadcast on BBC 2 or
Channel 4. In the past, some high-profile small-scale arts organisations have had
full-length programmes made about them.

Where you might get coverage

General magazine programmes and arts programmes may be interested in your
story. It is, however, increasingly difficult to get coverage as the programmes that
traditionally covered the arts and entertainment such as 'Arena', 'Omnibus' and
the 'South Bank Show' are now more concerned with high-profile popular
culture.

Saturday morning children's television and daytime magazine programmes
occasionally feature particularly spectacular and unusual arts events if they have
a flavour of popular culture. It is impossible to persuade them to cover unknown
bands and comedians as the major record companies and promoters have spotted
the potential of these programmes and cornered the market. It is increasingly
rare to get arts and entertainment coverage on national television news.

Why you might get coverage

Producers and editors may be interested in your information if it is newsworthy,
particularly visually interesting and appropriate to their programme's style and
content. Again, the *Radio Times* is a good starting point for your research.

Who to send your information to

Send your press release to a researcher, producer or editor on the programme you
are aiming at. BBC researchers do consult the bulletins produced by Forward
Planning, so it is worth sending them your information.

When to send your information

Magazine programmes need the information three to six weeks before the anticipated broadcast date. Full-length programmes plan about six to nine months ahead.

LOCAL TELEVISION

Local television takes the form of regional programmes, broadcast on BBC 1, ITV and cable networks. Some ITV companies have occasional cultural strands but these are increasingly more concerned with popular culture than with the arts and entertainment.

Types of coverage

There are opportunities for listings in a 'what's on' format as well as shorter items.

Where you might get coverage

Arts coverage may occur on any news or magazine programmes that cover local events, such as the local early evening news programme. In addition, some regions now produce magazine programmes aimed at young people which may cover rock and pop, comedy and particularly accessible contemporary arts.

Why you might get coverage

The main criterion for possible coverage is that your story has a strong local angle.

Who to send your information to

Send your information to a named researcher, producer or editor.

When to send your information

For magazine programmes send information three to six weeks before the anticipated broadcast date. For news programmes send it one to four weeks beforehand.

A sample press release appears on the opposite page.

earthfall, chapter, market road, cardiff, wales, uk CF5 1QE   tel 02920 221314 fax 02920 342259 email: earthfall@earthfall.org

PRESS RELEASE

Dancing, bleeding, laughing, lusting ... boxing clever

earthfall, internationally acclaimed and BAFTA award-winning dance theatre company present:

Rococo Blood

Earthfall, Wales' leading dance theatre company, are performing their sell-out show **ROCOCO BLOOD** at --- on ---------, at ----.

ROCOCO BLOOD, created by the award winning director-choreographer team, Jessica Cohen and Jim Ennis, fuses superb radical dance with exceptional live music and stunning visual imagery in a dynamic dance theatre work. Memories of first fights and first love are unmasked as extreme dance and extraordinary music expose the tyrannies within human relationships and tell of the personal histories and tensions in a fusion of tenderness, violence, pathos and humour.

During rehearsal the company trained with Cardiff based professional boxing coach, Clive Williams and developed a style which mixes superb new wave dance with Muhammad Ali's 'poetry in motion'. Break-dance and boxing, rapping and ranting, guitars, trumpet and hip-hop combine to make **ROCOCO BLOOD** an unmissable piece of total theatre shot with sharp social comment.

Internationally acclaimed *earthfall*, recent winner of the **1998 BAFTA Cymru Award for Best Short Film** for Too Old To Dream, is an outstanding exponent of pioneering dance theatre. The company of 6 multi-talented performers have worked with many notable performance and film companies. The live music is composed by Bristol-based musicians Jon and Paul Wigens and Roger Mills, who have worked with The Wood Children, The Blue Aeroplanes, Travis, Onalee from Reprazent and companies such as Blast Theory and Circomedia alongside *earthfall.*

ENDS

FOR FURTHER INFORMATION CONTACT THE ADMINISTRATIVE DIRECTOR, ON (02920) 221314, FAX (02920) 342259, mob (07930 40 28 20) email: earthfall@earthfall.org

3 SENDING OUT PRESS RELEASES

The aim of a press release is to give information to the press and media for publication or broadcasting. A press release should interest the reader sufficiently for them to consider publishing or broadcasting the information it contains or to want to find out more.

A press release is not always the best way to get coverage. If you are trying to get a journalist to write a feature story, start with a personal letter saying what you want them to write, and why they might be interested. Enclose your press release to back this up.

> A press release is more like a prayer in church than an advert – you have no real control over how an editor will use what you tell them. *Dispatches* is a short (2,000 word) snappy read in which my editorial voice (some might call it prejudice) is pretty strong so I will rewrite anything that comes and do not feel obliged to take things as seriously as the people writing press releases might. This means that being pompous is always a bad idea.
>
> **Bill Thompson, Editor,** *Dispatches*, **bill@andfinally.com)**

3.1 PRESS LISTS

> It is essential to make sure you send the right sort of information to each journalist.

Your press list should be divided up into sections so that you can write a separate press release for:

- listings publications
- specialist arts publications
- general interest magazines
- local newspapers entertainment pages
- local newspapers' news and general pages
- local radio
- local television
- national daily newspapers arts pages
- national Sunday newspapers arts pages
- national newspapers' general interest pages
- national Sunday newspapers' general interest pages
- national radio
- national television.

This will also enable you to send your press release at the right time – women's magazines need information four to six months in advance while listings publications only need ten days' notice.

Keep your press and media list up to date by regularly telephoning round to find out the names of the appropriate editors, producers, researchers, staff and freelance journalists to whom to send your information.

You can buy a press mailing list and a press contact list on CD-Rom and as hard copies from the Arts Council of England's Press Office. These lists contain English and Scottish national newspapers, television and radio plus the major daily regional newspapers. You could consult directories such as *PIMS*, *Willings Press Guide*, *BRAD* and *PR Planner* which are available for reference in large public libraries. Some arts organisations have used copies borrowed from businesses that sponsor them.

Keep telephone and fax numbers as well as addresses.

> People just automatically send us listings of their shows. We're not a listings publication and they should know that. We can't make use of the information so it's a waste of their resources and annoys our postman – it goes straight in the bin. It is very important that people segment their press list and think carefully about what they are sending out to each publication.
>
> **Brian Whitehead, co-editor,** *Arts Business*, **tel. 01954 250600**

3.2 WRITING A PRESS RELEASE

STYLE

- Try to limit the press release to one side of A4. If you cannot get all the important information onto one page then put 'more/...' or 'continued/...' at the bottom of the first page and '.../continued' at the top of the second page.

- Reflect your organisation's corporate identity by using your logo and choosing a good quality paper. Use coloured paper for more impact if this is appropriate but make sure that it can be faxed and photocopied.

- Type the press release. Keep block capitals to an absolute minimum as they are more difficult to read quickly.

- If you are sending your press release to publications that may reproduce it verbatim, such as local newspapers, use 1.5 or double spacing. This will allow sub-editors to mark it up ready for publication.

- Use bold and large typefaces to make sure that the important information stands out.

- Use short paragraphs.

CONTENT

> *Dispatches* is put together from stuff I get sent – mostly by e-mail, because I tend to forget to look at printed press releases when I'm writing it – and whatever else I can dredge up from the papers/radio/gossip from friends.

The single most annoying thing for me is a press release or e-mail that does not tell me everything I need to know. I tend to put *Dispatches* together on Sunday evening or Monday evening, and I don't have the time/resources to call people up. So if I don't know something, it doesn't go in. Sometimes it's just that the writer assumes that I already know who people/organisations are. Sometimes they forget to put dates, contact details or even names.

As a hard-pressed hack I need to be able to get all the info from either the release itself or a website that I am pointed to by the release. **Bill Thompson, Editor,** *Dispatches*, **bill@andfinally.com**

- Start with the heading 'Press Release' or 'Media Release' at the top of the page.
- Sum up what you have to say in a short, factual headline (do not try to be clever – that's the sub-editor's job).
- Target your information – only say things that are likely to interest that particular type of publication.
- Do not include irrelevant information. Most biographical facts belong in a programme, not in a press release. Only include it if it gives the story an interesting angle.
- Include all essential information in the first two paragraphs as this may be all your reader has time to look at. Tell them what is happening and when, where it is happening, why it is happening and who is involved in it. Include your box office telephone number in this part of the release to make sure that it gets included in any write-up.
- Include tour dates when writing to the national press and media. Some people like to put these on a separate sheet.
- Include a contact name and telephone number.
- Be factual and objective; do not use lots of adjectives and superlatives.
- Include details of your press night.
- It is not usually necessary to say that photographs are available as the press will almost certainly expect them to be. However, if the photographs are remarkable in some way or if there are colour transparencies available for magazines, do say so.

A press release should be concise. You should be very clear as to when and where – you wouldn't believe it, but some people bury when and where their event is on, and when you get loads of stuff you just don't want to plough through it … What you really need is a pithy way of summing up what the show or group is about, in a well-written way, without going over the top, without doing a hard sell. **Local newspaper journalist**

An example of a press release is on the following two pages.

Hijinx ▪ **Bay Chambers** ▪ **West Bute Street** ▪ **Cardiff Bay** ▪ **CF1 6HG**
01222 300331 ▪ **Fax: 01222 300332**

PRESS RELEASE

Theatre Company to Re-create Historic Occasion

Hijinx Theatre Company will be re-creating a piece of history on Friday when it brings its latest production, *Paul Robeson Knew My Father* to the Grand Pavilion, Porthcawl.

The production has been inspired by Paul Robeson, one of the greatest black actors and singers of the twentieth century and fans of Paul Robeson will not be disappointed as the production contains plenty music and film.

One of Robeson's most famous fans, Tyrone O'Sullivan of Tower Colliery, will be Hijinx' special guest at the performance.

Paul Robeson had a very close relationship with Wales, especially the miners of south Wales, and visited Wales during the twenties and thirties, often to raise money for miners during the economic recession.

In the fifties he was not allowed to travel outside of America due to his political activism, and had his passport withdrawn, like so many other leading Hollywood stars of the period. But the Welsh miners stayed loyal to him, and in 1957 invited him to sing at the Miners' Eisteddfod in the Grand Pavilion, Porthcawl.

Unable to visit in person, he spoke to the packed hall over the telephone, and sung over the wires with the Treorchy Male Voice choir. This was the final nail in the American Government's persecution of Robeson. The next year he visited in person.

The transatlantic telephone communication is the climax of *Paul Robeson Knew My Father*. The play received a standing ovation when playing at the Sherman Theatre over the weekend.

Director Greg Cullen said

> *"The performance at the Grand Pavilion will have an especial emotional significance for me and the Company as it is here that Robeson spoke to the Miners' Eisteddfod over forty years ago, especially as we are playing as part of the Miners' Eisteddfod itself."*

The performance stars at 7.30 PM. For tickets phone 01656 786996.

FOR FURTHER INFORMATION, CONTACT LOWRI JONES ON 01222 300331.

DATE: 4 OCTOBER 1999

Pafiliwn y Grand
Rhondda
Porthcawl
CF36 3YW

Ffôn : 01656 **783860**
Ffacs : 01656 **772111**

THE 5...
30th 1999

The Grand Pavilion
The Esplanade
Porthcawl
CF36 3YW

Telephone : 01656 **783860**
Fax : 01656 **772111**

History is repeated in new Robeson play

PAUL Robeson has been the inspiration for many people.

Legendary film star, singer and political activist, he established a relationship with the miners of Wales during the 1920s and came to Wales frequently, the high point being his visit to film *Proud Valley* in Rhondda in 1939.

Hijinx Theatre Company will be recreating history on October 8 at 7.30pm when it performs *Paul Robeson Knew My Father* in Porthcawl's Grand Pavilion as part of this year's Miners' Eisteddfod.

The Pavilion was at the centre of Welsh and world interest during 1957 when Robeson made a transatlantic telephone broadcast to the Eisteddfod.

He had been invited to sing at the Pavilion but due to his political stance on behalf of black Americans, his passport was withdrawn and he could not travel outside America.

The climax of *Paul Robeson Knew My Father* happens in that very same 1957 Eisteddfod.

Writer and director Greg Cullen said: "This performance will have special significance and will be an emotional one for us, and hopefully the audience as well. Paul Robeson has been a hero of mine since childhood."

The performance will star Melissa Vincent from Blaengarw in her first major tour.

Tickets for the show cost £4 and are available on 786996.

HISTORY RELIVED: Paul Robeson *in Proud Valley.*

Hijinx's press release and resulting coverage in Porthcawl

> Instead of getting a piece of A4 with everything the same size, I do like the
> title to stand out more and the date. The names of the cast usually mean
> nothing … but I would want to know if it involves twenty young non-
> professional actors or is a three-hander. The snappier the better … a sharp
> little sentence makes you think it will probably be a sharp little play. **Arts**
> **correspondent on a national newspaper**

3.3 FOLLOW-UP TELEPHONE CALLS

You will probably need to follow up your press release with a telephone call if you want to achieve anything longer than a listing. The press and media may contact you when they receive your press release but you can be sure that you have produced a remarkable one when this happens!

Make sure that you telephone at a convenient time, when the person to whom you wish to speak is not up against a tight deadline. For a national Sunday newspaper, some days are much better than others:

> Monday is a bad day. Only the secretaries come in. Tuesdays and
> Wednesdays are pretty good days. Thursday is a terrible day because it's
> layout of pages. And Friday's bad because the paper goes to press.
> **Arts Editor's Assistant, national Sunday newspaper**

Have an argument for coverage worked out beforehand and a copy of your press release in front of you so that you can refer to it if necessary. If possible, introduce a new piece of information at this stage as your trump card.

> Someone rings up and says 'Hello, have you got my press release?' And I
> just think I'm going to die. They think they are the only ones sending me
> press releases. It drives me mad if they don't say 'This is X from X and I
> want to know if you will be coming to the opening of X on X date.' **Arts journalist,**
> **national newspaper**

4 INTERVIEWS

Interviews can take place by telephone or face to face. If you manage to get an interview with the press or media, you will need to work out a good time and place for it. You may need to suggest a suitable interviewee. Anyone involved in your organisation can talk about their particular input. Most journalists prefer to speak to performers, directors and writers about specific events.

Contact the interviewee and explain what the interview is for. Tell them what you know about the publication or programme and the interviewer. Explain why the interviewer is interested in speaking to them. Interviews can be quite daunting so it is often a good idea to telephone the interviewee afterwards and discuss how the interview went, You may also want to speak to the interviewer and check that they have all the information they need.

5 PRESS NIGHT AND REVIEWS

It is standard practice to hold a press night for a performing arts event. A press night is a performance to which critics and other influential people are invited to see your work. Small-scale touring companies usually hold a press night near the start of their London run and regionally, as appropriate.

Send out a separate press invitation to all the critics and other influential press and media people you would like to attend. It is general practice to offer people a pair of complimentary tickets. Send your invitation about three to four weeks before the press night.

You will usually need to check who is attending by making a follow-up telephone call to the arts desk of each paper. Make your follow-up call about one week before your press night. Make it clear that the tickets will be kept for them; check with the box office that they are already earmarked. Some people prefer to send out tickets in advance once they know that someone is attending.

It is a good idea to invite other VIPs to the press night as well; you can make the evening into a special occasion by having lots of influential people together at the same time. Some organisations start their press night one hour earlier than normal (e.g. at 7pm rather than 8pm) so that critics have time to write their reviews for the following day's newspaper. However, few newspapers now actually print reviews overnight. An exception is London's *Evening Standard.*

You may find that several other shows are opening when you wish to have your press night. In London, the Society of London Theatres (SOLT) operates a press night chart, to make sure that press nights do not clash; this chart includes venues that are not in the West End.

It is important that your press night is full or nearly full to create a good atmosphere. Some venues 'paper the house' (offer free tickets) to make sure that the theatre is full, while others offer reduced price tickets or two tickets for the price of one. Provide critics and VIPs with a free drink if possible. Offer them a free programme. Make sure that there are black and white photos available, complete with hard-backed envelopes, and check that there is a telephone they can use if they need to.

There should also be someone available to answer any questions that critics may have. Some people think it is a very bad idea for you yourself to ask critics direct questions such as 'Are you enjoying it?' or 'What do you think of the show?'

Most national critics are based in London which is the heart of the press and media; however, many national newspapers also have regional critics. Many local newspapers also send reviewers to performances. As with any other sort of coverage, different sorts of publication will want to convey different sorts of information to their readers. The following shows the difference of approach between a reviewer from a local paper and one from a national newspaper when reporting on a performance by a children's theatre company.

A more demanding hour was provided for older children … The show follows the adventures of a runaway and illustrates the dangers and delights for children abroad in the big city. Their skilled combination of music, masks, puppetry and mime put over with an assured, humorous touch, proves just how far children's theatre has moved in the last decade. Energy and commitment have always been by-words, but high production values and a confident professionalism are evidence of a greater stability. **National newspaper**

Half term was great fun for these kids thanks to the new friends they made at the library on Monday. Mark and other children met up with a performer from the company and some of her more unusual-looking pals.
Local newspaper

Some reviewers are reticent about seeing non-traditional performances:

I don't think reviewers have the language to talk about mime … and, partly, that's why they don't come to performances. It's true that – at the moment – many reviews do begin with 'mime is no longer about a person who's not talking, trapped in a glass box' but they haven't got beyond that yet. They don't have enough awareness of what mime is – and we need to do something to change that situation. **Representative, lobby group**

Display any good reviews in the front-of-house area as soon as they appear. Promoters should send copies of reviews to companies for their records. Companies should send reviews to promoters later on in the tour.

The main problem with venues is that they hardly ever send reviews unless you ask them: 'Were there any reviews? Could you please send me copies?'
Marketing Officer, Asian theatre company

6 PRESS CUTTINGS

It is important to keep records of your press and media coverage for future reference. There are agencies that will send you copies of cuttings, which may save you considerable time and effort. You can mount cuttings on A4 paper. You can also keep cassette copies of radio interviews and videos of television coverage. There are also broadcast monitoring agencies which will make transcriptions for you, although these tend to be fairly expensive.

7 EMPLOYING A PRESS AND MEDIA REPRESENTATIVE

As getting press and media coverage is complicated, time-consuming and requires some specialist knowledge about who to contact and what to say, you may wish to employ a press and media representative, also known as press reps or PRs.

Read the papers, watch television and listen to the radio regularly to spot organisations that seem to be getting a lot of coverage and find out who generated it. Talk to other organisations to see who they use and what they are like to work with. Choose someone with a specialist knowledge of the area of the press and media on which you want to concentrate. The daily rates charged by press reps and PR agencies vary considerably depending on their level of expertise and overheads.

Brief them carefully so that they understand your target audience and your event, and specify exactly what kind of coverage you want. Ask for regular updates about how their work is progressing, so that you know who they have contacted and how much coverage to expect. They cannot guarantee coverage, however, as that depends on the nature of your event, how cooperative your performers are and what else is competing for journalists' attention at that time.

> We decided to employ a publicist for the first project as we are launching the company as well as a national tour, and whilst it is a big outlay for a new company, and inevitably involves some risk, if we establish the company now, it will save us time and money with future productions.
>
> **Producer, unfunded theatre company**

13 HOW TO SET UP AND RUN A PRESS PHOTO CALL

SEE ALSO CHAPTER
12. HOW TO GET PRESS AND MEDIA COVERAGE

1 LOCAL PRESS

1.1 THE LOCAL ANGLE

Local newspapers like images with a local angle. These are best taken by the paper's own photographers, although you will have to come up with the idea for the image.

Always ensure that the company knows about any photographers who will be shooting them. Some picture desks may need to be reminded that performers cannot work if they are unexpectedly interrupted in the middle of a workshop or fifteen minutes before a performance.

There must be a good story behind the image. Performers with local connections, a local setting for a play or characters with local connections are all possibilities. Outdoor locations are particularly popular – performers doing something unusual at a local landmark or even in the town's shopping centre. A story without a local connection can be given one with such a location, e.g. an actress modelling five outlandish costumes in the street outside the theatre, an actor whose first job was as a shelf filler stacking tins of beans in the local supermarket.

If you are not sure whether a particular photo call idea will be attractive, ring a sympathetic picture editor or photographer to test it out.

1.2 INVITATIONS

You can either make the photograph exclusive to one paper, or send an invitation to all the papers. Send the invitation to the picture editor.

The invitation should state clearly and briefly the story behind the planned photo call. Give the date, time and place of the photo call and a contact name and telephone number. Type it in 1.5 or double spacing so that the recipient can easily make notes on it. Make it brief. If the photo call is outside, make sure that you specify an easily found meeting point.

Send out the invitation about two weeks before the photo call. Ring everybody up the day before to check who is intending to come. This gives you time to cancel it if no one is interested. When you telephone, ask for the picture desk (the picture editor's office). The person on duty will have the diary in which all the next day's assignments are listed. If your photo call is in the diary and has a photographer allocated to it, it is likely that they will attend. If an unexpected major news event breaks the next day, then they may be needed to cover that instead. Make sure that the performer(s) are aware of this.

1.3 THE PERFORMERS

Ask the performer(s) verbally to take part in the photo call, explaining exactly which papers it is for and what the story behind the picture is. Then send them a written confirmation to ensure that they have the details of where and when it will take place.

1.4 LOCATIONS

Occasionally you will have to get permission to do your photo call in a public area, if, for example, you are likely to cause an obstruction. In these situations, a telephone call to the relevant local council department and the local police station will usually be enough. Obviously, the permission of the owner is needed if the location is on private property. A shopping centre is private property, and in any case it would be courteous to inform the centre management of what you intend to do. This will save embarrassment and ill feeling on both sides.

1.5 THE PHOTO CALL STEP BY STEP

1. Ensure that the performers arrive early so that they are ready on time. Photographers have tight schedules and will not wait around.

2. The performers will be nervous. Make sure that they know exactly what will be happening.

3. Greet the photographers when they arrive. Make a note of their names for future reference. Give each of them a typed press release containing a brief explanation of the story behind the photo call, the name(s) of the performer(s) and any relevant information such as the box office telephone number. They will take this back to their sub-editor who will use it to write the caption under the photograph.

4. Explain what you intend the performer(s) to do. Ask if this is appropriate. They will probably make additional suggestions.

5. Make sure that the performer(s) feel happy about any new suggestions. Act as a go-between, explaining to the performers what the photographers want them to do.

6. The photographers will probably have got what they want within 15–30 minutes. Check that they are happy with what they have. Thank them individually for coming to the photo call.

2 NATIONAL PRESS PHOTO CALLS

It is also possible to hold press photo calls for the national press. Unless you have a story of major national importance, you will not get any photographers to attend if it happens outside London or Manchester (where the national press have regional offices).

If you know of a freelance photographer who has good contacts with the national picture desks, contact them directly and ask if they would be interested in covering the story. If they think it is good enough, they will offer the picture to the nationals and get paid a fee if it is accepted. It would be much easier to interest them rather than a picture editor in any of the photo stories suggested below.

2.1 IDENTIFYING A PHOTO STORY

It is important to study the photographs that appear in the national papers over a period of time. You will then get a feel for the type of photograph that each paper prefers. Some of the broadsheet papers select images on the basis of their photographic interest, particular the *Guardian* and the *Independent.* Others are only interested in the story behind the image.

Unless your story is news of major national importance, the tabloid press and major regional dailies want images that will immediately be understood by their readers. This is also the policy of some of the broadsheet papers such as the *Daily Telegraph.* The picture editors of these papers will tend to think in terms of the stereotypes their readers are used to. Consider carefully whether you wish your organisation to be depicted in this way.

These are some of the types of story that are likely to attract interest:

- an amusing photograph, e.g. performers in incongruous costumes in a serious setting, any image with a visual joke

- a dangerous or unusual stunt – this often works best in an outside setting, e.g. riding a unicycle, breathing fire, being particularly athletic, working with a snake (especially if it goes missing), etc.

- performers playing famous people where there is a strong resemblance, e.g. Marilyn Monroe, Laurel and Hardy, Margaret Thatcher, Groucho Marx, etc.

- a young performer (preferably with a hard luck story) getting their big break against all the odds.

The tabloid press in particular will respond to the following type of photo call involving a pretty young actress. Overt sexism is usually involved and the performer should be made aware of this. Again, consider whether this type of publicity is appropriate for your organisation before pursuing it:

- an actress sitting in the park or by the river on a sunny spring or summer day

- an actress with some sort of attractive animal, e.g. feeding the ducks or a lamb or cuddling a kitten or a foal

- an actress wearing a pretty costume from the production (some tabloids will want the actress to reveal as much flesh as possible).

This particular type of photo call is most likely to succeed if you involve a local freelance with good contacts with the national press rather than sending out invitations. You will probably have to send the freelance a photograph of the performer in advance.

It is virtually impossible to interest the popular tabloids in a photo story that does not involve a well-known television personality.

2.2 THE PHOTO CALL STEP BY STEP

The process for inviting the national press to a photo call is much the same as for the local press:

1. Before fixing a date, ring up the Society of London Theatres (SOLT) which keeps a photo-call and first-night diary to prevent date clashes. Do not forget to ring them back to tell them the date you finally decide. This will increase your chances of a good attendance.

2. Send invitations to the picture editors of the appropriate types of newspaper. It is unlikely that the popular tabloids would be interested in anything other than a very famous face. The *Daily Telegraph* will be interested in a different sort of picture to the *Daily Mail*. Look at the newspapers over a period of time to get a feel for what each paper's interests are.

3. The invitation should state clearly and briefly the story behind the planned photo call. Give the date, time and place of the photo call, and a contact name and telephone number. Use 1.5 or double spacing. Make it brief. If the photo call is outside, make sure that you have specified an easily found meeting point.

4. Send out the invitation about two weeks before the photo call. Send it to freelance photographers and press agencies as well as the picture desks.

5. Inform the performer(s) verbally and in writing where and when it will take place. Make it clear that no photographers will turn up if, for example, a major news story suddenly breaks.

6. Get permission for your photo call if necessary.

7. Ring the picture desks up the day before to see if they are going to turn up.

8. Ensure that the performers arrive early at the photo call and are ready on time.

9. Brief the performers.

10. Greet the photographers when they arrive. Make a note of their names and the papers they are working for. Give them a typed press release with the story behind the photo call, the name(s) of the performer(s) and any relevant information such as the box office telephone number. They will take this back to their sub-editor who will use it to write the caption under the photograph.

11. Explain what you have asked the performer(s) to do. Ask if this is appropriate. They will probably make their own suggestions too.

12. Make sure the performer(s) feel happy about any new suggestions. Act as a go-between the photographers and the performer(s).

13. The photographers will probably have got what they want within 30–45 minutes. Check that they are happy with what they have. Thank them individually for coming to the photo call.

2.3 NATIONAL PHOTO CALLS FOR REVIEWS

National newspapers and freelance photographers will also be interested in taking their own pictures to accompany reviews. This photo call usually happens before or after a dress rehearsal. National photo calls are only suitable for productions that will be reviewed by the national press. Regional dailies occasionally like to take their own photographs for reviews.

The process is exactly the same as that for other national press photo calls except:

1. Only send invitations to the picture desks of newspapers that you expect to review your show and to freelance photographers.

2. You will probably need to liaise with the director/choreographer to decide on the best section(s) to show.

3. You will need to choose very short sections and repeat them several times.

4. Liaise with the technical staff to make sure that they are aware that the photo call is taking place and that they can provide a very bright lighting state.

5. You will need to allow at least 45 minutes to ensure that everybody has had the opportunity to take the pictures they want.

6. The photographers will be moving around the front of the auditorium, so make sure that it is clear of debris from the dress rehearsal.

14 HOW TO CREATE AN ADVERTISING CAMPAIGN

SEE ALSO CHAPTER
3. HOW TO WRITE COPY

Advertising is a marketing communication method just like sending out a direct mail package or getting editorial coverage in the press and media.

It is, however, one of the most traditional methods of publicity – many people immediately think of advertising when planning their marketing activity. The main advantage of any sort of advertising is that you retain a lot of control over getting information in the press and media: you can choose exactly what you want to say and how and where you want to say it. But advertising is usually expensive. You may not get value for money because a lot of people who see your advertisement simply will not be interested in your product. It is very difficult to change people's minds through an advertisement, so this form of communication is most effective in communicating with the committed arts attender who already knows quite a lot about what you are offering or for telling people about a straightforward, high-profile event with wide appeal.

1 CHOOSING THE MEDIUM

You need to decide which medium will be most cost effective in achieving your objectives. This means considering these factors:

- which medium is most likely to be seen or heard by your target group
- which will reach the greatest number of your target group
- how much persuasion your target group will need to take action
- which medium will reflect your organisation's corporate identity
- which will reflect the content and style of your event
- which will get your particular message across most effectively
- how much competition there will be for your target group's attention
- the number of times a member of your target group needs to see your message for it to be effective
- how much it will cost to produce your advertisement
- how much it will cost to buy the space on the page or the slot on radio or television
- how easy will it be for your target group to respond to your message.

Your first step is to find out the readership, circulation figures and advertising costs from individual publications and television or radio stations. Many publications produce special packs which contain this information, usually known as rate cards. You can also refer to press and media directories such as *BRAD*, *Willings Press Guide* or *PIMS* in public libraries with good reference sections. These are comprehensive reference manuals which have lots of facts and figures about hundreds of publications and commercial radio stations.

1.1 COMPARING EFFECTIVENESS

	STRENGTHS	WEAKNESSES
NATIONAL NEWSPAPERS	Reach large numbers of people quickly	Expensive
	Different papers reach different kinds of people so you can choose the right one for your target group	Design and artwork can be expensive
	You can use pictures as well as words	Only some papers have regional editions which means that you can save money by just advertising in the geographic area you want, but even in these, the regions are very large, e.g. you can choose to advertise in the *Guardian* nationally, or just the North, the South or London
	You can choose when your ad appears	
	You can choose the size, shape, position and content of your ad	
	You can include lots of detailed information if you can afford the space	It is expensive to run ads in colour and the use of colour is usually limited to particular pages
	You can build in a way for people to respond, e.g. with a reply coupon or a telephone number	Poor reproduction which means you cannot use small type and detailed photographs
	People can keep your ad as a tangible reference and so can have the box office telephone number in front of them when they want to book a ticket	You will be reaching a lot of people who will not be interested in what you have to offer (high wastage)
		Your ad can easily be missed by readers

	STRENGTHS	WEAKNESSES
LOCAL NEWSPAPERS	You can advertise in a specific area	The information about readership and circulation, etc., is usually poor so you cannot be sure who you are reaching
	You can link yourself with the community in that area	
	Newspapers often link advertising and editorial (known as advertorial)	Design and artwork can be expensive
		Colour is limited and expensive
	Advertising sometimes means a more favourable attitude towards giving you editorial coverage	Poor reproduction
		Some have a poor visual style
	Less wastage so it is more cost effective than national advertising	Some have a low standard of journalistic content
	You can include lots of detailed information if you can afford the space	There is lots of competition for readers' attention
	You can build in a way for people to respond	Your ad can easily be missed by readers
	People have a tangible reference	
	You can pay for a leaflet to be inserted into the paper	
MAGAZINES	If you choose the right magazine, you can target accurately and reduce wastage	Expensive
		Long deadlines: up to four months in advance
	You can reach a lot of people in your target group	There is lots of competition for readers' attention
	You can include lots of detailed information if you can afford the space	Readers often do not look at the pages at the back where ads smaller than a whole page tend to be clustered (known as 'the graveyard')
	More than one person usually reads each copy	
	People have a tangible reference	Monthly titles take time to reach all their readers
	People tend to keep magazines for much longer	No sense of immediacy: 'book now to avoid disappointment' would be particularly
	You can build in a way for people	

	STRENGTHS	WEAKNESSES
MAGAZINES CONTD	to respond The surroundings can enhance your message You can use lots of colour and images and the reproduction tends to be better	incongruous in a monthly magazine Your ad can easily be missed by readers
RADIO	Low production cost You can choose the station and time of day to reach your target group effectively You can repeat your ad frequently	You are unlikely to reach as many people in your target group You cannot show them your product because you can only use sound High wastage You have to repeat your ad several times before people get the message
TELEVISION	You can reach lots of people very quickly You can use colour, movement and sound TV attracts people's attention People watch TV together so they can make the decision to attend your show then and there You can advertise just in your region It tends to have an immediate impact on sales A good way of reaching social groups C1, C2 and D	Very expensive to advertise Very high production costs High wastage You have very little time to get your message across More affordable ad packages tend to be at the times of day and night when few people in your target groups are watching Viewers have nothing tangible to refer to later You have to repeat your ad several times before people get the message

2 UNDERSTANDING RATE CARDS

Rate cards are produced by newspapers, magazines and television and radio stations to tell the potential advertiser everything they need to know to book, design and place an advertisement. Rate cards from printed publications contain:

- a list of all the shapes, sizes and positions of advertisement possible along with a price for each
- technical details about the precise measurements and specifications for artwork
- copy deadlines
- cancellation deadlines
- information about circulation and readership.

Rate cards from television and radio stations contain:

- standard options for packages of advertisements that set out a combination of the number of times the advertisement is repeated and at what time of day and how long the advertisement lasts in seconds
- a price for each package
- deadlines
- the number of people listening or viewing at particular times
- a profile of the viewers or listeners.

BRAD (*British Rate and Data*) contains a rate card from all the media it lists.

If you are a registered charity, you may get a discount off the rate card price. Ring the relevant advertising sales department to find out.

You may be able to get sponsorship in kind for advertising. Publications and radio stations may give you free page space or air time in return for having their name associated with your organisation or event.

2.1 RATE CARD TERMINOLOGY

Bleed | An advertisement that is printed right to the edge of the paper rather than surrounded by a blank margin. Advertisements that bleed are charged for at a higher rate.

Classified | A style of advertisement consisting of simple text with no line breaks or design element and appearing under classified headings such as 'Theatre' or 'Entertainment'. They are charged for by the word.

Colour | An advertisement reproduced by the four-colour process method in which the picture is printed as a mass of dots of varying sizes in cyan, magenta, yellow and black, giving the optical illusion of full colour.

Yorkshire Post Display
Direct Advertising Rates
(Excluding VAT)

Per single column centimetre	£
Standard Rate	12.90
Financial Rate	17.85

Colour Rates - in addition to standard rates
Full Colour / Multi Spot Colour
Plus 25% on mono rate
One Spot Colour
Plus 15% on mono rate

Special Positions

	£
Solus Front Page (per scc)	18.40
Title Corner	76.55
(Fixed size) 32 mm x 75 mm	
(Back Page, TV Page or Business Post)	
Share Page Solus (Tues - Sat)	
543.60	
Solus TV (per scc)	14.15

Mechanical Data

Column Width	36mm
Column Length	560 mm
Number of Columns	9
Screen Mono	100
Screen Colour	100

Payments and Deadlines

Regular Account Holders: Payment required within 30 days of invoice date.
Non Account Holders: Payment required within 7 days of invoice date.
All Agencies: Space order numbers must be produced with copy before insertion.
Booking Deadline; 3 days prior to publication.
Copy Deadline: 2 days prior to publication
Cancellation: ROP - 2 days prior to publication
　　　　　Special Positions / Colour - 28 days prior to publication
　　　　　Solus Positions - 10 days prior to publication

Rate effective from 1.1.2000

Yorkshire Post Newspapers Ltd, Registered Office P.O. Box 168, Wellington Street, Leeds, LS1 1RF.
Tel No. Leeds 0113 2432701. Fax 0113 2388535. Ad Doc DX 25151 Leeds 4. Registered No. 2899, England.
Yorkshire Post Newspapers Ltd. is a Regional Independent Media company.

YORKSHIRE'S

NATIONAL

NEWSPAPER

**YORKSHIRE POST
NEWSPAPERS LTD**

Column

Text in newspapers and magazines is laid out in a series of narrow columns running down the page. The width of these columns and the number of columns on each page varies from publication to publication and even from one section of the same newspaper to another. The dimensions of an advertisement are usually given as the length downwards in centimetres and the width as the number of columns it stretches across. The display advertisement below appeared in *Time Out* and measures 14cm by 2 columns (in June 2000, *Time Out*'s columns were 48mm wide). It would be referred to as 'fourteen by two' for short. (*See left*)

the BOC
covent garden
festival
of opera & music theatre
17 May – 5 June 1999

Bank Holiday events...

• **The Ring** by Richard Wagner
The entire Ring cycle
condensed into one evening
Fri 28, Sat 29 May
Peacock Theatre

• **Let Him Have Justice**
A new musical drama about
the Derek Bentley case
Fri 28, Sat 29 May
Cochrane Theatre

• **Trial by Jury**
by Gilbert & Sullivan.
Fri 28, Sat 29, Mon 31 May
Bow St Magistrates' Court

• **La Senna festeggiante**
by Vivaldi
Sat 29 May
Freemasons' Hall

Box office **0171 413 1410**
website **www.cgf.co.uk**

THE BOC GROUP

AMERICAN EXPRESS Cards

Copy date	The deadline for the advertiser to submit copy or artwork.
Display	A style of advertisement that contains a variety of typefaces se out as the advertiser wants and with illustrations if required. (*See below*)
DPS	Double-page spread, charged at a premium rate.
Extra positioning	Any other criteria on the positioning of the advertisement, e.g.

bottom right-hand corner – charged at a premium rate, usually a percentage on top of the normal cost.

Facing matter	Opposite a page containing editorial.
FFM	Facing full matter – opposite a page with only editorial.
First site	The first advertisement inside the supplement, charged at a premium rate.

PEACE (Public Electronic Art Commission Exposition)
Alberto Duman and David Cotterrell

July - October 2000
Queen Victoria Square · Hull
Launch 29th July at 1pm
For more information contact HTBA (01482) 216446 / PEACE@htba.demon.co.uk

voice
Over

Fractionals	Advertisements that are fractions of a page, e.g. half page or quarter page, as opposed to being measured in single column centimetres
IBC	Inside back cover, charged at a premium rate.
IFC	Inside front cover, charged at a premium rate.
Mono	A black and white advertisement.
OBC	Outside back cover, charged at the highest rate.
OTS	Opportunities to see: the number of readers who have the opportunity to look at your advertisement.
Press date	The date when the newspaper will be printed.
RH	Right hand.
RHP	Right-hand page.
ROM	Run of magazine – see *run of paper*.
RON	Run of news – an advertisement that the newspaper can put anywhere in the news pages only at its discretion and charged for at a slightly higher rate than for run of paper.
ROP	Run of paper – an advertisement that the newspaper can place on any page it likes and charged at a basic rate.
Run of week	An advertisement that the newspaper can insert on any day during a specified week at its discretion and which is slightly cheaper than if you want it inserted on a specific day.
scc	Single column centimetre – the standard way of measuring advertisements in newspapers. The display advertisement below measures 8 cm by 3 columns (an 'eight by three') and so is 24 scc. (*See below*)

Semi-display

A style of advertisement appearing in the classified section but laid out with a variety of typefaces. Occasionally illustrations are permitted. (*See left*)

Solus

The only advertisement on a page.

Spot colour

An advertisement that is mainly black and white but has an element picked out in a standard colour, e.g. with the title in red.

National and regional newspapers usually have different sales departments for classified and display advertising so when you ring up with an enquiry or to get a rate card, make sure you know which you want.

3 TYPES OF ADVERTISEMENT

3.1 DISPLAY ADVERTISING

Arts organisations often think first about display advertising in newspapers. Possible reasons are that:

- it is relatively straightforward – you get a specific amount of space at a specific time
- you can use images
- your display advertisement is likely to be noticed by other arts organisations which is perceived as bringing prestige and certainly boosts the ego.

However, it is expensive and there may be more cost-effective ways of communicating with your target group. Out of a sample of 134,886 audience members at a wide range of events, 13% said that they had heard about the event through an advertisement in the press compared to 25% who had a leaflet or brochure posted to them.[1] You need a big enough budget to create an impact with your advertisement and to repeat it in more than one issue to ensure that enough of your target group sees it. If you can only afford a small advertisement, you may find it is barely noticeable beside others on the same page.

[1] Peter Walshe, *Research Digests for the Arts* (Arts Council of Great Britain, 1992)

DISPLAY ADVERTISING COSTS: JUNE 2000

	Rate per scc	5cm x 2 columns	12cm x 2 columns
Guardian Run of main paper + 10% for fixed day	£38	£418	£1,003.20
Friday Review	£41	£410	£984.00
Yorkshire Post	£12.90	£129	£309.60
Stamford Mercury	£4.20	£42	£100.80
The List (a listings magazine based in Exeter)	£6.50	£65	£156.00

As well as the cost of the page space itself, you will need to pay for the production of the advertisement. Production costs usually include graphic design, artwork and typesetting. Some publications will artwork simple advertisements for you, but you will probably have to pay for this facility and may not end up with satisfactory results.

The advertisement below was placed in the *Fulham & Hammersmith Chronicle* and the *West London Post* and cost £50 to produce at £20 per hour for the designer's time.

I work with a freelance graphic designer called Annie Rushton. We have a mutual understanding – I almost don't have to brief her. We've got the corporate identity looking so strong that we don't have to waste time passing paper to and fro. The first visuals need so little tweaking.

Paul Gray, Marketing Manager, Covent Garden Festival

CREATING YOUR DISPLAY ADVERTISEMENT

- When choosing the size of your advertisement, remember that it must be big enough to include all your essential information and to be noticeable on the page.

- Focus on your organisation's corporate identity when deciding what to put in your advertisement. Consider including your logo and repeat any imagery you have used on other publicity materials. If you have employed a graphic designer to produce other publicity for your event, ask them to design your advertisements as well.

- Make sure that your advertisement communicates the relevant benefits for the target group at which you are aiming.

- Choose an image that communicates the key benefit.

- Use a by-line that explains the key benefit or makes a promise to your target group.

- Use simple, succinct copy.

- Newspapers do not have high standards of reproduction – if you include complicated imagery or a lot of copy it may not be legible.

- Make sure that it is easy to respond to your advertisement. Test a mock-up on other people, preferably someone in your target group.

- If you get any editorial coverage about your event and/or organisation, place your advertisement on the same page to give people the information they need to take action.

- People tend to notice the right-hand page of a publication before the left, so it is better to position your advertisement on the right-hand page where possible.

SYNDICATE GROUPS

Many local newspapers are produced in syndicates. This means that there are several different editions, each with a different title and covering different geographic areas. The main content of the paper remains the same but a few pages carry information relevant to the particular community. It is relatively cheaper to place an advertisement in all of the newspapers in the group and you will only need to produce one set of artwork for the advertisement to be reproduced in several different newspapers. It costs £4.20 per single column centimetre to place an advertisement on the entertainment pages of the *Stamford Mercury* and £1.60 in its sister paper, *The Citizen*, but just £5.25 per single column centimetre for both.

COMPOSITE ADVERTISEMENTS

These are advertisements where the style and layout remains the same but the content alters each week. Some venues produce composite advertisements known as 'ladder ads'. These are long and narrow in shape and contain a simple listing for each forthcoming event – usually the date, time, company and show title.

Composite ads are particularly useful for promoters as they are simple to use and relatively cheap. Some organisations get a graphic designer to create the standard format and they then use simple desktop publishing to change the information. Others send the new copy to the newspaper which typesets it in the agreed style. Some organisations simply telephone newspapers to change copy. This involves careful attention by the arts organisation to ensure that spellings, dates and use of upper or lower case is correct.

It is easy to make mistakes in composite ads, whoever creates the artwork, particularly when typing new information on top of the old. I saw a ladder ad in a local listings magazine which announced that Bodger and Badger were starring in *Macbeth*!

> We take a weekly ladder listing in our local paper, with the name of the company and four lines of copy. We did an audience survey which showed that the majority of our audience found out about the show from the paper. We advertise in English for English-language productions and Welsh if the show is in Welsh and they appear side by side. **Administrator, mixed programme venue, Wales**

3.2 CLASSIFIED ADVERTISING

Many larger venues place regular classified advertisements in the larger regional newspapers and sometimes in the national papers as well. They are most effective in communicating with audiences who have decided they want to go out and are consulting the paper to find out what is on that night. This means that classified advertisements need to be in every issue of the paper.

CLASSIFIED ADVERTISING: COSTS IN MAY 2000

National daily (the *Daily Telegraph* theatre listings Monday to Friday)	£4.80 per line + VAT
Regional listings magazine (*The List*, in Exeter)	50p per word

> Most weeks our classified advertisement appears next to 'Pick your own raspberries'. It has no impact at all … We are trying to get together with the other arts venues in our area and places like the cinema complex to take a block that we book jointly and all use so that people know where to look for everything to do with the arts. **Administrator, arts centre, England**

3.3 RADIO

Radio advertising enables you to market your organisation using words, sounds and music. It is well worth considering for productions with a broad appeal where the music is very important. The main disadvantage of radio advertising is that listeners cannot refer back to the advertisement and have to write the box office telephone number down as they listen.

- Make sure that your advertisement communicates the relevant benefits for the target group at which you are aiming.
- Get the listener's attention at the start of your advertisement.
- Use a short sentence at the beginning that explains the key benefit or makes a promise to your target group.

- Use very simple, short sentences.
- Repeat the important information, particularly the key benefit and the box office telephone number.
- Read your advertisement aloud to other people, preferably from your target group, before you give it to the radio station.

All the Independent Local Radio (ILR) stations offer radio advertising. The costs vary depending on the time of day and the length of the advertisement. You will also have to pay for the production of the advertisement.

A Midlands radio station suggests that arts clients take out four or five 30-second slots a day for three days. They sell air time in packages, and the price varies according to the package you choose.

> Radio advertising is the best way to get to the Asian community. **Arts marketing consultant**

PIRATE RADIO

Many illegal pirate radio stations also offer advertising slots. This is considerably cheaper than advertising on licensed stations, but there are several risks involved: the station probably will not be able to provide you with much information about its audience; the quality of the broadcast may vary considerably; and the station might suddenly disappear from the airwaves altogether! However, there are usually fewer advertisements on pirate stations, so your advertisement may be played many times more than on a licensed station.

A small-scale black theatre company appeared at an arts centre in the Midlands with a reggae/soul musical. Because of the nature of the show and some of the target groups at which it was aimed, the company decided to advertise on pirate radio. A 30-second advertisement was broadcast approximately 12 times over each 24-hour period for the week of the performances. Although no formal audience research was done, informal questions showed that a large percentage of attenders had heard about the show through the advertisement. The company's administrator says that the cost of advertising on pirate radio depends largely on personal contact with the radio staff.

4 PLACING YOUR ADVERTISEMENT

1. Get a rate card from the publication or television or radio station.
2. Decide how big/long you want your advertisement to be, taking into account the amount of information you need to include and the impact you need to make to be noticed by your reader.
3. Decide whether you want a colour advertisement, to use spot colour or to stick to mono (black and white). Do you want additional impact by having an advertisement that bleeds (goes right to the edge of the page rather than having a margin).

CASE STUDY

ADVERTISING RATIONALE FOR THE BELFAST FESTIVAL AT QUEEN'S FESTIVAL DATES FRIDAY 27 OCTOBER – SUNDAY 12 NOVEMBER 2000

Advertising, and indeed the marketing of the Belfast Festival, operates at two levels.

1. **Brand investment:** The Belfast Festival is keen to get to a position where our brand is recognised as standing for high quality international arts presented alongside the best of Northern Irish work in a unique and exciting atmosphere.
2. **Events promotion:** Each festival is different and shaped by the events of that year. Each event needs to be marketed separately to the appropriate target audience using appropriate messages.

In 2000 we have to convey the following:

- **BRAND:** The 2000 Belfast Festival is innovative, has a major international theme, is commissioning new work for the first time and is increasing access opportunities in a number of ways, i.e. website and reaching new parts of Belfast.
- **EVENTS:** There are almost 200 different events, mostly paid for by the Festival but there are others that are co-promoted by the Festival.

So what are we trying to say?

- The Belfast Festival is for you and it is everywhere in Belfast.
- Stop doing what you normally do from 27 October – 12 November and go to the Festival.
- Here are specific events we know you will like and this is why.

The advertising schedule (overleaf)

Radio: persuasive medium. Reminds people that the Festival is happening.
Outdoor: In-your-face, creates atmosphere in the city.
Press: more detail, actual events.
Postcard advertising: quirky, trendy, suits 18–35 year olds.
Washroom advertising: new ambient media, suits 18–35 year olds.
Specific targeting is limited using above-the-line advertising, so this will be supported through direct mailing.

Most advertising will take place in Northern Ireland, but a combination of press, radio and direct marketing will be used in the Republic of Ireland to target city break buyers with an arts interest, particularly in the Dublin area where rail links to Belfast are excellent.

It is intended to commence advertising activity from the launch of the Belfast Festival on 6 September and until the end of the festival on 12 November. Particularly important is the period after the initial launch interest until the opening of the festival (27 October) when booking patterns show a dip in ticket sales. The Belfast Festival must create a sense of expectation and urgency to get tickets in this period. Margaret McKee, Sales and Marketing Manager, The Belfast Festival at Queen's

Client: Belfast Festival at Queen's

Subject: Media Schedule 2000

Media	Size	Sep 4	11	18	25	Oct 2	9	16	23	31	Nov 6	13
									Festival dates: 27/10 - 12/11			
Northern Ireland: c£20k		Programme launch 6/9										
Events Press												
Belfast Telegraph; Irish News;	c15 cm x 2 cols, mono											
News Letter; Belfast News	5 insertions per title						x	x	x	x	x	
Outdoor												
48 sheets	20 sites x 4 weeks						▓	▓	▓	▓		
Radio												
Cool FM; Belfast Citybeat	10 seconds (5 versions) x 3 weeks						▓	▓	▓			
Republic of Ireland / Additional media: c£10k												
Generic Press												
Belfast Telegraph; Irish News;	10 cm x 1 cols, mono		x	x,x	x,x	x	x	x				
News Letter; Belfast News	7 insertions per title											
ROI Radio												
Lyric FM, Lite FM	30 seconds x 3 weeks				▓		▓		▓			
ROI press												
Sunday Times (Culture)	20 cm x 2 cols, mono				x	x	x		x			
Hot Press	Quarter page, mono				x							
Additional Media												
Guardian	Sizes tbc							x	x			
Internet	Sites tbc							▓		▓	▓	▓
The Big List	Size tbc							x	x	x	x	x

Week commencing dates 2000 — September, October, Nov

4. Decide which section of the newspaper or magazine will reach your
    target groups most effectively. Do you want your advertisement to
    appear on specific pages or in a specific position? If you want to
    advertise on radio or television, what time of day will reach your
    target groups best? Are there any specific programmes that your
    target group listens to or watches?

5. How many times do you want your advertisement to appear to ensure that
    you reach as many as possible of your target group and they
    understand and remember your message?

6. Check the rate card to see if you can afford what you are planning.

7. Decide when you want your advertisements to appear. Do you want
    to bunch them together for impact or spread them out over a period
    of time? Do you want them to appear on a particular day of the
    week each time, perhaps to coincide with a particular programme or
    section of the publication that is likely to appeal to your target group?

8. Decide whether you want the publication to prepare artwork for the
    advertisement or to organise that yourself. Most television and radio
    stations will want to take responsibility for producing your
    advertisement as a guarantee of quality.

9. Telephone the sales department of your chosen publication or station.
    Many newspapers have separate departments for display and
    classified advertising so the switchboard will ask which you want to
    talk to.

10. Tell the sales representative what you are planning. Check the price.
    If you want them to produce the artwork or the radio or television
    advertisement, find out how much this will cost.

11. Find out what the copy deadlines are (this is when you have to deliver
    the artwork or give them the copy for them to produce the
    advertisement).

12. Find out to whom you should address the artwork or copy and
    exactly what address you need to put on the envelope, including the
    department and floor if appropriate.

13. If you are organising the artwork, find out precisely what size it needs
    to be in millimetres and how they want the artwork presented. Write
    this down carefully as you will need to give it to the graphic designer
    if you are using one.

14. Ask the sales representative if there is anything else you should know.

15. Type up all the information you have collected and send the sales
    representative a confirmation fax. This means they can spot anything
    you may have misunderstood or that they have forgotten to tell you.

16. Brief the graphic designer by telling them exactly what you are trying
    to achieve and giving them the copy you have written and the
    technical information you have collected. Make sure that they are
    aware of the deadline.

17. You will also need to brief the television or radio station or the publication's graphic designer in the same way, although they should know the technical information already. The sales representative usually acts as a go-between in this process so it is important to give them everything in writing.

18. Check the final artwork before it goes to the paper. If you are placing a radio or television advertisement, you will want to check the script thoroughly before it is recorded as well as the final result before it is broadcast.

19. Telephone your graphic designer before the deadline to check that the artwork is going to arrive on time.

20. Check that your advertisement has appeared correctly in the newspaper or magazine or in the appropriate slots on television or radio.

21. Keep a copy for your records.

22. Check the invoice when it arrives to check that the amount and insertion dates are correct.

REMEMBER ✳

Monitor the response to your advertisement by comparing daily sales before and after it appears or by asking box office staff to find out where people heard about the event. You could even use a different telephone number in the advertisement and keep track of the number of calls on that line.

15 HOW TO SET UP A WEBSITE

SEE ALSO CHAPTER
3. HOW TO WRITE COPY

Consult www.netlingo.com for a glossary of terms used by web designers and consultants.

A website is a marketing communication method like any other. You should only set one up if it is the most effective form of communication with one or more of the target groups you have chosen. Websites are not a targeted medium so arts organisations should not overestimate their effectiveness. Direct e-mail is more powerful as it can be targeted precisely.

Identify what it will provide for your target groups that they cannot get more effectively elsewhere. Too many organisations set up a website that is nothing more than their brochure on-line and the only people they tell about it are the readers of their event programmes or leaflets and season brochures. These are some of the ways a website can offer your existing and potential audiences a unique service:

- Provide the very latest information about events including recent reviews and up-to-the-minute ticket availability.
- Give potential attenders the chance to read feedback from people who have already seen the event.
- Provide one or more members-only sections where particular groups of your audience and participants can chat, ask questions, share information and exchange opinions.
- Offer a chance to sample the event through video and sound clips.
- Give background information and insights into the creative process through interviews with artists, performers and staff members.
- Answer questions through a live interview with the director or choreographer of the event a few weeks before the show.
- Quizzes and competitions.
- Take them on a virtual guided tour of the venue – including the opportunity to see the view from the seat they are thinking about booking.
- Send people highly targeted e-mails which offer them a direct link to the information in which they are interested – you simply go to the right page on your site, copy and paste the web address of that page into the e-mail and when they receive it, they can click on the address and go straight there.

- Give access to image and sound archives.

- Order and pay for their drinks, programme and ice cream in advance.

- Web-casting actual on-line events.

So what makes a good site?

- fast access

- accessible to people with slow modems and low resolution screens

- easy to navigate

- accurate and up-to-date information

- an obvious name

- a warm welcome to visitors

- easy to find the answer

- essential information is at the top of the screen

- minimum scrolling around screens.

The main decision you need to make is whether to create and maintain your site internally, or to delegate responsibility to an outside organisation or individual.

I think it's better to do something very simple in-house and then you can afford to update it at least weekly. If you can cope with desktop publishing software, then you can design a site. Just go on a course. The main thing is not to over-design it. Instead of flashy graphics, concentrate on dividing your information into small chunks and keep people moving through it. Above all, get on line and surf like crazy. **Dan Pinchbeck, Hull Time-based Arts**

[1] Bill Thompson, *Super Activ: Your Own Website* (Hodder Children's Books), £3.99

Try Bill Thompson's book *Super Activ: Your Own Website* which is written primarily for children so even a complete novice can follow it.[1]

1 THE PLANNING PROCESS STEP BY STEP

1. Decide which target groups will be best served by the website.

2. People are using the Internet far more in their working lives and free Internet service providers means that more people have access at home. One of the fastest growing sectors is retired people. Even so, wherever possible, you should research to find out what proportion of your target groups have easy access to the Internet. One website aimed at 16–18 year olds in school foundered because the young people only

had access at a brief time-tabled period during the week and the computers had insufficient processing capability to interact with the site.

3. Decide how the website will integrate with your overall communications strategy.

4. Identify the information needs and wants of your target groups. Unless you offer useful information, activities and services, no one will look at the site more than once. Different parts of the same site can be aimed at different target groups.

5. Decide what your website is *for*. What do you want browsers to think and do? Do you want your site to give your target groups additional information not available elsewhere? Do you want to provide them with an easier way to buy tickets? Do you want to help them plan their night out? Do you want to enhance their understanding of the art form? Or do you want to have a two-way conversation with them?

6. If you are working with other organisations on a collaborative project, clarify who owns the site and who is responsible for its upkeep.

7. Decide who in your organisation will be responsible for deciding strategic issues about the site and who will be in charge of its day-to-day running (they can be the same person, although it is a good idea to have a small steering group who take an active part in making strategic decisions).

8. Now decide what process you are going to use to set up and run the site. Will you work with a consultant? If so, how will you choose them? Will you liaise directly with a web designer? Or will you design and create the site in-house?

9. Identify who will be contributing information to the site.

10. Think about how that information will be presented online. Focus on your target groups who will have different levels of understanding and technical ability, different hardware and software and different access needs.

11. How are you going to evaluate the site's effectiveness? You will need to monitor this throughout the active life of the site.

A good website is a usable website. If it's a showcase then put the show behind a simple, fast-loading and easy-to-follow home page – that gives people the option to miss the show and just find out the stuff they want to know. **Bill Thompson, bill@andfinally.com**

2 CHOOSING CONSULTANTS AND/OR DESIGNERS

It seems to me that people's common sense goes completely out of the window when it comes to website design. Surely, you should go about it in the same way as you would go about doing anything like this – you would always write a design brief for your brochure and it should be the same for your website. **Jonathan Goodacre, Marketing Development Manager, Eastern Touring Agency**

1. Compile a brief. This should include:

(a) Introduction to the project.

(b) Background information about the organisation.

(c) A summary of the aims and objectives of the project.

(d) What you want the site to achieve.

(e) Information about the target groups and the type of hardware and software to which they are likely to have access.

(f) How you see the scope and style of the site.

(g) How you want people to be able to navigate and search for information within the site. This is often sacrificed in favour of creative design.

(h) Any stipulations you have about readability and accessibility. Large files are expensive and time-consuming to download for those with slow modems.

(i) Information about the proposed Internet service provider.

(j) Your technical requirements, e.g. about two-way communication.

(k) The content you want on the home page and how this should link with other pages. Complex home pages are slow to access.

(l) Tell them if you want the consultant, designer or agency to be responsible for the maintenance of the site, future design developments and/or updating of information, or if you will do this in-house. Say how you plan to go about this.

(m) Specify who you want to be responsible for registering the site with search engines.

(n) You can include guidelines for good practice set up by other organisations. Current useful sites include:

 i) The Web Content Accessibility Guidelines endorsed by the RNIB and developed by the Web Accessibility Initiative (WAI), a project group of the Worldwide Web Consortium (W3C): www.w3.org/WAI (May 1999).

 ii) Guidelines for the use, management and design of public sector websites available on www.citu.gov.uk

2. Make a shortlist. You can find a list of web designers searchable by speciality and geographic area on **www.webresources.co.uk**. Find out who was responsible for sites you have seen and admired. The Arts Marketing Association newsletter contains a 'Webwatch' column that reviews arts websites, good and bad, and the Theatrical Management Association's magazine *Prompt* carries a list of its members' websites.

3. Ask the designers, consultants or agencies to send you a CV listing live websites that you can look at on-line. It is very important to talk to the people in the organisations behind those sites to see how satisfied they are with the service they got both during and after the development process. How efficient and reliable were the web designers and account handlers? Did they have enough staff to respond quickly to any problems, even in busy periods?

4. Now narrow down your shortlist, send them the brief and ask them to make a presentation to your steering group. You should ask them to show you pages from sites they have designed that illustrate the issues set out in your brief.

5. When you have chosen your designer or consultant, contract to pay them less than half of the agreed fee up front and hold back a significant percentage until the site is up and running efficiently and they have provided everything you specified to help you maintain and update it. Make sure that you specify that your organisation will hold the copyright on design, not the designers.

6. If you are contracting an outside organisation to be responsible for maintaining the site, the contract should specify:

    (a) the length of the contract

    (b) number, timing and promptness of updates

    (c) number of templates to be provided by the contractor

    (d) number of site redesigns to be made during the period of the contract

    (e) potential cost of additional design work outside that specified in the contract.

7. Make sure that the contract gives you and your colleagues access to the server and passwords so that you can update the site whenever you need to.

Make sure that the sections of the site that need updating are very simple and do not use complex graphics. This means that you and your colleagues can update the information with the minimum of training.

Dan Pinchbeck, Hull Time-based Arts

3 PROMOTING YOUR SITE

- Register with all the key search engines.
- Set up hot links with as many related sites as you can, e.g. tourist information, the local authority, and other leisure, entertainment and educational sites.
- Run an advertising campaign in your local listings magazine or gig guide.
- Send out press releases.
- Send e-mails to on-line magazines.
- E-mail your e-mailing list and any other key contacts.
- Send out direct mail to your target groups.

4 EVALUATING YOUR SITE

- Designers and site managers should view sites alongside members of the target group and listen to their comments.
- Statistical reports (known as log reports) from the server including hits, how long people are spending on the site, the most popular pages and the number of different people looking at the site (known as hosts).
- Incoming e-mails.
- Content of e-mails.
- Press reviews of the site.
- Income from ticket sales.

5 INTERNET TICKETING

This is an area that is constantly changing. For up-to-date information, contact the Arts Marketing Association. In June 2000, arts organisations had five options:

1. An e-mail booking service similar to the fax service operated by many box offices where the customer orders their tickets by e-mail and the box office responds to confirm the booking. (This is not really Internet booking but is better than nothing.)

2. Offer a link to a third-party site that has direct access to your ticket inventory. This can involve a booking fee for the customer as well as a charge to your organisation. The link can be seamless so that the customer feels that they are getting the full on-line reservation and payment service from your organisation.

3. Your customer goes to a third-party site and buys tickets through a live link into your ticket allocation.

4.   Give a ticket allocation to a third-party site. This usually involves a booking fee for the customer but the site may not make a charge to you. This offers no advantages to your organisation beyond those of the normal ticket agency sale as your box office staff will have to enter the customer's name and address manually into your system.

5.   Offer customers an integrated on-line reservation and payment service that does not involve a third-party server.

16 HOW TO CREATE EFFECTIVE DISPLAYS

SEE ALSO CHAPTER
12. HOW TO GET PRESS AND MEDIA COVERAGE

Displays are a communication tool that can serve several different purposes:
- to attract attention and raise awareness of an event, company or venue
- to give additional information to persuade your potential audience to attend
- to enhance the audience's understanding of your organisation's work
- to make a space more interesting.

Most venues have some display space in their foyers or front-of-house areas, but you can also put up displays in shop windows, libraries, shopping centres, schools and colleges, town halls and other public buildings.

REMEMBER

Effective displays are time-consuming to create so consider the cost in terms of both time and money before choosing locations – they should give you the potential to communicate with a large section of your target groups to be worthwhile.

Touring companies often invest significant resources in preparing ready-made displays to send to their venues as this is an effective way of persuading existing attenders at the venue to see their show. These displays should aim to remind people about an event they may have already seen in the season brochure, to give them additional information about the event and what it will be like through images as well as words, and to prompt them into taking action to buy tickets. If you are sending them to venues through a parcel delivery service, you will need to pack them well to avoid damage. You may also be able to deliver them during your marketing visit to the venue. To get the most use out of display boards, stage managers can collect display boards at the end of a performance and send them on to another venue. This may take some careful planning, but will considerably reduce the number of displays you need to create.

1 DISPLAY MATERIALS

You can display your information on free-standing or hanging boards or in lockable display cabinets or cases. Information that is not covered is usually more inviting to look at, as there is no glass or plastic to reflect light or show the dirt, but any uncovered photographs or posters may get damaged or stolen. Companies will find it easier to transport display boards rather than cabinets.

A wide range of free-standing display boards are available from the larger catalogue stationery firms and direct from manufacturers. These are expensive but good quality stands are long lasting. Choose a design that is easy to erect and dismantle, packs down into a carrying case that will fit into a car boot and is stable without presenting possible trip hazards. Be aware that some display systems are unsuitable for use with some of the possible methods of fixing your display such as drawing pins and staples or Blutack.

You can make your own value-for-money displays by buying materials from builder's merchants. Consider strawboard, fibreboard, chipboard, hardboard or large cork tiles. It is best to choose a material that is both durable and lightweight, takes pins or staples and also retains a good surface after they are removed. The builder's merchant will cut your board to size for you. You can then paint it or cover it with fabrics like felt, velvet, brocade or hessian to improve its appearance.

You can get material for less robust but cheaper and lighter display boards from graphic art shops. These come in A1 or A2 sizes and in a range of colours. Choose from: mounting board; foam board (which is light but dents easily); polyboard or chromaluxe which comes in vivid colours and a glossy surface but is rather thin. You can mount chromaluxe on a stronger board.

You can use a variety of materials to fix your information in place: double-sided sticky tape, drawing pins with small plain heads, map pins with coloured heads, sticky fixers, aerosol adhesive or Velcro. A staple gun is quick and easy to use. Choose methods that are not going to damage your display materials. Liquid glue will buckle paper, card and photographs. You will not be able to remove double-sided sticky tape, adhesive pads or Velcro dots from photographs without damaging them.

Make sure that your display is appropriately lit.

1.1 WHAT TO DISPLAY

This will depend on the purpose of the display, the amount of space available and its location. A display that aims to attract attention and raise awareness should be bold and simple and carry less information than one designed to enhance audience understanding. This also applies to locations in which people will be unwilling or unable to stop and look for long.

Displays should always reflect the organisation's corporate identity by using graphic identities such as logos, communicating in an appropriate tone of voice and reflecting the quality of its work.

Choose textures and colours that complement your information. It is generally less effective to use too many colours and textures in the same display. Use strong-coloured paper or card to mount photographs and press cuttings, giving you an attractive border round each.

With all displays, place information at an appropriate height for people to look at it. If at all possible, repeat similar information at different heights: low for children and people in wheelchairs, higher up for others.

It is usually best to use simple, striking shapes like strong verticals or diagonals. Repeat images to reinforce your message, but do not cramp the information together. Enlarge written information with a photocopier. It is worth spending time and effort – an untidy display will make your organisation look cheap.

PRINT

You can display posters, leaflets and programmes. You are unlikely to reduce programme sales by displaying them – in fact, people might be tempted to buy one as a result. Display the inside and back of leaflets and programmes as well as the front.

PHOTOGRAPHS

For maximum impact it is better to use a few large photographs, perhaps 12″ x 16″, than several small ones. Choose a variety of landscape and portrait formats for interest. You can get a repro house to turn colour transparencies into prints, or if you cannot afford this, use colour photocopies and colour laser prints. Caption photographs with details of the characters and/or performers as appropriate – repro houses can provide captioned photographs for you or you can make captions yourself and stick them on.

You may be able to afford to laminate photographs to make them last longer. Some larger organisations get photographs of performers in costume enlarged to almost life size, mounted on chipboard or thick, dense cardboard and cut them out to create 'standees'. Cinema distributors often provide these for blockbuster movies. Chain them down, however, or fans will steal them.

PRESS CUTTINGS

It is worth displaying interesting preview pieces and good reviews to provide an independent endorsement of your organisation and event. You can enlarge cuttings with a photocopier, perhaps using coloured paper. Mount the cuttings on card or paper to stop them getting tatty. Cut out especially good quotes such as 'a marvellous production' and display them in slash format (placed diagonally across a corner) for maximum impact.

OTHER INFORMATION

You can put up any information that is relevant to your event or organisation. For example, you may want to show costume or set design sketches or initial research notes. All this 'behind the scenes' information is likely to be of interest to the general public and to enhance their understanding of the creative process.

BANNERS

Look in Yellow Pages for a specialist printer who can provide a range of colours and sizes on weatherproof plastic, or you can make fabric banners to use indoors and get a signwriter to add the copy. You are likely to need planning permission from the local authority to display signs and banners outside as well as permission from the owners of the buildings to which you want to attach them.

3D DISPLAYS

3D displays are usually very effective. You can exhibit a model of the set design of a particular production. It is probably best to put this in a display case as it could easily get damaged. You can also display costumes and props.

VIDEOS

Videos can be used as 'moving displays'. They are especially useful for telling people about non-text based events which are hard to describe in words.

The most effective videos tend to be those that actually tell a story and do not just show the work that you do. These can include footage of previous or current productions by the same organisation, or of audiences or participants engaging in activities that your organisation puts on such as workshops. It is best to keep videos short as people usually have a limited attention span. You will need a video player that automatically rewinds and restarts the video unless you have a member of staff standing by to do it manually.

Make sure that your video is of adequate quality – a poorly produced video is more likely to persuade people not to see the event as it implies that it will be of low quality. It is a good idea to put up a notice on or next to the video monitor saying when and where the company shown can be seen live.

1.2 WHEN TO MOUNT DISPLAYS

Do not mount your displays too early or they will lose impact. Generally, put up information about a particular production about two to three weeks in advance of a performance date. However, it is useful to put up a display at events with a similar audience to your own, even if these take place two or three months earlier. You can also put up a small amount of information about six weeks in advance of your event and then replace it with a full display nearer the time.

CASE STUDY

LEICESTER COMEDY FESTIVAL: DISPLAYS IN LEICESTER CITY CENTRE

Leicester Comedy Festival, now in its eighth year, takes place over a ten-day period in February. The Festival involves a host of art forms, ranging from stand-up comedy to poetry and takes place at nearly thirty venues throughout Leicestershire.

Leicester city centre is the geographical focus for the county and the Festival, so it is vital to display unmissable publicity material in this area. Because the Festival covers such a range of art forms and involves so many venues, the brand needs to embody all that the Festival stands for within one striking logo that appears everywhere.

The Festival has used street banners in the city centre for a number of festivals. The four busiest city centre streets are used to host the banners. In addition, the Festival encourages all participating venues to display a venue banner, which features the Festival logo and the number of that venue as it appears in the Festival brochure.

The Festival produces posters in a range of sizes which are distributed by a display team throughout the city centre and county. Libraries, shops, pubs, cafés, bars and community centres are the principal outlets for both Festival posters and brochures.

This year, the Festival also introduced another display idea.

We persuaded a variety of high street stores either to provide window displays for the Festival or to display posters inside the shop. Participating shops included Marks & Spencer, Woolworths, Virgin Megastore and Waterstones.

We planned that the cumulative effect of our efforts would ensure that anyone in the city centre would know that the Comedy Festival was taking place and would have immediate access to the information they needed to follow up that awareness, including the dates of the Festival and the hotline number to call for more details. **Trudie McGuinness, Marketing Officer, Leicester Comedy Festival**

17 HOW TO MANAGE YOUR BUDGET

As you will see, managing a budget is simply common sense combined with careful record keeping.

1 A STEP-BY-STEP GUIDE

1. If you have simply been given an overall marketing budget figure, divide it into headings based on the broad categories of what you spend your money on. Find out what your marketing budget is supposed to cover, e.g. will your travel expenses and the cost of any training you go on be deducted? If so, include them as a budget heading. If you can, base this on what was spent last year, making adjustments according to your overall plans for the year. For example:

	£
Advertising	6,000
Design	3,000
Printing: brochures	12,000
overprinting, etc.	1,500
Film publicity	2,500
Postage	12,000
	37,000

    This organisation has not included a contingency. This is the figure, often 10% of the total, that is set aside to act as a buffer in emergencies. It would be a good idea to have one just in case.

2. Now decide when you are likely to spend the money. It is best to divide it up on a monthly or a show-by-show basis depending on what kind of organisation you work for. This organisation spends roughly the same on advertising every month but only produces two brochures every year. Put the budget for large items of expenditure in the month when the invoice will arrive:

In the management accounts, your finance officer is likely to spread large items of expenditure like this over the months to which they apply – in this case the period covered by the season brochure (see accrual in the glossary below).

Budget		April	May	June	July	Aug	Sept	Oct	Nov	Dec	Jan	Feb	Mar
Advertising	6,000	500	500	500	500	500	500	500	500	500	500	500	500
Design	3,000						1,500				1,500		
Brochures	12,000						6,000*				6,000*		
Overprinting, etc.	1,500	100	100	100	150	150	100	100	100	300	100	100	100
Film publicity	2,500	750			50	750		50	50	750		50	50
Postage	12,000	500	1,000	500		4,000		500	500	4,000		500	500
TOTAL	37,000												

This budget breakdown is meant as a guide only. If you spend more than you have allocated one month, do not worry too much as long as you can spend less in the future or under another budget heading to make up for it.

3.   Every time you order something, make a note of it on your spreadsheet or in a book. Larger organisations may have official purchase order forms with one copy going to the supplier and one to the accounts department. You should keep the third copy. The purchase order will fix the quantity, quality and price of whatever it is you are buying.

4.   Make sure that you see every invoice that will be counted as marketing expenditure. You should check them against your purchase orders. Write down everything in a book or on a spreadsheet like this:

Invoice Date	Supplier	Item	Total Actual	Advertising	Design	Brochures	Over-printing	Film publicity
02/08/00	Post Office Counters	Franking machine	4,000					
12/08/00	Housemouse Design	Brochure design	1,700		1,700			
17/08/00	APL Printing	25,000 brochures & leaflet overprinting	5,675			5,600	75	
21/08/00	APL Printing	Leaflet overprinting	75					
24/08/00	Kempsford Mercury	Season ads	380	380				
		Total Actual	11,830	380	1,700	5,600	75	0
		Budget	12,900	500	1,500	6,000	150	750
		Variance	1,070	120	-200	400	75	750

The 'variance' column is the difference between the total expenditure for that heading in that month and the budget. Over the whole period covered by your budget, you should aim to keep the total variance to nil (or at least to a minimum). If you achieve this, you have successfully managed your budget.

5.   Every month, check that your figures and your accounts department or finance officer's figures are the same. If they are not, find out why by going through the copies of invoices and purchase orders kept by each department and matching them up.

2 UNDERSTANDING YOUR FINANCE OFFICER: A GLOSSARY OF TERMS

Accrual	If you spend a lot on something that you use over an extended period of time, your finance officer may want to spread that cost over the whole period in the management accounts. An example would be the season brochure – in the example above, the organisation pays £7,500 for design and printing in August and December. The brochures cover September to January and February to June. The finance officer may decide to make an accrual of £1,200 for each of the five months that each brochure covers.
Actual	This is what you or your organisation have actually spent as opposed to what you were planning to spend when you drew up your budget.
Audit	This is the most important point in your finance officer's year when the firm of accountants appointed by the board of directors come to inspect the way that your organisation goes about its business to ensure that the financial records are accurate. They check a sample of everything – including the receipts in the petty cash tin in your bottom drawer.
Audited accounts	The version of the accounts approved by the auditors as a 'true and fair' record of your organisation's finances.
Budget	A set of guide figures for you and your colleagues to work to. They are not set in stone – if your organisation is facing a deficit, everyone may be asked to reduce their budgets.
Carry over	If you have not spent all your budget, your finance officer may occasionally allow you to carry it over from one financial year to the next. Usually they do not because it is needed to cover someone else's overspend! Some organisations divide up their budgets on a show-by-show basis and you may be allowed to carry over any money that you have not spent on one show to another.
Cashflow forecast	This is your finance officer's attempt to chart exactly when money is likely to be received and paid by the organisation. This is important as it ensures that the organisation does not spend money that, at that moment, it has not got.
Deficit	The word used by non-profit making organisations

when their expenditure is more than their income. A commercial organisation that seeks to make a profit would call this 'a loss'. Deficits are shown either in brackets or with a minus sign in front of them.

Earned income
The money coming into your organisation through ticket sales, royalties, merchandising, catering and sponsorship. It specifically excludes grants from funding bodies, bank interest, etc.

Expenditure
All the money that your organisation spends.

Financial accounts
A more formal version of the accounts which shows who owes your organisation money and what money your organisation owes other people (debtors and creditors). It may include a balance sheet which is a statement of the organisation's overall financial position and indicates whether it is solvent or bankrupt.

Fixed cost
A cost that does not change regardless of how many performances or events your organisation does. You have to pay a designer the same fee for creating the set regardless of whether you do 10 performances of that show or 200.

Income
All the money coming into your organisation including grants as well as earned income.

Management account
Accounts designed to give your senior management team and/or board of directors the information they need to make responsible decisions. They may include a breakdown which matches the income and expenditure for each event to show the surplus or deficit.

Overhead
Expenditure that you cannot easily allocate to a particular event or activity. It might include salaries, rent, lighting and heating.

Pre-payment
A payment made in advance in one period when you will get the service or goods in the next. An example is paying for a whole season's advertisements in a newspaper in advance in January when the season does not end until May. Your finance officer may ask you to work out how much of that pre-payment is for advertisements before the end of the financial year and how much is for advertisements that will appear after.

Purchase order
A record of an item of expenditure to which a member of staff has committed the organisation. This means that your finance officer can keep track not just of what money has actually been spent, but what will be spent in the near future.

Surplus
The word used by non-profit making organisations

when their income is more than their expenditure. A commercial organisation which seeks to make money would call this profit.

Turnover   Strictly, this refers to your organisation's total earned income excluding VAT but without making any kind of allowance of what it spent to earn that money. Many arts organisations use it to refer to their total income including grants from funding bodies.

Variable cost   A cost that changes depending on the number of performances or events your organisation puts on. Your season brochure will cost less to print if you only have three shows in it rather than eight because you will need fewer pages.

18 HOW TO PREPARE A MARKETING PLAN FOR A LOTTERY APPLICATION

This is a framework for a marketing plan suitable for small- and middle-scale companies, promoters and venues.

1 CURRENT MARKETING PRACTICE

What role does marketing play within your organisation? How can you demonstrate that it is seen as important? Who is responsible for marketing and how much time do they spend on it?

1.1 BUDGET

What is your marketing budget? Is this more or less than in previous years?

1.2 MARKETING INFORMATION

What information do you have about your end users (audiences, participants, teachers, etc.)? If you rely on other organisations such as partners, co-producers or venues to market your work, then talk about them too. What are they like? What are their needs? Summarise that information here.

1.3 MARKETING COMMUNICATIONS

What marketing communications methods do you currently use? How effective are they? What do you want to improve? This section should include printed material, advertising, public relations, press and media relations, etc. Here is an example:

PRESS AND MEDIA EDITORIAL

The key role of our Press and Publicity Officer is to maintain Kempsford Playhouse's high profile in the local and regional press and media. Kempsford Playhouse has a comprehensive media list and sends out press releases to launch each season as well as to promote each event.

Press and media coverage has three priorities:

- to raise awareness of Kempsford Playhouse within the community
- to promote community involvement and participation
- to sell tickets for events.

PRESS ADVERTISING

We regularly advertise in the following publications: *Chronicle & Echo, The Citizen, Evening Telegraph, Herald & Post* and the *What's On* magazine. We also occasionally place advertisements in other newspapers.

2 ISSUES

Describe briefly the major challenges and opportunities that you want your marketing plan to address. This should make clear links to the issues you raise in the rest of your application.

3 MARKETING PLAN

3.1 AIMS

What are the broad aims of your marketing plan? Here is an example:

- To increase the number of people attending and participating in events at Kempsford Playhouse.

- To broaden further the range of people attending and participating in events at Kempsford Playhouse.

- To increase the number of people using Kempsford Playhouse building outside performance times.

- To raise awareness of Kempsford Playhouse's activities within the community of Kempsford District.

- To further develop audiences and participants to support the elements of Kempsford Playhouse programme expanded as a result of a successful lottery bid.

3.2 TARGET GROUPS

List your target groups here. Be as specific as possible, for example:

- Local authority arts officers in Lincolnshire, Leicestershire and Northamptonshire

- People who have not attended dance but have attended at least two other arts events in the past 12 months living within a 30-minute drive of each venue on the tour.

3.3 STRATEGIES AND OBJECTIVES

Describe how you will achieve your aims. Strategies are broad, less specific ways of tackling an issue; objectives are the specific ways that you will achieve your strategy. An example is:

> **Key issue:** to resolve the problem of the falling population of 16 to 24 year olds who have been the main market for albums and singles.
>
> **Strategy:** to encourage a higher spend on music by the 31–45 age group
>
> **Objective:** to re-release albums by major bands of the 1970s and 1980s on CD and achieve sales of £8m in the UK within two years.

You may want to organise this bit according to your areas of activity and then according to your target groups.   Here is an example.

Film programme

This is an important element of the programme that will be used to bring into the building for the first time:

- young people aged 16–24
- parents with children under 12
- other non-attenders all living within a ten-minute drive time of Kempsford.

Objectives:

- Years 1 to 3: To produce a separate two-colour cinema flyer in the style of cinema rather than theatre print.
- Years 1 and 2: To analyse the database to identify people who have only attended film events and direct mail the cinema flyer.
- Year 1: expand the print distribution system to include at least 30 sites visited by young people aged 16–30 and by families with children under 12 within a ten-minute drive time; identify existing sites that should have a separate rack for the cinema brochure.

Visual arts

There will be a significant increase in the number of national exhibitions and of visual arts and crafts evening classes and workshops.

Objectives:

- Year 2: To undertake a Test Drive the Visual Arts project aimed at one of the priority target groups selected according to the availability of appropriate exhibitions. The project will use the results of the New Audience Fund projects which seek to test various test drive methodologies and identify the most appropriate for this community, venue and art form. It will seek to persuade a minimum of 150 people to attend an exhibition for the first time and a further 50 people to try out a practical session for the first time.
- Year 3: To write to members of visual arts and crafts groups within a 45-minute drive time to inform them about events and classes on offer.

3.4 DEVELOPING AUDIENCES

Describe how you intend to increase access to the arts by particular priority groups (think social inclusion!). Talk here about your end users: these could include the 5–12 age group, young people aged 16–24, people in isolated rural communities, people from particular ethnic communities, etc. Be specific. Here is an example:

South Asian community

Objectives:

Identify a co-promoter within each of the following communities and identify an appropriate product to be promoted on a quarterly basis resulting in 400 new attenders per year (100 attenders at each of four events). This is likely to mean adding events in other South Asian languages to the existing programme which is predominantly in Hindi.

Year 1:

KP8 1 (22% of population Asian)

Year 2:

KP8 4 (6%)

KP8 5 (4%)

Year 3:

KP3 3 (4% Ambridge)

KP16 8 (4% Emmerdale)

3.5 OTHER MARKETING ISSUES

List the other strategies and objectives that you have for your marketing activities – this will probably include some strategies and objectives for collecting information about your target groups and improving your database.

4 MONITORING AND EVALUATION

Describe in detail how you will monitor whether you achieve your objectives. How will you evaluate your work (e.g. handing out evaluation forms at workshops)? Do not forget to describe what you do with the information from these – make it clear that they are not just collecting dust on a shelf.

19 HOW TO COPE WITH AN EMERGENCY

In all emergencies, consider the short- and long-term implications for your organisation. Do not do anything that might significantly impair your corporate identity.

1 A MISTAKE ON YOUR PRINT

If there is an error on your print, consider having a reprint. If the printer is at fault, you should not have to pay for a reprint, but if it is your mistake you will.

If time and/or money prevent you from reprinting, you can use sticky labels to correct the information. Your printer can print sticky labels for you in the background colour of your leaflet and/or poster, so that the change hardly shows. This is the best option but is relatively expensive. Alternatively, your printer can simply ink out the mistake and print the correct information alongside it, using the same process as overprinting.

You can correct errors yourself, using a felt pen. This is the most time-consuming option, but also the cheapest. If time is very short, it is probably better to simply delete the wrong information rather than supply misinformation.

2 A CANCELLED PERFORMANCE

If your organisation has to cancel a performance, perhaps because of illness, the most important thing is to work with box office staff to telephone ticket buyers as soon as possible, explaining why the performance cannot take place. It is important to send out refunds promptly once you have spoken to them together with a letter explaining the problem once more.

Make sure that the box office does not take any more bookings for the show. If there is enough time, use stickers or a stamp saying 'cancelled' on the relevant page of the season brochure.

Put up notices in the foyer to tell people the reasons for the cancellation. If you cannot contact all ticket buyers, make sure that there is someone on hand to explain the situation as they arrive for the performance. You can minimise the loss of good will by offering people complimentary tickets for other performances to make up for the inconvenience caused as well as refunding the price of their ticket.

If any reviewers are expected, make sure that you inform them too. Suggest an alternative date for them to see the show.

3   THE EVENT IS NOT SELLING

There are some short-term strategies that are effective in generating ticket sales quickly. Tactics involving ticket deals should not be used too frequently as you will create an audience that expects money off and will consistently book at the last minute to get a deal.

3.1   TELESALES

Analyse your box office computer system to identify people from your main target groups who have not yet bought tickets. Give the list to a freelance telesales specialist. The regional marketing agency might offer this service themselves or have a list of others who do.

3.2   PRESS AND MEDIA

- Most local newspapers offer an insertion service and need as little as one week's notice.

- Get coverage in the local paper or on television and radio with a photo story or by raising a controversial issue.

- Put a ticket offer in the arts pages.

- Place a competition in the local newspaper or on the local radio station.

3.3   LEAFLETING OTHER EVENTS

Some venues will leaflet their audiences for you in return for a future favour. If not, stand outside the venue and hand out leaflets as the audience emerges. It is usual to notify the venue that you will be doing this.

3.4   TARGETED DISCOUNTS

Offer discounts to easily accessible target groups such as members of a fitness centre, teachers in local schools (as individuals, not as people who might bring school parties) or groups meeting in a nearby hall.

3.5   TARGETED DIRECT MAIL OFFERS

Make absolutely sure that you do not send these to people who have already bought tickets for the show as this can cause intense ill will. Instead, choose people from your box office computer system who have shown themselves to be price sensitive, perhaps by buying bottom price seats, and have attended a similar type of show in the past. Avoid people who have attended the venue in the past three months or so, as they are less likely to reattend than people who have not been for a while.

3.6   STAFF DISCOUNTS

Big employers will sometimes distribute information about exclusive offers to staff in the internal mail or in pay packets.

3.7 ARTS PROFESSIONALS

People who work in the arts in some way are usually very frequent attenders. You may be able to get lists from marketing agencies and regional arts boards.

3.8 PRINT DISTRIBUTION

Pay someone to go round key shops, offices and public buildings in the locality distributing print.

4 TOURING COMPANIES

4.1 A LAST-MINUTE BOOKING

What you can do depends on how last minute the booking is. There are several steps you can take to help promote the date.

If you have any print, despatch it immediately, by courier service if necessary. If it needs overprinting, photocopy the overprinting details onto self-adhesive labels and then stick them on the leaflets. Photocopy the overprinting details directly onto the posters if possible. If not, use your word-processing software to set out the information in a suitably sized panel, print copies on a good quality printer and glue them on. Consider engaging casual help to assist you.

If you have no print in your office, but your printer can supply you with some quickly, make an order immediately. Ask the printer to send it direct to the venue. If you do not have any print, write a direct mail letter and send it to people who have seen your company before or who have seen similar events at the venue. Do not try to develop new audiences in these circumstances.

You may not have enough time to use the standard systems of print distribution, but you can slip the programmes of other shows at the venue in question and at other local venues.

You could employ a freelance arts marketer on a contract basis to help distribute your print for one or two days. This may be cost effective if you have a lot of seats to fill. Send the venue any displays you have. You could also employ a freelance press and media representative. Make sure that there is really enough time to obtain some press coverage – ask the representative's advice about this. The costs of employing a freelance can be shared between the company and promoter.

4.2 CANCELLATION OF A TOUR

If you have to cancel your tour, make sure that you tell everyone concerned as soon as possible. Telephone venues and agencies that are involved in supporting you and the venue. Follow up with a letter of explanation and apology. It is very important for companies to inform promoters of cancellations promptly so that they can try to fill the gap in their programme with another event. Tour cancellations cause venues major problems which will take time and money to resolve, especially if your event has gone on sale to the public, so be prepared for disappointment and even anger.

PART II The big ideas

20 TALKING TO THE RIGHT PEOPLE

SEE ALSO CHAPTERS
23. MARKETING PLANNING
24. MARKET RESEARCH
25. AUDIENCE DEVELOPMENT

1 TARGETING

Chapter 1, 'Getting Started', looked at the process of developing a campaign plan. A very important part of this process was talking to the right people about the right things and in the right way.

You cannot possibly communicate effectively with every single person in the communities you serve so you need to divide the population into bite-sized chunks. These groups of people must have something in common which means that you can talk to them about the same things and in the same way and all of them will be likely to respond.

Choosing who to talk to involves examining your organisation's audiences and comparing them with the people in your community to decide on which groups you want to focus your resources. The process is also known as targeting or market segmentation.

You cannot choose the most appropriate target groups unless you know something about the people who make up your audiences, and about audiences for other events. It is unwise to assume that you know from experience alone what your audiences are like. Your guesses are very likely to be inaccurate.

People who work in arts organisations often make some disastrous guesses:

- They think that their audience is made up of people who are all the same. They talk about 'the typical audience member'. In fact, their existing audience is made up of lots of different kinds of people with different interests, aspirations and motivations for attending.

- They think that these typical audience members are just like them with the same attitudes, lifestyle and level of knowledge and understanding about the arts. Most attenders know very little about the arts – they just like attending.

- They think that their audience is committed to the arts and will actively seek out information in order to attend. In fact, most arts attenders do not attend very often at all. Research tells us that 25% of all the people who said they attended any performance in a theatre attended less often than once a year and 28% say they attend just once a year; 55% of contemporary dance attenders attend less often than once a year.

These misconceptions means that they assume that only a small proportion of their community will be interested in what they have to offer and market the work on that basis so, of course, only a few people attend. They talk about their organisation's work in a way that will appeal to a knowledgeable few and leave all the potential attenders feeling baffled or even thinking that the arts are not for them.

You need to put aside your own myths about your audiences and use hard evidence:

- to find out which sections of your potential audience should be your priority target groups

- to find out what elements of your organisation and its events appeal to each of these target groups

- to find out the best methods of communicating with each target group.

2 THE BIG DECISIONS

Before you start choosing target groups on which to focus your marketing efforts, you need to make some over-arching decisions about what your organisation's long-term approach should be. Here are your options:

- Specialise in providing one kind of arts activity to one particular target group (e.g. The Drill Hall specialises in presenting work by and for London's gay and lesbian communities).

- Specialise in two or three different areas, focusing each activity on a different target group.

- Offer a wide range of activities, but all of them aimed at one particular target group (e.g. The Junction in Cambridge presents gigs, clubs and live dance and theatre all aimed at the 15–30 age group).

- Offer one particular type of activity but target them at a wide range of target groups (e.g. The Place in London only offers dance performances, participatory and services for dancers but targets them at a wide range of groups from Middle Eastern businessmen attending Raqs Sharqi performances to professional dancers setting up their own companies via the under 12 year olds attending beginners' classes).

- Offer something for everyone in your community but ensure that each type of activity is focused on a specific section of the community (many mixed programme presenting venues strive to achieve this).

- Offer something for everyone in your community but without distinguishing between target groups (this is the least successful strategy because not everyone likes the same things so talking to everyone about everything in the same way just simply isn't persuasive enough to get them to attend).

3 MAKING SENSE OF THE INFORMATION

You need information in order to choose the target groups you want to focus on. You need to understand your existing audience, the audience for other cultural events in your community and the people who do not attend at the moment.

3.1 SECONDARY INFORMATION

This is information that has been collected by someone else about audiences for events similar to yours. Look at the information available and try to answer these questions:

- What age ranges are predominant? You could use this information to identify age groups that are underrepresented in your own audiences.

- What occupations are most common? You could use direct mail to reach other members of the predominant occupations.

- What other art forms do they attend? You could sell your shows to audiences at these types of event.

- Why do audiences say they attended a particular event? Reflect these 'benefits' in your publicity material.

- How often do they attend your particular art form? You could compare the information with the results of research into your own audiences to see what sort of people your loyal attenders are.

- How far do people generally travel to see a performance? Use this to identify the area in which to distribute your print.

The information made available through Target Group Index is essential as a standard against which to compare your own audiences. Peter Verwey, Senior Marketing Officer at the Arts Council, has prepared summaries of this information including analyses by region and by art form. (See Chapter 24, 'Market Research', to find out more about TGI.)

3.2 LOOKING AT THE INFORMATION ABOUT YOUR OWN AUDIENCES

Now think about the information you have collected about audiences at your events. Try to answer the following questions:

- What sort of people attend your shows frequently? These are the 'enthusiasts' who make up your most important priority target group.

- How often do they attend?

- Why do they attend?

- Are they mainly from a particular age group?

- What other art forms are they interested in?

- Do they attend events by other companies from your art form? If so, how frequently? Do they attend other events at other venues in your area?

- Are there organised groups in the audiences? What sort of groups are they?

- Are there particular occupational groups that are well represented within the audiences?

- How old are the audience members? What is the predominant age range?

- Where do people come from? How far did they travel to attend the performance?

- What postal sectors are particularly well represented?

- What other art forms do people attend frequently?

- Do they attend performances by other companies from your art form or other venues in your area?

- Why did they attend the performances?

- What proportion of the audiences was new to the venue? Why do they say they attended a performance at the venue? How did they find out about the performance?

- What proportion of the audience had never seen the company before? Why do they say they attended the performance?

- How did they find out about the performance?

It is important to compare this information with the secondary information you explored earlier. This will highlight some of the important facts about your audience. The TGI data show us that attendances at contemporary dance performances are higher than average for people aged 15–19 and 20–24. If you found that other age ranges are common in your audiences, you would know that these other age ranges represented significant target groups. When interpreting the information you have collected, be aware of the audience members who did not fill in the questionnaire. Some sections of the audience may be underrepresented because of a tendency not to respond to forms of this sort.

Students usually made up 40% of the audiences of a small theatre based in a northern university town. In 1988, after some research, they discovered that this figure had dropped dramatically. The theatre is now looking at ways to target students in ways not felt necessary before. It is taking a stall at the Freshers' Fair to raise the profile of the theatre as a venue and as a resource for all those involved with performing arts societies. It has also programmed a small-scale circus/music company to perform for three days during the fair on the lawn between the theatre and the students' union.

4 DEFINING TARGET GROUPS

You can use a wide range of factors to define possible target groups. The people in the target group might have the following in common:

Purchasing behaviour	• how often they buy tickets
	• what events they buy tickets for
	• what else they buy – workshops, meals in the café, postcards and so on
Demographics	• their age
	• where they live
	• their gender
	• their income
	• their social grade (an official definition of class and status – see below)
Attitudes and opinions	• their attitude to the arts in general, e.g. going to the theatre is something to do to celebrate a special occasion or the arts are not something they connect with their own lives, it is what other people do
	• their attitudes to other aspects of life
	• the relationship they feel with your organisation, e.g. they are enthusiasts and persuade other people to get involved
Their stage in life	• they have a family and how old their kids are
	• they have retired, their children have left home and they have time on their hands
Lifestyle	• what else they do with their leisure time
	• what their aspirations are, e.g. self-improvement, three holidays a year, emotional fulfilment, etc.

You might have to market your organisation's work to people who are not potential audience members such as teachers, local authority arts officers, venue managers and promoters. You can divide these up in the same sort of way. If you work for a small-scale touring company, you might divide venues up into target groups using these criteria:

- whether the venue books your company regularly, occasionally or not at all
- what else the venue programmes
- geographic location
- number of seats
- size of stage
- quality of facilities for performers

- quality of facilities for audiences
- level and quality of marketing activity
- the attitude of the venue manager or programmer
- what kind of deal they usually do with companies (fee or box office split, etc.).

The more the people or organisations in your target group have in common, the more effectively you can communicate with them. Most of the factors we have just looked at are rather broad – there is a big difference between a 16 year old who has just left school and got their first job and a 16 year old studying the violin to Grade VIII standard. You cannot talk to them about classical music in the same way.

Most arts organisations combine factors to narrow down their target groups, for example:

- people with at least one child under 5 living in postal sector KP4 3
- existing attenders who have bought tickets for at least three events in the past year but not contemporary dance
- venues with 200–350 seats in the Midlands where the venue manager or promoter has seen the company's work but never booked them.

The more the target group has in common, the more effectively you can communicate with them and the more likely they are to respond.

This approach means that, instead of mailing everyone who has attended a particular art form, you need to separate out the informed art form enthusiasts, people who like seeing a bit of everything and the people who would be adventurous if they were given a bit of encouragement. Then you can communicate effectively with each group by giving them the specific information they want and need. You will have to take a painstaking approach to making mailing selections from box office computer systems based on audience members' frequency of attendance at the venue and at specific art forms, attendance at a range of different art forms and how recently they attended. As most dance attenders buy tickets for dance less often than once a year, there is little point in repeatedly mailing everyone who has attended dance within the past twelve months.

4.1   ATTITUDES AND OPINIONS

It is relatively easy to define target groups according to what they are like and what they buy. This often is not enough. People behave in particular ways because of their attitudes and beliefs. There is a lot of secondary qualitative research available which tells us about attitudes and beliefs and, increasingly, larger arts organisations are carrying out qualitative research into their own audiences' perceptions and attitudes. There follows a summary of some of the results of qualitative research carried out by Anne Roberts for Warwick Arts Centre.

Attenders at contemporary performing arts events
Nothing by Chance, Anne Roberts, Arts Management Services, 1996
This research identified three key target groups among attenders of
contemporary performing arts events at Warwick Arts Centre. The
factors they had in common were that they were:

Embracers
- seeking something different
- proud of being risk-takers
- mostly under 35
- not influenced by price or promotion
- loyal and uncritical of Warwick Arts Centre.

Cautious toe-dippers
- needing reassurance and careful nurturing
- easily put off by bad experiences
- not confident
- looking for a whole package (a night out)
- equally under and over 35.

I know what I like
- confident in making decisions
- over 50
- enthusiastically critical of the programme and promotional material
- strongly influenced by price and word of mouth.

Andrew McIntyre from Morris, Hargreaves, McIntyre has also been talking to
audiences about their attitudes and beliefs. He divides up the people in our
communities like this:

At the bottom of the pyramid are Rejectors who will never come to what we
put on. Above them are the Resistors. There are lots of education and
outreach schemes which try to persuade them that they want to come to
the arts, which you could broadly characterise as missionary work. At the
top of the pyramid you have Attenders who you could divide up into
friends, advocates, subscribers, frequent attenders, occasional
attenders and infrequent attenders.

In the middle you have a gap inhabited by a group which a lot
of people describe as Intenders. There is a problem with this
label, though. If they are Intenders, how can we explain why
they aren't coming? The difference between the people
who are coming and the people who aren't is that the
former group have been persuaded that what we have
to offer will fulfil their needs. The people who aren't
coming haven't been persuaded yet.

Attenders

Open to
persuasion

Resisters

Rejectors

We call the group in the middle Open to Persuasion. They are a group of people who are open to what we do and at the top end of the group they are actually trying it out, so the line between Attenders and Open to Persuasion is blurred.

Andrew argues that arts organisations will be able to communicate much more effectively with audiences if they define target groups rather than just describe them:

[1] Andrew McIntyre, *'Understanding Customer Behaviour'* in *Revolving Doors: Increasing Audience Retention* (Arts Marketing Association, 1999)

Usually we try to segment by age, social grade, lifestyle, postcode, attendance habits, newspaper readership and so on. These approaches are better than asking the queue at a bus stop if they want to come to an arts event. But they don't get to the heart of what drives people's arts attendance. Not all over 55s like classical music. Not all teachers like contemporary dance.[1]

4.2 SOCIAL GRADE

You will often see references to social grades in the press and in literature produced by arts organisations and funding bodies. They talk in particular about arts audiences being predominantly ABC1s. This is what the different categories mean:

GRADE	SOCIAL STATUS	OCCUPATION	GB POPULATION TGI survey
A	Upper middle class	Higher managerial, administrative or professional	2.7%
B	Middle class or professional	Intermediate managerial, administrative	15.1%
C1	Lower middle class managerial, administrative	Supervisory or clerical, and junior	23.8%
C2	Skilled working class	Skilled manual workers	28.1%
D	Working class	Semi- and unskilled manual workers	17.8%
E	Those at lowest level of subsistence	State pensioners or widows (no other earner, casual or lowest-gradeworkers	12.3%

There are some drawbacks to this system of classifying people:

- It was set up decades ago and is based on some old-fashioned ideas about class and status.
- It is based on the occupation of the head of household and it is difficult to define who that should be as the structures of families have changed over the years.
- It does not take into consideration households with two breadwinners.

The government is introducing a new way of classifying people according to status from the 2001 census which they hope more accurately reflects today's society. This is how it is likely to work:

- Social Class 1: Professionals such as lawyers, doctors, vets, teachers, librarians, social workers, police inspectors and above, business people who describe themselves as employers, etc.

- Social Class 2: more junior managers, journalists, police below the rank of inspector, hospital nurses, etc.

- Social Class 3: clerical workers, secretaries, skilled manual such as computer technicians, auxiliary nurses, etc.

- Social Class 4: employers of fewer than 25 people, self-employed

- Social Class 5: supervisors of people in categories 6 and 7, craft and related occupations, etc.

- Social Class 6: semi-routine occupations such as drivers, assembly line workers, sales assistants

- Social Class 7: routine occupations such as domestics, porters, refuse collectors and all labourers.

5 CHOOSING WHICH GROUPS TO FOCUS ON

The 'enthusiasts' are the most important section of your audiences. They have made their interest in what you have to offer very clear by their frequent attendance. This means that out of the whole population, they are most likely to respond to any approach you make to them. You should now have a very good idea of what sort of people they are.

Other important sections of the audience will stand out in the information you have collected. They will be different for every organisation. A small mixed programme venue in Wales has selected the following target groups: a core group of adult audiences who support drama; young people, especially through the youth theatre; schools supportive of drama and especially of Welsh-language work; students from the local college of further education; tourists. They stopped targeting party bookers after they discovered that most of their audience prefer to come as individuals.

You may find that sections of the audience that stand out are too large to target with your resources. A solution would be to combine factors that define groups.

The University of Surrey discovered that a significant proportion of their audience for dance events was made up of off-duty teachers, and that Woking and Guildford were key areas across all audience types. They therefore decided to target teachers of all types in Woking and Guildford. They also made improvements to their distribution systems in these areas. However, they found that specialist dance teachers in schools and colleges were bringing groups to performances from a much wider area, even from as far away as Bognor Regis. They decided to build up a mailing list of specialist dance teachers from Surrey, Sussex and Hampshire.

Think about the following things before deciding that it is worth targeting a particular target group:

1.   **QUANTIFY THE TARGET GROUP:**

    (a) How many people?

    (b) How much are they likely to spend?

2.   **IS IT WORTH TARGETING?**

    (a) Would targeting this group fit in with your long-term aims and objectives?

    (b) Is it big enough?

    (c) Will they spend enough in the short and long term to give you a return on your investment of time, energy and money?

    (d)   If not, are they an important group in terms of access issues to make your investment worthwhile?

    (e) Is there something they all have in common so you can talk to them about the same things in the same way and still be likely to get a good response (i.e. is it homogenous)?

3.   **IS IT ACCESSIBLE?**

    (a) Is it possible for us to get hold of these people effectively?

    (b) Can we provide them with what we have to offer in an effective way?

4.   **CAN WE AFFORD IT?**

    (a) Do we have enough money and staff to communicate effectively with the target group?

Below are the target groups identified by an arts centre which planned to set up a crafts project working with disabled artists and young people. They wanted to employ disabled artists-in-residence and offer demonstrations, workshops and work experience opportunities for disabled young people and evening classes for both able-bodied and disabled people living in the area.

ACTIVITY	TARGET GROUP
Demonstrations or workshops by visiting artists	Headteachers of special schools within a 20-mile radius
	Teachers in charge of special needs units in mainstream schools within a 20-mile radius
	Teachers with an interest in special needs in the region
	Young members of clubs and societies offering services for disabled people within a 60-minute drive time
	People interested in crafts living within a 20-minute drive time.
Work experience and tasters	Headteachers of special schools within a 20-mile radius
	Teachers in charge of special needs units in mainstream schools within a 20-mile radius
	Teachers with an interest in special needs
	Careers services within the catchment
Evening classes	People interested in crafts living within a 20-minute drive time.
	People attending other evening classes within a 20-minute drive time
	Artists working in other media

6 SETTING OBJECTIVES

It is very important to be able to see which of your marketing activities actually work. To do this you need to set yourself goals.

Look at the target groups you have chosen and set goals for the number of people from that group that you want in your audiences. Probably the best way to state each goal is as a percentage of the audience at each performance for the season or for the year.

Setting the goals is not straightforward because the target groups overlap to some extent. Some of the enthusiasts may have attended as part of an organised group, or come from one of the targeted occupations.

Peter Verwey from the Arts Council of England has devised a very simple way of setting goals through audience surveys using self-completion questionnaires. His method involves sorting the questionnaires into heaps according to a sequence of criteria and then counting the numbers in each heap. These figures are then turned into percentages per performance. If you wanted to set a target for the number of under 25 year olds coming to the venue for the first time, you would sort your questionnaires into four heaps:

1. First-time attenders under 25.
2. First-time attenders 25 and over.
3. Repeat attenders under 25.
4. Repeat attenders 25 and over.

Count the number of questionnaires in each heap. Calculate the percentage like this:

Number of questionnaires in heap 1	÷ Total number of questionnaires in all the heaps X 100 =	The percentage of questionnaire respondents who are first-time attenders under 25

Now you know what your organisation currently achieves so your next step is to decide what a realistic increase would be. This is your objective.

TALKING ABOUT THE RIGHT THINGS

You now need to combine the information about your priority target groups with your knowledge of your organisation and the shows it presents. By pooling all this information, you can match up your priority groups with all the things about your organisation and shows that will appeal to them.

Different target groups will be interested in different things about your organisation and its shows. It is crucial to communicate the right things to the right group.

A metropolitan studio theatre booked a new play about love and *glasnost* written by a local woman and performed by an internationally connected women's company. The staff identified their targets as women's groups, political groups, writers' groups, political studies courses and the Workers Education Association. They decided that the principal benefits were: the political angle (especially the examination of the way that political movements affect individual lives), the examination of women's issues, the woman writer, the feminist theatre company, the local connection, the new writing and the international connection. They were careful to match these benefits to the target groups: the writers' groups would be interested in the local connection, the fact that the play was new and, perhaps, the international connection; the feminist theatre company would be interested in the woman writer, the examination of women's issues and the general political atmosphere of the piece would appeal to the women's groups and so on.

1 WHAT ARE WE OFFERING?

The reason that people come to an arts event centre is the arts event itself – without the event there would not be an evening out. What they are buying, however, is much more complicated than that. We are offering people an experience which might involve:

- their intellectual and emotional response to the event itself
- the social experience of being part of a crowd
- escape from routine
- something to talk about with friends or family
- their sense of spiritual well-being
- a sense of self-improvement
- the opportunity to do something together as a family.

Different people will feel that they are buying different elements of this experience.

[1] Mike Paxton, The Research Practice, *Expanding the Audience for Jazz: a report of the findings from a qualitative research study* (Arts Council of Great Britain, 1990)

The event is the core product but all these other elements of the experience are part of the product surround, and they are just as important. This is how jazz attenders described what they were buying when they went to see jazz:[1]

Arts organisations always tell potential ticket buyers about the core product, but they rarely tell them about what they might experience as part of the product surround. Audiences at a Shakepseare production who participated in a series of focus groups emphasised how important it was to them. Everyone felt aggrieved because the interval had been cut to 15 minutes. There was no time to have a drink and to discuss what they had seen so far with their companions. They felt cheated of a very important part of their evening and that affected what they thought about the quality of the production.

2 WHY PEOPLE ATTEND

² Denis Robb, The Research Practice, *Results of Research into the Contemporary Visual Arts* (Arts Council of Great Britain, 1992)

Here are the reasons that people say they go to the contemporary visual arts, taken from a report by The Research Practice.[2]

> It's relaxing ... it's a time to yourself ... you get away from all the hassles.
> **Norwich attender**

> You go into the Mappin with all your worries ... and you see something that jolts you ... it pulls a switch and your head is on a different plane ... The outside world channels you ... it forces you to think and do things, and you get rooted that way. But an art gallery can show you the other side ... the alternative potential within yourself. **Sheffield attender**

> You come out and you feel completely different. It's very liberating. Your mind is on a different plane ... yes I think 'spiritual elevation' is a good term. **London attender**

> I'm very interested in how things are produced, the technical side, techniques ... it's the mystery of how they are constructed or how they are made which interests me most. **Sheffield attender**

> I've no idea what I get out of it ... something warm inside ... I can't explain ... it's a sense of recognition, of accord ... for example, I find Francis Bacon disturbing, but that's what's great about him ... the reaction inside you ... so it's something that might make me happy or sad. It's something that affects my emotions. **Sheffield attender**

When did you last see any marketing communications for the visual arts that reflected these kinds of motives?

One of the difficulties is that different people have different needs and wants that going to a gallery can help fulfil. Some of the motives described here are contradictory, just as some of the jazz attenders wanted to concentrate on the music and others wanted to socialise with friends. This is why targeting is so important as it helps us decide which motive is most relevant to which target group.

Unfortunately, marketers' lives are made more complicated still by the fact that some people find it difficult to talk about the arts and why they like them:

> Funny, I've never talked about this before in public ... I've always felt that other people wouldn't relate to it. And if you did talk about it people would put you down as a pretentious name dropper. **Norwich attender**

Many people who have never been to an arts event simply do not know what to expect and have no idea what they might get out of it. Arts organisations do not tell them that they will enjoy it because it will make them feel happy or sad or serene, or that it will make them think, or that they will recognise aspects of themselves in the characters, or that the sheer energy of the performers will make them feel breathless, or that they are allowed to make a critical judgement about the event for themselves and then talk about it with the friends they are with. Instead they give them information about the event saying things like:

> Throughout the process there is a reopening, a constant repetition of the cut and breaking the boundary of the skin. The differentiation between 'making' and 'performing' becomes confused and redundant as the body persists in its own methodology ... This performance contains nudity.

3 DECIDING WHAT TO SAY

A feature is a fact about the performance, but a benefit is a reason that someone should attend.

Feature: 'See the Mali Theatre from St Petersburg'

Benefit: 'Decide for yourself whether this is the greatest theatre company in the world.'

Make a list of all the points about your organisation and the event that might appeal to your target groups. These are the benefits you have to offer. Look at all possible aspects of the core product and the product surround.

1. List all the benefits along the top of a square (see the example opposite).
2. List all the target groups you have selected down the side of the square. This kind of grid is known as a matrix.
3. Look at each target group in turn. Decide which of the benefits are most relevant for that target group and place a tick against it. You may find that several of the benefits are relevant for some target groups, but select only three or four really important ones. The information you collected from your audience research should help you do this.
4. Put a circle round the tick for the benefit you think is the most important to that target group.

This main benefit will become the promise you make to the reader in a direct mail letter and the central topic of your press release and the headline in your season brochure and the subject of the line of copy in your display advertisement. You will talk about the other benefits you have ticked to back up your main benefit.

All you are doing when you approach the potential ticket buyers in your target groups is telling them why they would want to come and see your show or visit your venue. You are communicating the relevant benefits to them. Therefore the matrix will help you decide on the content of your press releases, direct mail letters, brochure copy, the images on your poster, etc.

TARGET GROUPS/BENEFIT MATRIX

TARGET GROUPS

BENEFITS	Regular arts attenders at venue	25-plus age group arts attenders elsewhere	6th form students	Amateur dramatics groups	Local history groups	Literary groups
Prize-winning novel popular in the region	⊗	⊗				X
Up-market, literary work						⊗
Premiere of the adaptation	⊗	X				X
Good, gripping drama	X	⊗	X	X	X	X
Adult subject	X	X				
Suspense/mystery	X					
Local history			X?		X	
Educational						
Director well-known in area	⊗	⊗				

TARGET GROUPS/BENEFIT MATRIX

TARGET GROUPS

BENEFITS						

4 HOW PEOPLE MAKE DECISIONS

¹ Based on Anne Roberts, *Nothing by Chance: Qualitative Research into Attendance at New and Contemporary Film and Theatre at Warwick Arts Centre* (Warwick Arts Centre, 1997) and Midlands Arts Marketing, *Qualitative Research into the Attitudes of Audiences at Nottingham Playhouse* (1998)

In order to know what to say to your target groups, it is important to understand how they make the decision to attend.

How existing attenders use the season brochure to choose what to see.³

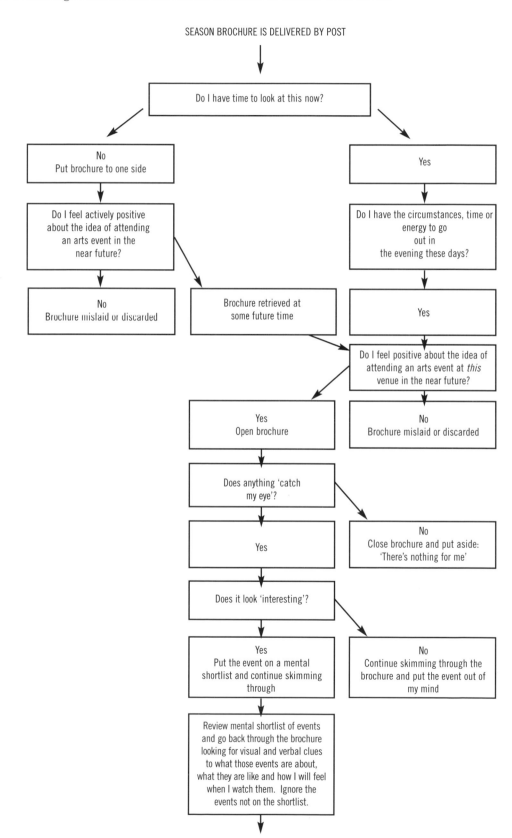

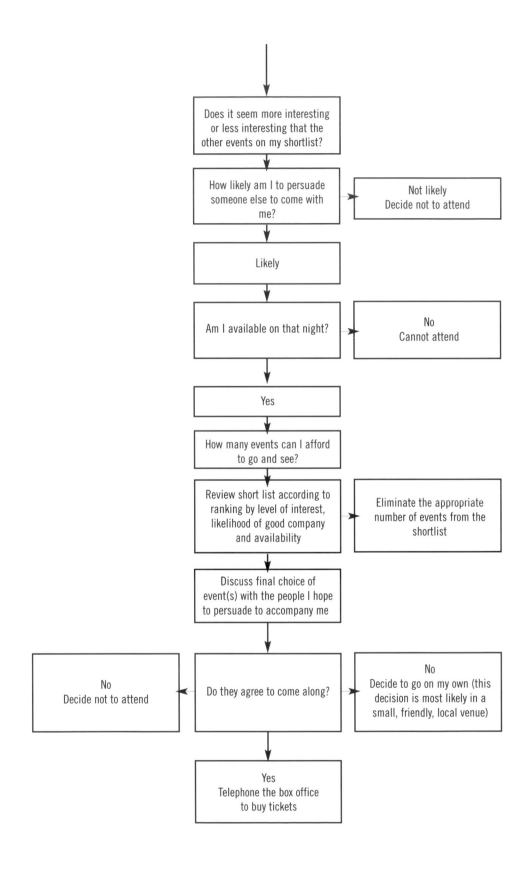

This decision-making process has implications for the design and content of the season brochure. You can make it easier for readers to decide to buy a ticket by the following:

- Big, bold images are important in catching the attention of readers skimming through.

- Readers will find it easier to decide whether to shortlist an event if the image conveys what the event is like and what it is about.

- A headline describing what the event is about in six or seven words will encourage them to shortlist it and then go back and read more.

- A summary of the programme in diary form will help the reader remember their shortlist and to decide their availability.

V-TOL DANCE COMPANY have identified through research that their potential audience, like most audiences for contemporary events, does not respond to over-selling. They dislike hype and simply want to know more about the production and the company. They do respond to recommendations from other audience members and critics. Tiffany Evans, the freelance marketer who works with V-Tol, writes a newsletter for each of the venues on the tour that they send to people who have attended dance or adventurous theatre events to follow up the season brochure and tour leaflet. (*See overleaf*)

CASE STUDY

Vtol
Dance Company

WITHOUT TRACE

When someone you love disappears all you have left is your imagination

V-TOL Dance Company returns to Theatre Royal Bury St Edmunds this Spring on Thurs 3 and Fri 4 February at 7.30pm. **V-TOL Dance Company**'s new production **WITHOUT TRACE** tells the story of Beth, a woman who leaves home and never returns.

WITHOUT TRACE combines filmed images and live action to create an account of Beth's journey and the impact of her disappearance on the lives of the people she leaves behind. The set is used as a large film screen which enables the story to be told from different perspectives.

Cutting into these images is the dance: edgy, electric, evocative movement which reflects the internal emotions of these characters. Two actors form the bridge: speaking the inner thoughts of the characters, voicing their memories, fantasies and secrets.

This thought provoking and moving tale is driven along by a haunting soundtrack, performed live. With four dancers, two actors and three musicians, **WITHOUT TRACE** is a breathtaking assault on the senses and compelling to the last.

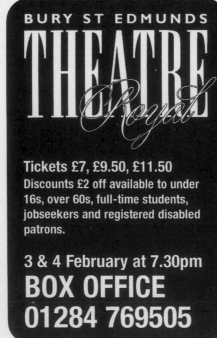

BURY ST EDMUNDS
THEATRE
Royal

Tickets £7, £9.50, £11.50
Discounts £2 off available to under 16s, over 60s, full-time students, jobseekers and registered disabled patrons.

3 & 4 February at 7.30pm
BOX OFFICE
01284 769505

Video stills: Mark Murphy

Dance
Cinema with moves

V-TOL Dance Company
Gardner Arts Centre, Brighton
★★★★

"Is it a film? Is it a dance?" is the question often asked when Mark Murphy's V-TOL takes to the stage. Actually it's both.

The idea of combining filmed images and live movement is not that new, but whereas in the past choreographers have used the screen as a prop or a mere backdrop, Murphy elevates the cinematic element of his work to the status of equal partner. Switching the action between screen, stage and a magical limbo in between, he creates what can only be described as dance cinema.

V-TOL's latest, Without Trace, is the company's most sophisticated exploration of this brave new genre to date. Part mystery, part thriller, with a dash of gore for good measure, the central story concerns the sudden disappearance of a 30-next-month woman from a stable and happy relationship. At least that's the way her deserted

partner looks at it. It's at this point that all previously held notions about the wanton inaccessibility and abstract opaqueness of modern dance should be set aside.

Murphy is in the business of telling stories and uses every device at his disposal to rush the narrative along: filmed sequences set the scene, actors articulate the internal motivations of the dancers, a voiceover links the action between past and present.

There's a line between accessibility and spelling things out and, in his anxiety to sidestep the security blanket of ambiguity which masks so much dance, Murphy sometimes crosses it. The classic Dutch thriller The Vanishing is a major influence on Without Trace, but where the movie revelled in guessing games, Murphy seems reluctant to leave as much to the power of his audience's imagination.

As a result, Without Trace is not quite the exercise in psychological exploration it promises at the start. What begins as an enigmatic mystery turns into a high-speed road movie, but it's an exhilarating spectacle for all that.

Driven along by a live score by Graham Cunnington, of post-industrial drum thumpers Test Department, the pace never flags as the story of the runaway Beth and her pining lover Jim unfolds in a cunning juxtaposition of dance and film.

The human element is the key to Murphy's success. Without that all the tricksy camera angles and back projections would be so much showing off. But not only does he have the technology, he also knows why he's using it.

The Guardian 19.10.99   **Keith Watson**

Patrons - Helen Mirren and Taylor Hackford
V-TOL Dance Company 92-94 Judd Street London WC1H 9NT *tel* 020 7278 2432 *fax* 020 7278 0883 *e.mail* info@vtol.demon.co.uk *web* www.vtol.demon.co.uk

22 TALKING IN THE RIGHT WAY

Different target groups are best reached in different ways. You have a wide choice of methods to use, so you need to choose the one that is going to get your message across most effectively to each target group.

Consider:

- which medium is most likely to be seen or heard by your target group
- which will reach the greatest number of your target group
- how much persuasion your target group will need to take action
- how much time and money you will have to invest
- how much it will cost to reach each person in your target group
- which medium will reflect your organisation's corporate identity
- which will reflect the content and style of your event
- which will get your particular message across most effectively
- how much competition there will be for your target group's attention
- how easy it will be for your target group to respond to your message.

Different target groups have different approaches to buying a theatre ticket, and you will also have to take this into consideration when planning. Experienced theatre-goers are most likely to buy subscription packages. People under 25 and new attenders tend to buy their tickets on the day of the performance. A regional arts centre programmed a series of Asian dance events with the aim of increasing the proportion of their audience from Asian ethnic groups. The performances sold out. However, many of the Asian people who wanted to attend did not buy tickets in advance and the arts centre had to turn away large numbers of the very people for whom they had staged the events. The arts centre now reserve a proportion of the tickets for such performances for sale on the door.

CASE STUDY

**SCOTTISH OPERA AND THE THEATRE ROYAL, GLASGOW: IS IT REALLY
NECESSARY TO PRODUCE SKIP LOADS OF LEAFLETS AND BROCHURES?**

Just think how much money you could save if you simply halved the number
of leaflets and brochures you produce. Does the thought of doing this send
you into a blind panic? Where else could your valuable pennies be placed
without harming ticket sales while maximising income? During our busy days
it is very hard to find time to sit and discuss what we do and why.

About five years ago, here at Scottish Opera and the Theatre Royal, we
decided to cut back on all our print. Not only did we reduce the number of
brochures, we also slimmed down their size and contents. After studying
daily ticket sales over a matter of months and mapping them against specific
dates of direct mail campaigns, advertising and print distribution, etc., we
found that when new print was distributed the effect on sales was minimal.

We had thousands of leaflets speeding around the country in shiny vans on
the way to their final resting places – literally! Snuggled up against hundreds
of other leaflets – all competing against each other. How many times have you
seen people peruse those racks and pick up a leaflet only to replace it again?

When we saved money on print, we saved on distribution too. Now our
budget stretched to cinema advertising and 48-sheet poster campaigns. The
very least we hoped was that our box office income would remain constant.
In fact, since we changed our ways:

- many of our performances continue to sell out and ticket sales
  have not suffered
- more of our budget is allocated to the productions that are
  considered 'difficult' to sell
- we have broken the £1 million barrier at the box office
- Scottish Opera subscribers are spending more than ever on
  their tickets.

Now we only print enough leaflets to supply current, lapsed and potential
subscribers, Friends of Scottish Opera and our constantly updated mailing
list. Special print – in limited numbers – is also working well. Postcards,
which are mailed or distributed by hand, are much more successful than
material left to fester in leaflet racks. If your box office sales staff are
regularly briefed on your productions, then the need for detailed and, dare I
say, boring print should be a thing of the past.

These days, not only do we save money on print and distribution, we also
have an extremely tidy store room. How many out-of-date leaflets do you
have lying around your print store? Go and have a look! Dianne McKechnie, Marketing
Manager, Scottish Opera and the Theatre Royal, Glasgow

1 COMPARING EFFECTIVENESS

Each communication method has different strengths and weaknesses.

	STRENGTHS	WEAKNESSES
DIRECT MAIL	More personal Easily targeted You can reach small target groups easily You can set up a campaign very quickly Most people open and read direct mail whereas they may not see other forms of communication, e.g. ads You can control the content You can include lots of information The potential ticket buyer can easily keep the information for further reference You can include a response mechanism such as a reply-paid envelope Easy to monitor responses	Labour intensive You need an accurate and clean list of the names and addresses of your target group Cost per person reached is high Must comply with the Data Protection Act
PRESS AND MEDIA EDITORIAL	Free These are mass communications so you can reach lots of people cheaply People see it as authoritative and you get an editorial endorsement Can target by choosing which publications or media	A lot of people from outside your target group will see your message Relying on someone else You can provide information but cannot control the way it is used Your information may not be seen by all your target group You can only communicate certain sorts of information Time-consuming You can only provide a limited response mechanism (i.e. if they publish box office telephone number) Hard to monitor

COMPARING EFFECTIVENESS contd

	STRENGTHS	WEAKNESSES
DISPLAYS AND POSTERS	Visual Attracts attention A good reminder Can target to some extent by putting displays in the right place Can reach lots of people Colourful and imaginative Can be mobile (e.g. buses and trains) Longer-term presence	You can only communicate limited information You are paying for a lot of people from outside your target group to see your message Either expensive or time-consuming or both No response mechanism Vandalism Hard to monitor
ADVERTISING	You can control the content (barring typesetting errors) Cost per person reached is low You can reach lots of people You can target by choosing the publication	Information limited by space You are paying to reach lots of people from outside your target group Not always seen or read Hard to monitor
PRINT DISTRIBUTION	You can control the content You can use colour, layout, etc. to increase impact Fairly targeted Can be creative and catch people's imagination Can include a response mechanism	Can be expensive Can be time-consuming
WEBSITE	You can control the content You can use colour, dynamic graphics, etc. to increase impact You can include a lot of information Flexible Can be used for many purposes, e.g. educational resource, web-casts, etc. Can include a response mechanism	Not targeted You can only reach people who are on-line It can be difficult to direct people you are not already in touch with to your site Visitors to the site can be passive Resistance by some box office system suppliers to enabling the selling of tickets on-line through your own site Technology can still be unreliable Expensive to set up Labour intensive to keep up to date

COMPARING EFFECTIVENESS contd

	STRENGTHS	WEAKNESSES
TELESALES	Very personal	Labour intensive
	Easily targeted	You need an accurate and clean list of the names and addresses of your target group
	Can get across complex information	
	You can control the content	Cost per person reached is high
	A two-way conversation	Must comply with the Data Protection Act
	Can tailor the information to the individual	
	Builds relationships	Can be intrusive
	Can reach small target groups easily	
	Easy to monitor	
NETWORKING	Very personal	You are relying on other people's commitment and enthusiasm
	A two-way conversation	
	Can get across complex information	Time-consuming
	Someone else is endorsing your event	Need to find the right people in the community to network for you
	Builds relationships	
	Can tailor the information to the individual	
	Very persuasive	
	Reaches parts of the community that other methods cannot	
	Inexpensive	
WORD OF MOUTH	Happens anyway	Can send out negative messages
	Very persuasive	Difficult to manage
	Does not cost anything	

A touring theatre company markets the productions designed to appeal to Asian audiences by contacting community leaders, direct mail to the Asian community, producing print in two languages and most importantly through radio stations. Radio seems to be able to reach the entirety of the Asian communities in many areas.

2 CHOOSING THE RIGHT COMMUNICATION METHOD

In order to select the most effective method of reaching your target groups, construct another matrix.

1. List all your target groups down the side of another square.

2. This time list all the potential means of communication with those target groups along the top (see the example).

3. Look at each of the target groups and decide which communication methods are most appropriate and put ticks against them. Again, you will probably find that several of the methods are appropriate for some of the target groups but keep to the most important two or three.

4. Put a circle round the tick for the communication method that you think is most effective in reaching that target group (see the example below).

We decided our principal method of getting an audience would be direct mail. Our research showed that a large number of people were here because they had been sent a brochure for the season. That confirmed we were doing the right thing in putting so much emphasis on that particular marketing tool. **Publicist, specialised venue, London**

TARGET GROUPS/MEANS OF COMMUNICATION
TARGET GROUPS

MEANS OF COMMUNICATION	Regular arts attenders at venue	25-plus age group arts attenders elsewhere	6th form students	Amateur dramatics groups	Local history groups	Literary groups
Venue's season brochure	⊗	X	X			
Company's own mailing list	X	⊗				
Direct mail			⊗	⊗	⊗	⊗
Local and national press	X	X				
Radio coverage	X	X				
Displays in foyer of venue	X					

The arts centre planning a crafts project working with disabled artists and young people chose the following as the most effective communications methods for each target group.

ACTIVITY	TARGET GROUP	COMMUNICATION METHOD
DEMONSTRATIONS OR WORKSHOPS BY VISITING ARTISTS	Headteachers of special schools within a 20-mile radius	Write a letter with an information pack and follow it up with a telephone call and a visit by the project manager to the school
	Teachers in charge of special needs units in mainstream schools within a 20-mile radius	Write a letter with an information pack and follow it up with a telephone call offering a visit to the arts centre
	Teachers with an interest in special needs in the region	Entry in the regional listings magazine for teachers
	Young members of clubs and societies offering services for disabled people within a 60-minute drive time	Write a letter with an information pack to the group organiser and follow it up with a telephone call offering a visit to the arts centre for their younger members
	People interested in crafts living within a 20-minute drive time	Send a personalised invitation and offer to put them on the mailing list so they can be kept up to date
WORK EXPERIENCE AND TASTERS	Headteachers of special schools within a 20-mile radius	Write a letter with an information pack and follow it up with a telephone call and a visit by the project manager to the school
	Teachers in charge of special needs units in mainstream schools within a 20-mile radius	Write a letter with an information pack and follow it up with a telephone call offering a visit to the arts centre
	Teachers with an interest in special needs	Entry in *Backstage* magazine for teachers
	Careers services within the catchment	Write a letter with an information pack and follow it up with a telephone call
EVENING CLASSES	People interested in crafts living within a 20-minute drive time	Send a personalised invitation and offer to put them on the mailing list so they can be kept up to date
	People interested in crafts living within a 20-minute drive time	Editorial in newsletters and magazines produced by arts clubs and societies
	People attending other evening classes within a 20-minute drive time	Distribute a letter with a tear-off booking slip which also has a tick box for people who want to be on the mailing list
	Artists working in other media	Send a personalised invitation

TARGET GROUPS/MEANS OF COMMUNICATION

TARGET GROUPS

MEANS OF COMMUNICATION

3 INTEGRATED CAMPAIGNS

In the most effective marketing campaigns, all the different communication methods work together to maximise the response. Different communications methods work best at different stages in the decision-making process:

AWARENESS

INTEREST

DESIRE

ACTION

Integrated campaigns ensure that people in the various target groups are given the information they need at the relevant stage in the process. Below is an example of an integrated campaign planned and implemented by a group of arts organisations in Colchester, Essex.

CASE STUDY

COLCHESTER ARTS MARKETING: 'YOU ARE HERE'

In February and March 2000, **Colchester Arts Marketing Exchange** (CAME) undertook a cutting-edge awareness-raising campaign under the slogan 'You Are Here' to promote the arts in Britain's oldest recorded town.

CAME commissioned media artists **muf architecture/art** to a make an interlinked series of five temporary site-specific projected images. The images were projected onto five arts venues in the town and ranged from a set of ghostly footsteps, which appeared and disappeared alongside Colchester Arts Centre, to giant celebrity look-alikes staring out from the windows of *firstsite* at the Minories Art Gallery.

The campaign followed on from the innovative Art Man Max promotion, organised by the group in 1998, which featured a commission from performance artist Richard Layzell under the slogan 'Choose Arts, Choose Colchester'.

The aim of 'You Are Here' was to make people more aware of the wealth of arts in Colchester, to refresh their interest and to make them see the arts in a new light. **muf** called the projected images 'a series of magical moments, to turn the everyday into something more beguiling'. This commission was to form the centrepiece of an awareness campaign with three basic underlying messages:

CONTINUED

- **ART IS FUN!**

- **ART IS HERE! (AS OPPOSED TO LONDON)**

- **ART IS FOR ME!**

The project was backed up by a set of four specially designed postcards, a series of three collectable badges and a six-week run of print advertising. These elements were all branded under the slogan 'You Are Here' and were time-released to achieve maximum effect. They served to stimulate curiosity in the campaign, as a way of sustaining interest and as a tangible longer-term reminder.

The campaign achieved remarkable local media coverage and some national attention. We estimate that through press editorial coverage alone we generated in excess of £6,000 worth of column inches. This does not include the distribution of over 20,000 postcards and 5,000 badges, many of which are still visibly in circulation. The response from the general public and our existing customers, although difficult to quantify, was nevertheless extremely positive. It is also important to recognise the immense benefit of projects such as these on the members of the group. They provide an invaluable learning tool and an opportunity for exploring new ideas and ways of working.

We feel that innovative campaigns such as 'Art Man Max' and 'You Are Here' are the most rewarding and effective ways of stimulating both the public and our member organisations. If the arts are about quality of experience then we feel this should be reflected in the marketing used to promote them. What better way is there to promote the diversity and excitement of the arts than through a series of original and vibrant art works? **Toby Oliver, Chair, Colchester Arts Marketing Exchange**

23 MARKETING PLANNING

SEE ALSO CHAPTERS
20. TALKING TO THE RIGHT PEOPLE
21. TALKING ABOUT THE RIGHT THINGS
25. AUDIENCE DEVELOPMENT
31. MONITORING AND EVALUATION

Planning is an unnatural process; it is much more fun to do something.

John Harvey Jones

1 WHY PLAN?

1 David Carson, *Some Exploratory Models for Assessing Small Firms' Marketing Performance* (1990)

David Carson looked at small and medium-sized businesses in the UK and identified these stages of marketing development.[1]

1. Reactive stage:

    haphazard use of some marketing elements aimed at existing customers

2. Tinkering marketing:

    haphazard use of some marketing elements aimed at increasing customer base

3. Entrepreneurial marketing:

    intuitive use of marketing which can achieve results but is high risk

4. Proactive marketing:

    (a) methodical, controlled marketing where each activity supports the others

    (b) clear, short-, medium- and long-term objectives.

Every arts organisation in the UK has developed excellent skills in reactive marketing and most are involved in developing audiences to increase their customer base. Arts marketers are also extraordinarily good at coming up with creative and innovative campaigns. But how many of us can say, hand on heart, that our organisations are engaged in methodical, controlled and integrated marketing with clear objectives?

The key to reaching this ultimate phase in marketing development is planning. Why, though, is planning so important?

We can tinker with marketing until we find things that work and we can carry on doing those things quite successfully. The problem is that the world around us is in a constant state of flux – and often the changes are dramatic (think how Best Value has changed arts organisations' relationships with local authorities). We have some options for dealing with change:

- see what happens and react accordingly (the trouble is that by the time we react it is usually too late)

- ignore change (and then it will definitely be too late)

- pretend to plan (also known as bluffing the funding body)

- plan secretly (if no one knows what you are trying to achieve, they will not notice if you fail)

- plan for a variety of outcomes (a waste of time and effort because what actually happens will be the one outcome for which you did not plan)

- plan to make the future happen (aka marketing planning).

We've actually gone quite far from a passive situation to a very interactive one. The model I like to use is rather like selling seats on an aeroplane. If the airlines just ran their flights on time and left it to people to turn up, buy tickets and get on them, they would go bankrupt. **Director, venue only operating part of the year, Scotland**

1.1 CREATING A MARKETING PLAN

Your organisation should aim to develop a marketing plan that covers the same period as its overall business plan (which should be at least three years). This is essential if you are going to get an overview of your journey instead of trying to complete it in short hops with little idea of your ultimate destination.

Your business plan and marketing plan should be integrated. Ideally, they should be developed side by side, but this is not always possible at first. Once you have developed your first plan, you can shift the planning cycles so that they are synchronised. At the very least, they should be trying to achieve the same goals for the organisation. There is no point in having a marketing plan that focuses on strengthening the organisation's corporate identity if the business plan has identified a £25,000 deficit which means insolvency within a year.

Your marketing plan is not fixed. Each year, you will evaluate whether you have missed, met or exceeded your objectives and amend the next year's objectives accordingly. Your original Year 2 will become Year 1 and you can then add more detail to that year's strategies and tactics. Then you will work out where you want to go in your new Year 3. This is known as a rolling three-year plan.

1.2 THE ROLE OF MARKETING IN THE DECISION-MAKING PROCESS

Your business plan and marketing should be closely related. This means that most arts managers and marketers believe that marketing plays an important role within the senior management team by:

- representing the point of view of audiences and participants in discussions
- telling the team what the impact of decisions might be on audience and participant numbers and on how the outside world sees the organisation
- making data available to their colleagues to help them make informed decisions based on hard evidence.

2 THE MARKETING PLANNING PROCESS

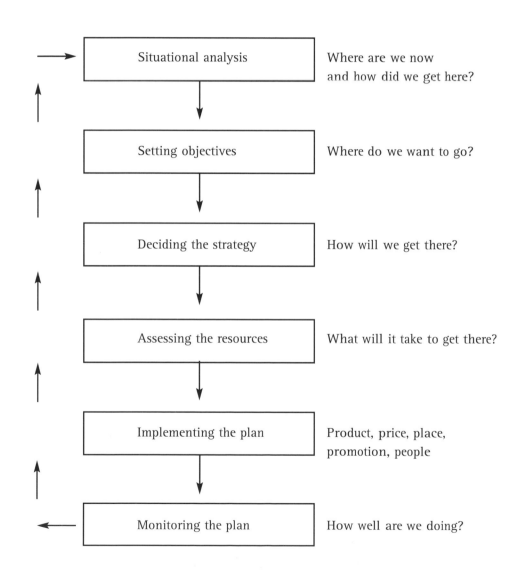

Situational analysis	Where are we now and how did we get here?
Setting objectives	Where do we want to go?
Deciding the strategy	How will we get there?
Assessing the resources	What will it take to get there?
Implementing the plan	Product, price, place, promotion, people
Monitoring the plan	How well are we doing?

It is like planning a journey. You find where you are now on the map, then you work out where you want to go. Once you have got your starting point and your destination, you can work out your route. You will also need to think about setting some milestones so that you can check your progress ('Berwick upon Tweed by lunchtime'!).

3 SITUATIONAL ANALYSIS

The situational analysis involves taking an objective look at where your organisation is now and how it got there. It consists of two stages:

- information audit
- marketing audit.

The information audit is designed to make sure that your judgement about where your organisation is now is based on hard evidence, not myth. It involves drawing up a shopping list of information you need in order to make your assessment of your organisation's situation. You can then collect the information you have available and assess how accurate and complete it is. Where you have adequate information, you can tick off the item on your shopping list. At the end of the process you will have to make plans about how you can collect the information left unticked on your list.

3.1 INFORMATION AUDIT

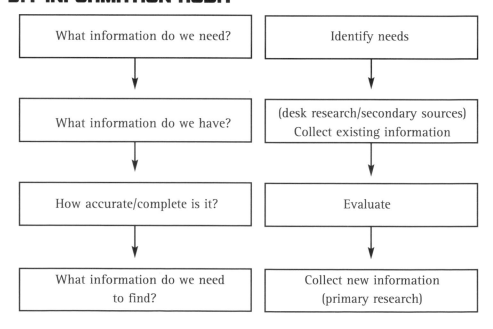

Peter Verwey of the Arts Council of England has drawn up an exhaustive list of the information that you could put on your shopping list in *Marketing Planning* (Arts Council of England, 1987). You will need to choose the items that are relevant to your organisation.

Here is a summary:

1. YOUR EVENTS:

(a) artistic policy

(b) past events

(c) audience perception of your building/organisation and shows

(d) touring/programming policy.

2. INCOME:

income from ticket sales, other earned income and funding bodies.

3. PRICING POLICIES:

(a) ticket yields

(b) top and bottom ticket prices

(c) concessions

(d) discounts.

4. TICKET SALES FACILITIES:

where and how tickets are sold.

5. NUMBERS AND TYPES OF TICKETS SOLD:

attendances broken down by show, by season, by year,
by price of ticket.

6. EXISTING AUDIENCE AND POTENTIAL AUDIENCE:

(a) existing audience analysed by geographic area, age, gender, social
classification, frequency of attendance, arts interests

(b) potential audience identified by looking at competition from similar
companies/ venues, comparing information with research from other
organisations

(c) the way the audiences are changing with time.

All of this is information about the organisation's relationship with its customers.
There are three other types of relationships to consider, however:

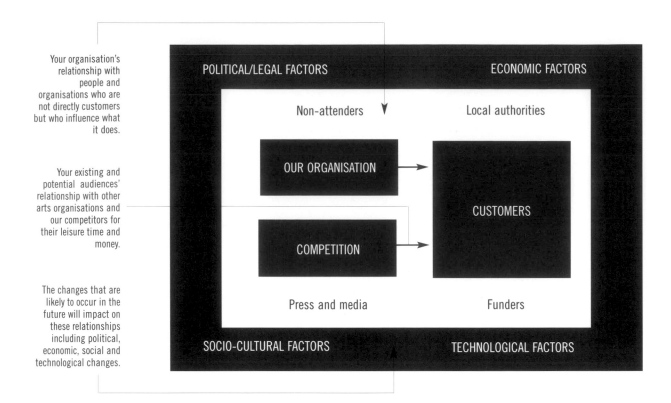

Your organisation's relationship with people and organisations who are not directly customers but who influence what it does.

Your existing and potential audiences' relationship with other arts organisations and our competitors for their leisure time and money.

The changes that are likely to occur in the future will impact on these relationships including political, economic, social and technological changes.

It would be all too easy to become overwhelmed at this stage. To prevent this, bear in mind the following:

- More data does not mean more information.
- Weigh the value of information against its cost.
- Accuracy is relative.
- Information is useless if it is not used.

Stick to this process:

COLLECT

↓

SIFT AND EVALUATE

↓

DISSEMINATE

3.2 MARKETING AUDIT

It is difficult for organisations and their staff responsible for marketing to be objective about what they do and why and how they do it. Often organisations employ someone else to make the assessment such as their national marketing agency, a marketer from another organisation in the area, a freelance marketer or a consultant.

The marketing audit will take into consideration the following issues and evaluate how effectively the organisation uses its marketing resources.

RESOURCES FOR MARKETING:
- number of staff hours available for marketing
- marketing budget
- additional help through volunteers, etc.

APPROACH TO MARKETING:
- benefits and targets, methods currently used, e.g. print, advertising, press.

3.3 MAKING SENSE OF THE INFORMATION: SWOT ANALYSIS

The next stage is to use the information to identify the key issues facing the organisation and their implications for the organisation.

SWOT analysis is the tool most commonly used to make sense of a lot of information. This is because it is simple to carry out and easy to put into practical use.

You need to look at all the information and use it to identify your organisation's strengths and weaknesses and the opportunities and threats that are facing it. Strengths and weaknesses are internal and opportunities and threats are external issues that your organisation cannot control. Only include important issues and make sure that your strengths and weakness are those perceived by your audiences, participants, funders, sponsors and other people in the outside world. The opinions of you and your colleagues are not enough.

BE SPECIFIC

If you find you have the same issue under more than one heading, examine it closely and be more specific about which aspects are positive and negative factors, for example:

Strengths	*Weaknesses*
A loyal core audience	A loyal core audience
↓	↓
A core audience of very frequent attenders	Have definite likes and dislikes
Have known the theatre for decades and are very proud of it	Unwilling to try adventurous events
Promote the theatre to their friends	Resistant to change in programming policy

Now take a look at your list and narrow it down to the factors that have important implications for your organisation. Now think about what your SWOT analysis means for your organisation. Concentrate on these ways of thinking:

- **Matching**: find strengths which you can use to take advantage of opportunities.
- **Converting**: think of ways of turning weaknesses and threats into strengths and opportunities or at least neutralising them so that they no longer hold any threats for your organisation.
- **Creative**: brainstorm innovative ideas.

INTERNAL	**STRENGTHS** Find matches	**WEAKNESSES** ← Convert or neutralise
EXTERNAL Out of your organisation's direct control	**OPPORTUNITIES** Find matches	**THREATS** ← Convert or neutralise

Summarise the key issues for your organisation and their implications for the future.

4 SETTING AIMS AND OBJECTIVES

An aim describes broadly what your project is trying to achieve:

> To bring 16–18 year olds into a theatre building and develop their understanding of how a dance work is created, staged and toured.

You now need to identify a series of long-term aims for your organisation which are designed to resolve the key issues identified in your situational analysis and tackle any other challenges highlighted during your organisation's general business planning process.

Objectives must be much more detailed – in fact, they are useless unless they are SMART:

Specific: Your objective must be as precise as possible, specifying exactly who you want to be involved and how many of them you want to do exactly what.

Measurable: Include numbers in your objective so that you can tell whether you have been successful or not. Make sure that you structure your measurement so that it ties in with the method that you are going to use to assess it, e.g. the percentage of attenders or participants that comes from your target group would be measurable by using the results of a survey.

Actionable: You must be able to take action to achieve your objectives, e.g. by having enough resources.

Realistic: You must be able to achieve your objectives – there's no point in being overambitious.

Timescale: You must say by when you want to achieve your objective – then you will know when to start measuring.

Here are some examples of SMART objectives:

- To increase the average frequency of attendance from 2.4 to 3.2 times a year within two years.
- To persuade 50 people who attended the Rock School last season to come to a gig this season.
- To increase ticket yield from £6.18 to £7.20 by increasing the number of full-price payers by the end of this year.

Your aims and objectives should cover in, for instance, a concert venue:

- your organisation's events
- audience size
- audience profile
- income
- how you will prioritise and collect the missing information you identified in your information audit.

5 DECIDING THE STRATEGY

Now decide on what, broadly, you need to do to achieve your goals. You will need long-term strategies that involve:

- your organisation's events
- target groups

- price
- place (how you get your events to your audiences and participants, including where the activities take place and how you make tickets available)
- the marketing methods you will use (also known as promotion)
- people: how your organisation develops a relationship with your audiences and participants and how you make them feel welcome
- market research.

6 ASSESSING THE RESOURCES

Marketing budget: what financial resources do you need to achieve your goals?

- staff
- other sources of help, e.g. volunteers, etc.

7 IMPLEMENTING THE PLAN

Tactics are the detailed ideas you will use to put your strategies into action. Here is an example:

Key issue:	55% of our audience is aged 55+ and overall numbers are likely to drop dramatically in the future.
Strategy:	Increase the number of 30–45s attending the venue.
Tactics:	• Develop a strand of music and comedy programming for the age group.
	• Produce a separate piece of print targeted at the age group and distribute to different sites alongside a press campaign.
	• Develop a 'bring a friend for free' sales promotion to audiences at other venues.

8 MONITORING THE PLAN

You will need to work out what methods you will use to evaluate how well you are achieving your objectives. These methods ought to be implicit in the SMART objectives you have set. For more information see Chapter 31, 'Monitoring and Evaluation'.

MARKET RESEARCH

SEE ALSO CHAPTERS
20. TALKING TO THE RIGHT PEOPLE
21. TALKING ABOUT THE RIGHT THINGS
25. AUDIENCE DEVELOPMENT
31. MONITORING AND EVALUATION

1   WHY DO RESEARCH?

There are three broad reasons for carrying out market research:

1. to collect information for a particular purpose or to resolve a particular issue;

2. to find out what your attenders or participants are like and what they do so that you can compare them with attenders and participants nationally, with attenders and participants at other events at your venue or with attenders and participants at other venues in your area;

3. to find out about different groups of your attenders or participants and then see if there are any significant ways in which they are different from or similar to each other, e.g. frequent participants and first-time participants.

> We've just finished putting together a sponsorship pack and the research has been built into this ... We're going to start approaching sponsors soon ... The research has enabled us to get a large grant from the Scottish Tourist Board to develop our café-bar and the front of house with a city-link box office.   The Tourist Board were very interested in those aspects because it brought tourists in. The fact that we could demonstrate we had got quite a large percentage of tourists made that money possible ... but also they liked the way we were doing the work and the fact that we had a marketing strategy. **PR officer, metropolitan venue, Scotland**

There are other benefits to doing research:

> As a result, word went back to the Arts Council that we roughly knew what we were doing, which was quite gratifying. **Press officer, specialised venue, London**

I have talked about audiences and participants but, of course, your organisation could deal with other sorts of 'customer' that you want to find out about including venues and promoters, community groups, local authorities and so on.

Whatever the particular interest of your organisation, however, doing research simply because you think you ought to is a waste of time, money and effort. You need to ask:

- What do I want to know?
- Why do I want to know it?
- What will I do with the information?

Clear answers to these questions will shape every aspect of the research you carry out and ensure that you end up with information that you can use. If you have carried out an information audit (see Chapter 23, 'Marketing Planning'), you will already have a shopping list of what you need to find out.

2 PLANNING RESEARCH

You must plan your research by deciding how you are going to tackle each of these stages before you start handing out questionnaires or organising customer circles. This will avoid you having to make embarrassing telephone calls like the one I got from a large organisation a couple of years ago: 'We've got about 6,000 completed questionnaires and we don't know what to do with them because we had our work experience student analysing them but he's just gone home in tears and he's only done 57.'

There are three sorts of market research that you need to build into your plan:

1. **Desk research**: information about your organisation and its audiences that is already available, including previous research into your audiences – all you have to do is gather it together.

2. **Secondary research**: information that someone else has collected about their audiences for an art form or target group similar to yours.

3. **Primary research**: information that you will need to collect about your audiences.

Think of primary research as a last resort. It takes up so much time and energy that it is much better to answer your questions through desk and secondary research if you can.

Go through your shopping list of what you want to know and why you want to know it. Which items of information might already be available in your organisation? Which can you collect by looking at secondary research?

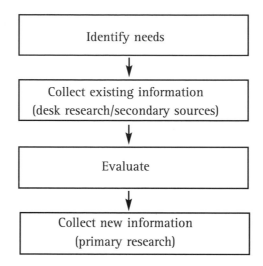

3 DESK RESEARCH

Gather together all the potential sources of the information you need within your organisation. These could include:

- finance reports

- information in funding applications

- daily, weekly and show returns from the box office

- seating plans for past shows (if you have not got a box office computer system)

- past season brochures

- annual reports

- past market research reports.

Talk to all your colleagues – they know what information they collect on a regular basis as part of their jobs.

Sift through the information that you have collected, looking for information that will help you answer your questions.

Make a judgement about the quality of each piece of information. How old is it? How complete is it? If you are looking at past market research, also look at the number of people that were surveyed (the sample size) and how they were selected. Is the sample too small to be reliable? Does the way they were selected mean that the research is biased? The research may give a good picture of part of your audience, e.g. regular attenders, but not reflect accurately the whole picture.

This could be a good moment to share your findings with your colleagues. Information is not much use if you keep it to yourself and they need to make informed decisions, just like you.

4 SECONDARY RESEARCH

The Arts Councils of England, Scotland, Wales and Northern Ireland and most regional arts boards hold audience research information about many different sorts of performance.   Look for information about your scale and art form – it may save you having to carry out expensive and time-consuming research of your own.

Secondary research is also important because you need to find out how your audiences differ from other audiences for your art form by collecting information for comparison.

It would be easy to collect vast quantities of information simply because it is available but you are unlikely to have the time to make sense of it all. Instead, concentrate on the shopping list that you drew up when you asked yourself 'What do I want to know, why do I want to know it and what will I do with the information?'

4.1 SOURCES OF SECONDARY INFORMATION

Arts Councils: see Arts Council of England publications list

- Index of Market Research for the Arts.
★ Research Digests for the Arts: Plays/Variety, Classical Music, Ballet, Contemporary Dance, Opera, Jazz, Visual Arts.
★ Target Group Index.
★ Area Profile Reports.
- Market research project reports for sale, e.g. Orchestral Concerts Quantitative Research, Selling the Contemporary Visual Arts, Youth Audience Research.
- Research reports held in the Arts Council of England Library (by appointment only).
- Other national research commissioned by the Arts Councils of Scotland, Wales and Northern Ireland.

Regional arts board

- May hold regional research and statistics.
- May hold lists of regional arts organisations (competitors).
★ Area Profile Reports.

Marketing agencies

- A wide range of research and statistics about regions.
- National market research data and project reports may be available for consultation.

Local authority

- Demographic statistics.
- Data on regional leisure facilities.

Trade directories

- Lists of arts organisations with information such as seating capacities, technical facilities, artistic policies, etc.

Marketing publications

- For example, *Marketing Pocket Book* – data on leisure spend, demographic information, etc.

- ★ = copyright data only available to organisations getting regular funding from one of the Arts Councils or a regional arts board

TARGET GROUP INDEX

This is a national survey completed by around 25,000 households across Great Britain each year, chosen to match the demographics of the population as a whole. The survey has been designed by the British Market Research Bureau to serve the needs of the commercial sector, but the Arts Council has paid for two questions about the arts to be included:

> About how often these days do you go to the following: any performance in a theatre; plays, ballet, contemporary dance, opera, classical music, jazz, art galleries or exhibitions?

> How long ago was the last occasion you went to the following: any performance in a theatre; plays, ballet, contemporary dance, opera, classical music, jazz, art galleries or exhibitions?

The answers to these questions have been cross-referenced to hundreds of others in the survey, giving information about other purchasing habits. e.g. a sherry drinker is twice as likely to attend performances of ballet as contemporary dance.

TGI is useful because it gives us a broad picture of how the whole population engages with the arts. Most of the information available to arts organisations is collected from people attending an arts event, but TGI surveys people who turn out to be non-attenders and potential attenders as well as existing attenders telling us in broad brushstrokes:

- what proportion of the population says they attend each of plays, classical music, ballet, contemporary dance, opera, jazz, visual arts and any performance in a theatre
- how often they attend each of the art forms
- what the cross-over is between art forms
- frequent and infrequent attenders' age, gender, social grade, occupation, when they left education, etc.

The Arts Council of England has compiled a suite of reports covering various aspects of the data and issues an update on the key information every year. A condition of the Arts Council of England being allowed to use the data is that these reports are only available to clients of the funding system.

AREA PROFILE REPORTS

Area Profile Reports, also produced by the Arts Council of England, are crammed with useful information about the population in particular localities. There are reports for the areas around over 100 towns and cities in England, Scotland and Wales. They cover the area within a 30-minute drive of the town or city centre and give data on:

- the whole population within that area
- how the statistics for that particular population compare with the average for Great Britain as a whole
- the population in each postal sector (e.g. KP12 1 or KP4 2) falling within the 30-minute drive time.

Use Area Profile Reports to:

- identify the key characteristics of your local community
- find out how many people in your community are likely to say that they attend a particular art form nowadays
- find out where there are concentrations of particular sorts of people, e.g. postal sectors in which there are well above the average number of households with children under 16
- compare the potential market for your work in different areas of Great Britain.

The reports come with a key explaining what each piece of data means, and a guide to how you can use them.

The Arts Council of England may be able to respond to requests for reports on additional towns and cities and for different drive-time areas.

MARKET RESEARCH INDEX FOR THE ARTS

This is an index of over 400 market research reports on the arts which were published between around 1975 and 1994. You can look up summaries of the research topic, report title, publication date and where it is available for consultation. The index at the back of the book is organised by art form, area and audience type so that you can identify reports that might answer the particular questions relevant to your organisation. Most of the reports in the index can be consulted by appointment in the Arts Council of England Library.

5 INFORMATION THAT YOU NEED TO COLLECT

If your desk and secondary research has not fully answered all the questions on your shopping list, you will need to carry out primary research.

This is where arts organisations could collaborate.   A single organisation is unlikely to have the resources to undertake all the research and analysis they need.   If organisations working on a particular scale or in a particular art form or with similar catchment areas pool their available staff time and money, a more extensive research project becomes possible.

5.1 EASILY ACCESSIBLE INFORMATION

Some information is readily accessible. All you have to do is analyse it. Postcodes on mailing lists will give information about where the audience lives or works. Computerised box office systems will usually give information about the number of tickets sold at each price, the number of concessionary or discounted tickets sold, how people pay for their tickets, how many tickets are sold in each transaction and so on.   A manual box office system may also have some of this information in the regular financial reports that it produces and on the seating plans.

INFORMATION FROM BOX OFFICE COMPUTER SYSTEMS

The amount of useful information that you can extract from your box office computer system depends on:

- which system you have

- how much information your box office collects

- the skills and knowledge of the system available in your organisation.

These are some of the more commonly run analysis routines:

Customer's purchasing patterns:
- what they buy
- when they buy it
- how many they buy
- how often
- how much they pay
- where they sit

About the customer:
- where they live
- gender
- children's ages
(if the box office staff collects this information)

Overall patterns:
- how many tickets you sell
- when they are sold
- income levels
- ticket yield
- which ticket price sells first

By:
- year
- month
- day of week
- season
- show
- performance
- type of show

6 PRIMARY RESEARCH

You can carry out your own research or you can employ a specialist consultant to do it for you. You will find a list on the Arts Council of England's consultants database.   The costs involved in employing a consultancy to undertake research are too high for small-scale organisations to cover on their own; however, the Arts Council and regional arts associations sometimes give financial support to this kind of project.

There are two sorts of information that can be gathered through research:

Quantitative research is essentially concerned with numbers – it counts things. You can discover the number of people responding to your survey who found out about the production through the venue season brochure, or the number of people aged between 16 and 18. These numbers can also be expressed as percentages: 55% of respondents found out about the production through the season brochure.

Qualitative research does not involve numbers at all. Qualitative research is used to gather in-depth information about people's perceptions, attitudes, opinions and behaviour. It can tell you what some audience members think of the performances or the venue, why they like or dislike what they see, the reasons for their attendance at the venue and so on. You can test the effectiveness of things like images or copy on print and so help you develop the right image for your organisation. Often members of the public see arts organisations in a completely different way to the people who work in them. Qualitative research allows you to look in detail at the benefits that your potential audience thinks are important rather than having to rely on your own or your colleagues' opinions.

6.1 QUANTITATIVE RESEARCH

There are various ways to obtain this type of information:

- **Postal survey:** this involves sending a questionnaire by post to all the households in a particular area. It is expensive, and because there is relatively little contact between you and the recipient, many people do not bother to send them back. It is impossible to tell if the results you get are balanced because only a limited type of person will respond.
- **Mailing list survey:** this involves sending a postal questionnaire to all the people on your organisation's mailing list. Touring companies may find it useful to survey some of their venues' lists. People are more likely to respond than for a postal survey because they already have an interest in the organisation, although a good proportion will not bother. It is much easier to carry out than a postal survey as all the names and addresses are to hand. However, it does mean that you can only find out about enthusiastic attenders within your catchment area.

- **Telephone survey of mailing list members**: this involves telephoning your enthusiastic theatre-goers and asking them questions. Most theatregoers have telephones which makes them easy to reach.   It is reasonably cost effective because the respondents are already interested in your organisation.   The survey can be done in the evenings when most people are at home and, because very little effort is required, the response rate is usually good.

We discovered that our audience is the alternative theatre/international theatre audience. They are AB mainly. They prefer to see dance at The Place and elsewhere rather than with us. They really enjoy the Indian music nights and meal package. **Marketing officer, Asian arts-orientated community theatre, London**

- **Self-completion audience questionnaire:** this involves distributing questionnaires to audiences on the premises. The audience is easily accessible and, because there are no telephone or postage costs, it is an inexpensive method.   The response rate is often good.
- **Interview:** this involves asking people for the information you need face to face. Interviews can take place on the street, at home, or in the theatre. This is the method that brings the best results but interviewing is highly skilled which makes the process very expensive. If the information is to be used in any formal way, e.g. for funding applications, professional interviewers must be used.

COMPARING QUANTITATIVE MARKET RESEARCH METHODS

Method	Cost	Response	Sample	Difficulty rate	Quality of information	Depth of information
Postal survey	high	low	unbalanced	medium	low	low
Mailing list survey	high	medium	frequent attenders only	easy	low	low
Telephone survey	high	high	mailing list members	medium	medium	high
Self-completion questionnaire	low	medium	attenders	easy	medium	low
One-on-one interviews: in the theatre, in the home, on the street	high	high	balanced	medium	high	high

SAMPLING

One of the most important stages in planning carrying out quantitative research is deciding:

- Who is to be surveyed?
- How many people should be surveyed?
- How will you choose which people to survey?

Getting your sample right will mean that you can avoid bias and achieve maximum accuracy for the money and time you have available.

Some jargon

- Sampling population: the group of people to be surveyed, e.g. everyone at this event tonight or attenders at all the performances by Stan's Café in March.
- Sample units: the clearly defined people you are going to take the sample from, e.g. people who have attended performances by Stan's Café at mac, but who have attended no other drama performance at this venue.

Sample size

The number of people you will want to survey (your sample) does not have to be linked to how many people are in your sampling population. This is because a reasonably large sample selected at random from a large population will be, on average, representative of what the population are like.

How many people you survey does depend on the staff, time and money you have and the degree of accuracy you need. Other things being equal, a large sample will be more reliable than a small sample taken from the same population. For example, if you survey 1,000 people chosen at random, you can be 95% certain that the answers they give are representative of the population as a whole within a margin of error of 3%. This is accurate enough for most needs.

REMEMBER

Be careful that enough people answer the survey. If less than 60% respond, then it is possible (and even likely) that what they say is not representative of the population because only particularly committed people (or people who like responding to surveys) have answered. One hundred completed from 200 handed out is more reliable than 100 completed from 2,000 handed out.

Sampling methods

- Simple random sample: completely random (e.g. using random numbers to choose people from a list). Everyone in the population has the same chance of being included.

- Systematic sample: random sampling with a system, e.g. every nth person is selected from a list, or a questionnaire is handed out to every nth person who comes through the door. This is easy to carry out but is not fully random. Some arts organisations use alphabetical order.

- Stratified random sampling: the population is divided into mutually exclusive groups or strata and a random sample is taken from each group, e.g. a random sample is taken from your box office computer system of people who live in six different areas.

- Quota sampling: the population is divided into groups according to a set of characteristics, e.g. men and women in five different age groups or frequent, occasional and first-time attenders. The researcher finds and interviews a set number of people in each of these groups.

- Area sampling: the area to be surveyed is broken down into smaller areas, e.g. postal sectors. A number of these are selected by random methods. Households within the selected areas are then chosen by random methods and these are surveyed.

- Multi-phase sampling: some information is collected from the whole sample (e.g. postcode) while additional information is collected from sub-samples (e.g. age and postcode).

6.2 QUALITATIVE RESEARCH

Qualitative research should always be carried out by professional researchers to get reliable results. The most frequent techniques they use are focus groups and one-to-one interviews. Focus groups involve bringing together a group of around eight people and encouraging them to talk about the issues that interest them. Researchers use a wide range of psychological techniques to get people to express the attitudes and beliefs that lie behind their opinions and behaviour. The biggest challenge is getting them to say what they really think rather than what they think you want to hear.

A London-based touring theatre company has undertaken quantitative research in previous years but in 1989 decided that it was necessary to do qualitative research in the form of face-to-face interviews. Thirty people were given interviews lasting about 5–10 minutes. Their marketing and development director described the reasons for doing the research:

> What the marketing audit done in 1981 threw up was a dated image ... We needed to consider our corporate image again ... It suggested we perhaps change our name ... So we got a copywriter to suggest five names and we've been testing these out in various areas on a face-to-face basis – talking to people to get their ideas. This wouldn't be very easy to do on paper.

Some attitudinal information can be gained from quantitative research if one or two questions are left open for people to answer in their own words, e.g. 'Do you have any comments you would like to make about the performance you have seen?' These comments are also useful for publicity material or even for promoting your organisation to possible sponsors.

Even though you should not try to carry out qualitative research yourself, it is useful to talk to your customers. These informal chats are often known as *customer circles*. You will get an idea about the opinions of some of your audience members, but you must not rely too much upon the results. Customer circles are simply a way for you to keep in touch.

SOME HINTS ON LEADING CUSTOMER CIRCLES

- Groups of around eight work best.
- Make sure that you do not mix incompatible people, e.g. non-attenders with frequent attenders or youngsters with your more traditional audience or people with English as a second or third language with confident communicators in English.
- Offer the incentive of wine, beer, soft drinks and nibbles.
- Make everybody feel at ease by using an intimate, informal space with comfortable seating.
- Make sure that everybody has their say.
- Keep to the point.
- Direct the discussion to where you want it to go but without stultifying it.
- Listen; do not talk.
- Try to be detached (even when they are trashing your print, never defend it).
- Ask open questions to encourage discussion.
- Do not ask leading questions.
- The session should last 45–60 minutes.

We discovered that people who were theatre-goers and who were being interviewed in our survey didn't see shows here although they went to other venues ... This was partly because of a lack of awareness of the show that was actually on ... because our shows change so frequently it's difficult to tell what's actually on that night when you are in the foyer – even with a big, board that says 'TONIGHT'. **Director, metropolitan mixed programme venue, England**

7 CARRYING OUT RESEARCH USING QUESTIONNAIRES

This is the first time we've done any audience research here for about five years. We've surveyed every performance for two weeks by going up to people in the foyer before the show with pencils and self-completion questionnaires. There's a prize draw with £45 worth of panto tickets. People ask us what we're trying to sell but we say we want to know what you think about the theatre. We've got boxes for completed surveys all round the theatre and we also collect them in person. We're averaging 45% response rate every night. We're going to put the results front of house so people can see that we are listening and responding. **Paul Griffiths, Press and Marketing Officer, Queen's Theatre, Hornchurch**

Before undertaking research yourself, you need to consider carefully what it will mean in terms of staff time and money. Answer these questions:

- Who is going to compile the questionnaire?
- Who will pay for it to be photocopied or printed?
- Who will distribute and collect it?
- Who will analyse the information (a very time-consuming task)?
- How will the information be used?

Unless everyone involved feels that they can cope with the extra work then it is best not to attempt it.

7.1 QUESTIONS TO ASK YOURSELF

We gave out the questionnaires rather than putting them on the seats ... I think it drew people's attention to them, because we said things like 'Please put them in the box after the show'. If you put them on seats, the house lights go down and people aren't going to look at them. We had a good return our way ... we had none that we had to throw away either. **Administrator, national touring mime company**

1. What's the problem?
   Talk to relevant colleagues at this stage.
2. What do you want to know? Why do you want to know it? What will you do with the information?

(a) It is not enough to say 'It's time we did some audience research'.

(b) Do not forget that you need specific objectives complete with time-scales.

3.   Who will you survey?

(a) A venue needs to decide whether to survey one production or a whole range to allow comparison between shows. A company needs to decide whether to survey one venue in depth, or several venues in order to make comparisons. Both types of organisation also need to ensure that they have a balance between performances on different days of the week as different sorts of people often attend shows at weekends than on weekdays. Consider whether to distribute it to the whole audience for a show or to sections. You could distribute to every fourth or sixth seat, or to selected areas of the auditorium if you wish to cover a large number of performances without overloading yourself with the sheer bulk of the responses.

(b) The number of performances that you survey will depend on the number of responses that you feel you have time to analyse.

4.   How many people will you survey?

You need to hand out a lot more questionnaires than you want responses. You will get a response rate of 20–60% depending on the effectiveness of the questionnaire and how you distribute and collect them. If you want to compare results from different sections of the respondents, e.g. new attenders, you will need a larger overall sample.

5.   How will you choose who you will survey?

6.   How will you analyse the results?

(a) Tallying the answers by hand: this gives basic results which may be sufficient for your needs. Simply count the number of people who have given each particular answer.

(b) Using a computer: there is relatively cheap software available, or you can buy the analysis from a commercial bureau. An Arts Council marketing agency may offer you a better service for a better price. Some organisations have used the resources of their local tertiary education institution.

(c) You must work out how you are going to analyse the results before you design the questionnaire, let alone hand any out. This ensures that you ask the questions in the right way.

7.   What questions do you want to ask?

(a) A long questionnaire means more work for you and a probable drop in the response rate.   An ideal length is one side of A4. Your questionnaire should certainly not be longer than four sides of A4 as audiences will become bored or run out of time at the interval and not complete it.

(b) Only include questions if they are essential to achieve your objectives.

(c) Make sure that your questions are structured so that you can compare the results with the available secondary research.

(d) It is very difficult to make the questions on a self-completion questionnaire simple and unambiguous. Peter Verwey, Senior Marketing Officer at the Arts Council, has constructed a list of 50 carefully formulated questions for you to choose from. Only select a small number of these questions, choosing those that will get the information you have decided you need.

(e) It is helpful to try out the completed questionnaire on colleagues and friends to check that it is easy to fill in.

8. How will you structure the questions?

(a) The order and structure of the questions will influence the results.

(b) The questions should be in a logical order with the less interesting personal questions last.

9. How will you word them?

10. What order should they be in?

11. How will you print the questionnaires?

12. How will you distribute the questionnaires?

(a) Handing out questionnaires gets a better response rate than leaving them on seats. Audiences need a reason for responding. The brief personal contact that audiences have with your organisation if they are handed a questionnaire can often make the difference.

(b) Ask the house manager to reinforce this by making an announcement before the show.

(c) Train the staff or volunteers handing out questionnaires so that they can answer audience members' queries.

(d) Staff or volunteers should check that respondents have something to write with and have plenty of spare pens to hand out.

13. How will you collect them?

(a) Staff or volunteers should ask for completed questionnaires as customers leave the auditorium.

(b) Put boxes labelled 'Please return your completed questionnaires here' in the foyer for people you miss, but do not rely on this as the only means of collection.

(c) A Freepost address may result in a few extra responses, but most people forget about the questionnaire as soon as they leave the building.

14. How can I increase the response rates?

(a) Offer an incentive such as a prize draw with an attractive and appropriate prize.

(b) Explain why you need the information.

(c) Only ask relevant questions.

(d) Use friendly, extrovert staff or volunteers to hand out the questionnaires.

(e) Make sure that the questionnaire looks attractive and is readable in the available lighting.

15. How will I present the results?

7.2 ANALYSING THE RESULTS

Analysing questionnaires is time-consuming. Specialised computer programs exist which enable you to record the information from each response and then cross-reference them, pulling out, for example, all the first-time attenders who heard about the show through the venue's brochure. There are a number of consultants (see the Arts Council's consultant database), arts marketing agencies and computer bureaux who offer this service.

The alternative is to tally the responses by hand. This method limits the amount of cross-referencing that can be achieved:

- Decide which groups you want to compare, e.g. people who have seen one of your events before and people who have not. Find the question that gives you this information. Sort the questionnaires into two different piles, one for all the people who say they have seen your events before and one for those who say they have not. Keep the piles separate. Now tally all the answers to all the questionnaires in the first pile. Next, tally all the answers to the questionnaires in the second pile. Compare the results.

- You can do this for as many different audience groups as you want but you must make sure that you have enough responses in each group. Do not pay too much attention to sub-groups with less than 100 respondents.

PERCENTAGES

You will end up with a series of figures. These are fairly meaningless until you turn them into percentages to allow for comparison between sets of results. The formula for this is:

No. of responses
―――――――――――――――――― x 100 = %
Total no. of questionnaires returned

REMEMBER ✳

Making sense of the results
- Look for differences that help to explain the patterns you can see in the data.
- Concentrate on the key issues rather than trying to report on all the data, whether it contains helpful information or not.

13c Have you ever been a member of Jump The Q?
☐ Yes
☐ No

14 What is your home postcode?

....

15 Are you currently...
☐ Employed
☐ In full-time education
☐ Retired
☐ Unemployed
☐ Not eligible for employment
☐ Other (please state) ....

Please state your current or most recent employment

job title ....

place of work ....

16 Are you...
☐ Male
☐ Female

17 Are you...
☐ Under 15
☐ 15-19
☐ 20-24
☐ 25-34
☐ 35-44
☐ 45-54
☐ 55-64
☐ 65+

18 Do you have children under eighteen years old?
☐ Yes
☐ No

If so, what are their ages?
☐ Under 5
☐ 6-10
☐ 11-14
☐ 15-18

19 Are you registered disabled?
☐ Yes
☐ No

Please enter your name and address if you wish to be entered into the FREE PRIZE DRAW

Name ....

Address ....

....

....

Postcode ....

Telephone (...........) ....

Are there any shows or performers you would like to see at the Queen's Theatre?

....

....

....

....

Do you have any further comments or suggestions?

....

....

....

....

....

Many thanks for your help

Audience Survey

To help us plan for the future, we would appreciate a few minutes of your time to complete this questionnaire. Each completed survey will be entered into a prize draw for a free family ticket (worth £45!) for this year's family pantomime *Cinderella* on Tuesday 12th December.

All answers will be kept strictly confidential and you need not give your name and address unless you wish to participate in the prize draw.

Thank you for your help.

1a Is this your first visit to the Queen's Theatre?
☐ Yes
☐ No

1b Which of these recent shows have you seen at the Queen's?
☐ The Beggar's Opera (Apr '00)
☐ Don't Dress For Dinner (Mar '00)
☐ The 39 Steps (Feb '00)
☐ Aladdin (Dec 99)
☐ Jack The Ripper (Nov 99)
☐ Brighton Rock (Oct 99)
☐ In The Midnight Hour (Sep 99)
☐ Having A Ball (May 99)
☐ Fings Ain't Wot They Used T'Be
☐ Misery (Mar 99)
☐ Our Day Out (Feb 99)
☐ Dick Whittington (Dec 98)
☐ Phantom of the Opera (Nov 98)
☐ Abigail's Party (Oct 98)
☐ From A Jack To A King (Sep 98)

2 How do you rate the Queen's?

		Very Good	Good	Poor	Very Poor
A	range of productions	☐	☐	☐	☐
B	quality of productions	☐	☐	☐	☐
C	ease of obtaining information	☐	☐	☐	☐
D	ease of booking	☐	☐	☐	☐
E	value for money	☐	☐	☐	☐
F	friendliness/ helpfulness of box office staff	☐	☐	☐	☐
G	friendliness/ helpfulness of usherettes	☐	☐	☐	☐
H	friendliness/ helpfulness of bar/cafe staff	☐	☐	☐	☐
J	auditorium facilities	☐	☐	☐	☐
K	toilet facilities	☐	☐	☐	☐
L	overall atmosphere	☐	☐	☐	☐

3 If you could change one thing at the Queen's, what would it be and why?

....

....

4 Which other theatres have you attended in the past 12 months?
☐ Civic Centre, Chelmsford
☐ Brentwood Centre
☐ Cliffs Pavilion, Southend
☐ Grays Theatre
☐ Kenneth More Theatre, Ilford
☐ Mercury Theatre, Colchester
☐ Orchard Theatre, Dartford
☐ Palace Theatre, Westcliff
☐ Theatre Royal, Stratford East
☐ Any West End Theatre
☐ Other (please specify) ....

5 Which of the following have you visited in the past two months?
☐ Cinema
☐ Sports Centre
☐ Pub/Nightclub
☐ Restaurant
☐ Bingo
☐ Other (please specify) ....

6 How many people (including yourself) are in your party tonight?
☐ 1
☐ 2
☐ 3
☐ 4
☐ 5-9
☐ 10+

7a Are you the person who booked the tickets for tonight's performance?
☐ Yes (go to Q7b)
☐ No (go to Q8)

7b How did you book your tickets?
☐ Telephoning the Box Office
☐ Visiting the Box Office
☐ Postal application

7c Did you have any problems booking the tickets for tonight's show?
☐ Yes
☐ No

If yes, please give details ....

....

8 What was your main source of information about A Chorus of Disapproval?
☐ Brochure
☐ Flyer/Leaflet
☐ Jump The Q
☐ Local newspaper advert
☐ Local newspaper article
☐ Local radio
☐ Poster
☐ Promotional letter
☐ Word of mouth

9 Which of these local papers do you read on a regular basis?
☐ Essex Courier
☐ Essex Chronicle
☐ Recorder Series
☐ The Herald
☐ The Post Series
☐ Yellow Advertiser
☐ Other (please specify) ....

10 Which of these national papers do you regularly read?
☐ Daily Express
☐ Daily Mail
☐ Daily Mirror
☐ Evening Standard
☐ The Guardian
☐ The Independent
☐ The Sun
☐ The Daily Telegraph
☐ The Times
☐ Other (please specify) ....

11 Which of these radio stations do you regularly listen to?
☐ Active FM
☐ BBC Essex
☐ BBC Radio 1
☐ BBC Radio 2
☐ BBC Radio 3
☐ BBC Radio 4
☐ BBC Radio 5
☐ Essex FM
☐ Other (please specify) ....

12a Do you have access to the internet?
☐ Yes
☐ No

12b Would you consider booking Queen's Theatre tickets via the internet?
☐ Yes
☐ No

13a Are you a member of the current Jump The Q subscription scheme?
☐ Yes (please go to Q14)
☐ No (please go to Q13b)

13b Are you aware of the Jump The Q subscription scheme?
☐ Yes (please go to Q13c)
☐ No

Please tell us a little about yourself:

How old are you?

Under 16 ( )   16-24 ( )   25-34 ( )   35-44 ( )

45-54   ( )   55-64 ( )   65+ ( )

What is your occupation? _____

How far have you travelled to see this evening's performance?

0-5 miles ( )   6-10 miles ( ) 11-20 miles ( )   21+ miles ( )

Do you have any other comments: _____

_____

_____

_____

Thank you very much for your time.

*Please give us your name and address if you would like to join the earthfall mailing list:

Name: _____

Address:_____

_____

Postcode:_____

Please tick this box if you would like us to pass on your name and address <u>to this venue</u> for
any mailing list they may have. ( )
* Your name and address will be kept strictly confidential

_____

We would be grateful if you could spend five minutes helping us with this survey. Any
response to the company and its work is always very useful.

Please give the completed survey to a member of staff or leave it at the Box Office.
Thank you very much for your time.

_____

Have you seen an earthfall performance before? Yes ( ) No ( )

If yes, did you see them at this venue? Yes ( )
at another venue? (please specify where) Yes ( ) _____

How did you hear about Rococo Blood?

- Venue Season Brochure   ( ) ~~~~~
- Leaflet   ~~~~~
- Poster
- Newspaper (if so, which paper?)   ( )
- Radio (if so, which programme?)   ( )
- Television (if so, which programme?)   ( )
- Venue contact
- Company contact   ~~~~~
- Word of mouth/friend told me   ~~~~~
- Letter   ~~~~~
- Other (please specify)

Why did you decide to come and see Rococo Blood? _____

Have you seen any contemporary dance/physical theatre productions before?

Yes ( ) No ( )

What other events do you attend regularly?

- Classical dance   ( )   Contemporary music ( )
- Contemporary dance   ( )   Classical music   ( )
- Jazz   ( )   Theatre   ( )
- Opera   ( )   Art Galleries   ( )
- Musicals   ( )   Other (please specify) ( )

Targeting audiences:

We've initiated some audience research for this production and have results from the previous tours of **Rococo Blood and Fabulous Wounds**. This has proved useful in attempting to ascertain who *earthfall* attendees are and how to target them. With this production, we're also very keen to develop new audiences. I've enclosed some of the results from audience surveys - I hope they're useful to you.

Rococo Blood is a good production for attempting to harness new audiences for physical theatre/contemporary dance. It's 'total theatre' - as much about the live music and drama as about the dance. It's dynamic and energetic, shot with humour but also full of emotional depth and intelligent comment. All these elements could be pushed to different target audiences.

Students - push the live music angle - Jon and Paul Wigens and Roger Mills are renowned musicians and have worked with Travis, The Blue Aeroplanes, The Wood Children, Onalee of Reprazent and companies such as Blast Theory and Circomedia. Specially composed live acoustic dub and trip-hop grooves form more than just a backdrop - the music and musicians are an integral part of the production. Contemporary music audiences can also be targeted. Music is always a major part of an *earthfall* production with the musicians being part of the performance and the dancers/actors speaking/rapping and playing instruments.

earthfall are available to do pre or post-show discussions if timing and availability allow. This has proven to be added incentive for student groups. *Please contact the earthfall office ASAP if you would like to try and arrange a formal or informal pre or post-show talk.*

Contemporary drama attenders/students - **Rococo Blood** has a strong drama element and it's worth pushing to drama students and contemporary drama attenders as a great example of how dance, drama and music can work together to create a stunning piece of innovative theatre.

earthfall are recent winners of the <u>BAFTA</u> **Cymru Award** for **Best Short Film** for *Too Old to Dream*. For venues equipped to show films, it may be possible to arrange a showing of the film as a double offer for audiences. *Please contact the earthfall office ASAP if you are interested.* This would also be a good press story.

We have a video comprising six minutes of excerpts from **Rococo Blood**, this is worth showing in the foyer, to groups to encourage them to book and excerpts can be offered to local television. The video gives a taste of the company's vibrant and powerful work and can also be loop- played in theatre foyers to interest visitors to the venue for several days leading up to the performance.

Colleges and Schools - To encourage colleges and schools to book, you could use the company information, performance information and the page highlighting 'themes' as an education pack, perhaps also arranging a pre or post-performance talk and pre-show rehearsal if appropriate. *The company also teach a comprehensive range of workshops.*

Suggested Target Audiences:	Reaching Target Audiences:
Previous earthfall attenders	Direct Mail - latest production from a BAFTA award winning company
Previous contemporary dance/ physical theatre attendees	Direct Mail
Attenders of contemporary music events	Print distribution/Direct Mail - live music; guitar, drums, trumpet, hip-hop, vocals throughout the performance.
Art exhibition and gallery attenders	Direct Mail - stunning visual imagery fused with live performance. Print Distribution
'Art-house' cinema attenders	Direct Mail - pushing the fact that its cinematic, multimedia, cutting- edge live performance
Contemporary 'avant-garde' drama attenders	Direct Mail - pushing the fact that it's not just dance - it's drama, music - total theatre
Local dance companies	Print distribution/letter/Company information
Local dance classes Community dance organisations	Print distribution/special group booking offer/Company information
Leisure centres which may run dance classes	Print distribution, Print Display Panels
Local Drama colleges which also have Performing Arts courses, Contemporary Music courses	Print distribution/special group booking offer, Direct Mail Letter to tutors Possible Post-Show Talk
Local art colleges - most Fine Art courses also have a performance art option.	Print distribution/special group booking offer, Direct Mail to Tutors Possible Pre/Post-Show Talk
Local schools, colleges & universities - most have GCSE/A'level courses in dance/drama	Print distribution/ special group booking offer/ involve student groups/ placements in show related marketing project, Direct Mail Teachers Pack / Education Pack Possible Post-Show Talk
People working in the Arts - from audience research undertaken, a high percentage of attenders work in the Arts, in various capacities.	Print distribution and letter to Arts Venues/companies. Ticket offers in exchange for poster display in other venues
Performers/Visual Artists	Word of Mouth, print, direct mail, offers
General students & lecturers	Print distribution and a letter - push the live music angle
General Public	Exciting, innovation with accessibility

From audience survey responses for previous works, students; school students and higher education (performance art courses, arts admin courses, music courses, drama courses etc.) made up a large part of the audience and earthfall are keen to further develop our student following. If you have specific promotion ideas to attract students, earthfall are keen to help in any way with poster give-aways, possible ticket offers etc.

25

[1] NOP Market Research, *Report on Qualitative Research into the Public's Attitudes to 'the Arts'* (Arts Council of Great Britain, 1991)

Many non-attenders of arts events have no understanding or familiarity with the arts. They fear that they will not understand, feel overawed, unintelligent and inferior and have no reason to believe that they are going to enjoy themselves.[1]

Many arts organisations want to incorporate the new and the challenging in the work they present to audiences. They need to develop audiences for that work by improving audiences' understanding of the arts, whether they are already involved in the arts or have never experienced an arts event before. This is audience development.

Even an organisation that does not charge for its events still has to convince funders to continue supporting it. This means that every arts organisation is trying to increase the number of attenders or participants, their frequency of attendance, the amount they pay to experience the event and to encourage people to see less familiar events. All of these activities involve audience development.

Many organisations are keen to ensure that different sectors of the community have real opportunities to attend arts events that interest them. For some, working with organisations in other sectors to tackle social exclusion is their reason for existence. This is audience development too.

As you can see, cultural organisations carry out audience development for different reasons but, overall, they always see developing audiences as a way of achieving their objectives. This means that the starting point for planning audience development must be your organisation's goals.

1 THE BIG DECISIONS

Projects only work if they are part of a long-term strategy for audience development which is developed jointly by the artistic, education and marketing functions of an organisation. The projects themselves, however, may be carried out by just one of those functions. Even though one person may be undertaking most of the work on a particular audience development project, every member of staff and volunteer needs to be involved and fully briefed.

The process of developing this long-term strategy involves deciding why the organisation wants to develop audiences and then focusing resources on achieving this goal. You then need to consider which of these four options will help you best:

1.   **Concentrate on developing your existing audiences' relationship with the activities that your organisation offers at the moment.** This could include targeting people who have stopped attending, encouraging

audiences to something different, persuading them to come more often, and so on.

2. **Develop new kinds of activities for your existing audiences.** An example would be introducing a new strand of monthly folk gigs to encourage the summer festival audience to attend all the year round.

3. **Develop new audiences for your existing activities.** This might include anything from asking your existing audiences to bring a friend through to concentrating a campaign on a particular postal sector where your organisation has few current attenders.

4. **Develop new audiences for new kinds of activities.** This is the riskiest option which needs significant investment of time and money from everyone in your organisation. An example would be introducing a whole new programme for the under 10s including 6pm cinema screenings, Saturday morning live events and weekday foyer performances for the under 5 year olds and their carers.

No organisation could undertake all four of these options with any hope of success, so you need to choose one or two at the most and commit to them at least for the duration of your organisation's three-year business plan.

Organisations can get confused about audience development. Various people within the organisation can have different views of what audience development is:

  • Education workers largely focus on the development of the individual and on the art form as a whole. Their work usually involves participation, although attendance at events may also be involved. When they evaluate projects, they tend to measure the quality of the individual participant's educational experience and the development of their understanding of the arts. The results they want do not necessarily involve the worker's own organisation but may benefit other arts organisations in the long term, e.g. 'creating the audience of tomorrow'. Many people see these long-term results as unmeasurable.

  • Artists tend to focus on improving audiences' understanding of their work. They wish to bring more people into contact with the work but are often particularly concerned with finding 'the right audience' who will best appreciate it. These projects often lack clear objectives and the results are not evaluated.

  • Marketers look for results that directly benefit their arts organisation. They aim to affect a change in the attitudes, understanding and behaviour of both existing audiences and non-attenders. Their aims almost always involve attendance although this may be in five or even ten years' time. Their projects tend to be carefully targeted at specific groups of people and have clear objectives. Most marketers are aware of the need to monitor and evaluate audience development projects but research shows that many do not do so because of time pressures.[2]

[2] Questionnaire and telephone research carried out in 1995 by Martin Kyne-Lilley for Eastern Touring Agency exploring the audience development practice of over 350 cultural organisations in all sectors.

All these activities are equally valid and none are mutually exclusive. The differences only exist because artists, education workers and marketers approach the concept of audience development from different directions. Each has a different set of experiences to offer audiences and participants and so each is the key to an essential part of the audience development tool kit. The activities of education workers can offer a highly personal, in-depth experience of the arts to relatively small numbers of people. Marketers can persuade very large numbers of people to get involved in the arts but cannot usually offer that depth of experience. You can see that both approaches are necessary to make a significant impact in a community.

Artists, education workers and marketers agree that audience development is a planned process which involves building a relationship between an individual and the arts. This takes time and cannot happen by itself. Arts organisations must work to develop these relationships.

All too many arts organisations develop projects persuading people to experience an art form, maybe for the first time, and then never get in touch with them again. This kind of poor practice happens because the organisation's staff do not work together. Artists, education workers, marketers and the staff who meet audiences such as box office assistants and stewards must all play their essential part in developing the relationships.

One part of an organisation can make contact with people and another part can pick up the relationship to follow it through.

2 WHAT DOES AUDIENCE DEVELOPMENT INVOLVE?

Audience development involves breaking down the physical, psychological and social barriers that stop people participating in or attending the arts. Lack of relevant information is also a very basic barrier to attendance.

STEP 1: CHOOSING WHO TO WORK WITH

Too many audience development projects seem to involve organisations first of all thinking up events or ways of working that appeal to them and only afterwards looking around for sections of the community to which to apply them. Audience development is about enhancing and broadening specific individuals' experiences of the arts and so we need to start with those individuals.

Ideally, identify the section of the community with which you want to work first (the target group). You need to identify a target group of people whose perceptions, behaviour and needs are sufficiently similar to allow you to talk to them effectively in the same way.

Then create or choose the arts event that is most likely to interest them and to overcome the barriers that currently stop them attending.

You may be in a situation where the arts event has already been chosen. Find a target group whose needs and interests closely match the benefits that the arts event has to offer. A close match is important – without it, you will not be able to persuade your target group to attend or participate. If you cannot find this match then it is better not to use this event to develop audiences.

STEP 2: FINDING OUT ABOUT YOUR TARGET GROUP

You need to collect the information that will help you plan an effective audience development project. Before you can choose your target group, you need to know what your existing audience and the local population are like. To overcome the barriers that stop people attending the arts, you need to know what they are. To help someone make an informed choice about attending or participating in an arts event, you need to know what information they need. You do not need limitless resources: your organisation will already have collected some useful information and much of what you need will be available through research published by other organisations. Besides, some of the smallest voluntary arts organisations regularly carry out effective audience research.

STEP 3: MAKING USE OF THE INFORMATION

You need to pull out the key facts from the information that you have collected. These will help you shape your project. Also find out about audience development projects carried out by other organisations and aimed at similar target groups – whether these were successful or not.

Your knowledge and understanding of your target group is the single most important factor in making your planned audience development project a success.

Use the information that you have collected about your existing audiences, attenders or participants and about your local population to:

- choose the right target group
- identify the barriers to attendance that you need to overcome
- choose the right product for your target group
- give potential attenders or participants the information they need to make an informed choice
- work out what you are going to say to your target group, how you are going to say it and how you are going to get your message across.

STEP 4: CHOOSING THE ARTS EVENT

You need to choose or even create an event that is likely to interest the target group and to overcome the barriers that currently stop them attending. Some of the most exciting audience development projects have taken an imaginative approach to the arts event at their centre.

Do not choose events simply because you are finding it difficult to reach your attendance target. If your existing attenders or participants are staying away in droves, you are unlikely to persuade a non-attender to come along.

STEP 5: PLANNING THE PROJECT

For your project to be a success, everybody involved must know why they are doing it and what, exactly, they are trying to achieve. Arts organisations often invest heavily in audience development projects but most are unable to say whether they were worth the investment, whether they are worth doing again or even whether they worked at all. The solution is to make sure that you plan effectively. Set clear aims and specific objectives, and work out beforehand how you are going to evaluate the results.

STEP 6: CONSULTATION

Before you carry out the project, you need to check that it stands a good chance of working. Try out your ideas on your own colleagues, your counterparts in other organisations and people with the relevant experience in your regional arts board or local authority.

Consult the target group. There are a number of ways to do this:

- Bring together a group of 8–10 individuals from the target group to talk informally about your ideas.
- Employ a professional to undertake more formal research.
- Talk to a number of community leaders or other key figures individually.
- Ask group leaders such as teachers or youth leaders to talk to small groups of their members.
- Visit a meeting of your target group in their usual gathering place.
- Try out your project on a small group of consenting 'guinea pigs' from your target group.

STEP 7: IMPLEMENTING THE PROJECT

Attention to detail is important at this stage. This will ensure that there are no unexpected problems that might prevent your target group attending or participating – or stop them coming back again.

There are seven areas about which you need to think:

1. Product: this does not just mean the art that is on the walls or on stage – audiences and attenders see every aspect of their visit as part of the product you offer.

2. Price: many audiences see comparatively high prices as an indication of good quality, while several target groups find that they cannot afford normal ticket prices. A good way of balancing these two issues is to set top-price tickets as high as the market will stand but then offer substantial discounts to the target groups who find that price is a barrier to attendance.

3. Place: where your event takes place can be a barrier to attendance by your target group. Many projects involve a special effort to make the first-time attender feel more at home.

4. Promotion: describes how you communicate with your target group and the offer you are making them. It is essential that you take into account everything you have found out about your target group to make sure that you are telling them the things that will persuade them to attend or take part in your event. Ensure that you have chosen a communication method that will be effective and that you are using an appropriate tone of voice.

5. People: many non-attenders feel alienated by theatres, concert halls, museums and galleries. Your front-line staff are the people who can make them feel at home. Some organisations have made sure that their youngest stewards are on duty to welcome participants in a project aimed at young people.

6. Process: you need to check every step of the process that your potential attenders or participants will have to follow to get involved in your event. Is it clear what they should do if they are interested? Will they be able to find the venue? Do all the box office staff know about any special offers?

7. Physical evidence: arts organisations offer an experience rather than a tangible product. Our attenders and participants cannot be sure that they will enjoy our event until after they have experienced it. This means that we must make sure that everything we do or say reassures our target audience that we are offering something that is of good quality, e.g. the quality of our printed material, the appearance of the foyer, the efficiency of the box office.

STEP 8: SUSTAINING THE RELATIONSHIP

Just because someone has been targeted by an audience development project does not mean that they have become an arts attender or participant. Becoming an arts attender involves a series of steps:

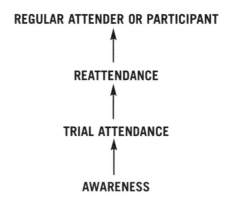

REGULAR ATTENDER OR PARTICIPANT

↑

REATTENDANCE

↑

TRIAL ATTENDANCE

↑

AWARENESS

We must actively persuade people to take the next step. This means keeping in touch so that we can develop our relationship with them.

STEP 9: EVALUATING THE PROJECT

Evaluate the immediate aftermath of the project. Did your project achieve its targets? Was it an effective use of your resources? How did it contribute to your organisation's overall artistic, social and financial objectives? Did it achieve any unexpected results – 'spin-offs'? What did your target group think of their experience? Is there anything you would have changed? Is it worth doing again? You also need to work out what have been the medium- and long-term effects on your target group's arts attendance or participation.

CASE STUDY

THE CASTLE, WELLINGBOROUGH: DEVELOPING AUDIENCES FOR WORLD MUSIC

World music was a relatively new part of the programme at **The Castle**, and audiences had little knowledge of the art form. They certainly had not heard of the bands on offer as there are few opportunities to hear world music on the radio. Marketing Manager Gordon Glass wanted to help past and potential attenders to form their own opinions about the music so that they felt that buying tickets was much less of a risk. He believed that by doing so, they would learn more about the art form and become more confident in their own judgement.

The Castle produced 500 sampler cassettes with an introduction to each band and extracts from the music, of which 216 were mailed to previous world music attenders and the rest were offered to customers at the box office and at music or ethnic souvenir shops within a 20-minute drive of Wellingborough. The objectives were to sell 75 tickets to each concert, increase first-time attenders by 25% and persuade 25% of that season's world music attenders to come to at least two gigs in the series.

The Castle's team felt that it was very important to monitor the project and so analysed the information held on their box office system to evaluate the results.

The best attendance of the series was achieved where the initial taster via the sampler cassette was backed up by a direct mail reminder and generous press coverage. The results of the project emphasised the importance of the particular style of the bands in attracting audiences. Although they did not achieve all their objectives, the team felt that they had learned a great deal about the audience which would enable them to strengthen the programming and marketing next season.

Heather Maitland's book *A Guide to Audience Development* (1997) covers this topic in full including case studies and is available from the Arts Council of England.

26

MANAGING INFORMATION

SEE ALSO CHAPTERS
8. HOW TO WORK WITH YOUR BOX OFFICE
10. HOW TO CREATE A DIRECT MARKETING CAMPAIGN
24. MARKET RESEARCH

1 DEVELOPING RELATIONSHIPS

Many arts marketers are convinced that their most important marketing tool is their mailing list. It is certainly easy to see why they think that information about their audience is so important. The group of people most likely to attend a particular event is the people who have attended something similar at the venue. If you have their names and addresses then you can very easily communicate with them in a persuasive way to encourage them to attend your event.

You can also encourage occasional attenders to come more often, regular attenders to become subscribers or to persuade their friends to attend and advocates to give up time or money to support your organisation. Think of this process of developing a sense of belonging between an individual and your organisation as a ladder. It is quite easy to go up a ladder just one rung at a time. Similarly most arts organisations have been highly successful in moving their audience up this ladder of loyalty.

| Donor |
| Volunteer |
| Advocate or friend |
| Subscriber |
| Frequent attender |
| Occasional attender |
| Repeat attender |
| First-time attender |
| Used to attend but doesn't any more (lapsed attender) |

You cannot do any of this unless you have the names and addresses of individual audience members.

2 COLLECTING INFORMATION

The people best placed to collect information about your existing attenders are your colleagues in the box office. The first question they should ask a customer on the telephone or in person is 'Have you bought tickets from us before?' If the customer says yes, they can pull up their details on the computer and enter the transaction in the right name. If not, they can search for the last name and postcode, in case the customer has forgotten a previous purchase. If this is unsuccessful, they can then collect the information you need.

A name and address is useful but a name and address of a customer linked with information about the events for which they have bought tickets is invaluable.

Buxton Opera House used to print at the top of the address labels used to send out the season brochure 'For speedy service, quote this number when you call' and add the customer's record number. They could find the right customer instantly simply by entering the number in the system at the start of the call.

Whether your mailing list is held on a computer or not, you must comply with the Data Protection Act when you collect information, otherwise you will not be able to use it for marketing purposes.

2.1 BOX OFFICE COMPUTER SYSTEMS

If you have a box office computer system, box office staff can collect the names and addresses of everyone who is booking for the first time as an integral part of the transaction.

Many venues, large and small, collect the names, addresses and postcodes of over 90% of ticket buyers. The absolute minimum that your box office staff should be collecting is 75% to ensure that you have a good overview of your audience. This is a question of training. Not everyone understands why the information is needed and so they do not collect the information in the right way or, worse, do not bother to collect it at all. Make sure that your organisation has a set procedure for each transaction that includes how names and addresses are collected and that everyone understands why this is important.

The question 'Have you bought tickets from us before?' at the start of the transaction is doubly important. It means that you can save time in the short and long term by finding the customer's existing record and entering the transaction in that name. If you do not ask it, staff will end up entering the name and address of existing attenders over and over again and then later having to find, merge and delete all the duplicate records.

The most difficult time to take down names and addresses is when people are queuing for tickets just before an event is due to start. Many venues manage it even then by having enough staff on duty selling tickets.

Other venues ask their box office staff to enter the bare minimum of information (last name and postcode) and write down the transaction code or customer code on a pre-printed postcard. Staff then ask the customer to fill in the rest of their details and hand the card back to a member of staff at the end of the evening. This is more time-consuming than entering the information during the transaction as someone has to type in the information at another time.

2.2 MANUAL MAILING LIST

If you do not have a box office computer system, you can ask box office staff to hand a mailing list card to everyone who is not already a member. The card should ask them what their interests are as well as for their mailing details. This means that you can send the right information to the right people at a later stage.

3 TOO MUCH INFORMATION

Organisations with box office computer systems sometimes worry that their database is getting too large and they cannot afford to mail the season brochure to everyone. One possible response is to start deleting customer records if they have not attended for a while. This is a very bad idea. If you start deleting people, you cannot:

- persuade them to come back to your venue
- analyse the database to find out useful information about them – are there lots of lapsed attenders from a particular area or who like a particular art form?
- get an accurate overall picture of your audience and how it is developing.

You do not need to delete people from your database because you do not have to mail your season brochure to everyone.

A much better approach is to select people from the database and only print labels for them. These are just some of the ways that a range of venues choose to which people to send their season brochure:

- everyone who has been to an event in the past 18 months
- everyone with a particular postcode
- everyone who has been to a live performance in the past two years
- everyone who has bought tickets for more than one performance plus all the people who bought tickets for the first time in the past year, even if they have only been to one show.

4 MANAGING RELATIONSHIPS

You will need to take an organised and methodical approach to the information on your mailing list. Some organisations do not and end up mailing the same frequent attenders again and again. One venue worked out that they were mailing frequent drama attenders more often than once a month. They only noticed because they wanted to know why drama audiences were falling. The reason was that these people felt bombarded with information and had stopped responding.

> With a database [as large as ours], it is easy to fill a 5,000 mail shot from within the core audience of frequent attenders. This meant that many records outside of the 'core' audience rapidly became redundant because they were never selected. Many customers were being mailed several times a month – they were effectively under siege from the Royal Festival Hall. When we compared our mailing activity with the sales histories of these customers, it became clear that our mailings had limited impact on the frequency of their attendance. We were preaching to the converted.
>
> This core group of loyal customers are valuable to us because they represent the bulk of our income but they have limited long-term growth potential. The real opportunity lay in the group we had abandoned. Infrequent attenders and new customers were only being given a couple of further chances to attend before our selection process was dumping them. We were making assumptions about their preferences and their loyalty at too early a stage in their relationship with us. **Chris Denton, Marketing Manager (Classical Music), South Bank Centre**[1]

[1] Read more about Chris's approach to his mailing list in *Revolving Doors: The Case for Customer Retention* (Arts Marketing Association, 2000)

An effective approach to this problem is to divide up your database or mailing list into boxes using the criteria in the diagram below by analysing your box office computer system or mailing list.

1. Photocopy the diagram so that you have three copies.

2. Decide what is an appropriate definition of 'occasional' and 'frequent' in your organisation. To help you, run a report giving you the number of people attending at each frequency during a 12-month period and compare this to the frequency of attendance in Target Group Index.

3. Run a routine to select customers from your database according to the criteria for one box on the diagram. On one copy of the diagram, write down in the relevant box the number of people you end up with in your selection. Repeat for all the other relevant groups.

4. Now note down in the boxes on the second copy what marketing activity (if any) you target at each group at the moment, e.g. you might send the season brochure and direct mail letters about live events about once a month to the frequent attenders.

5. On the third copy, write down your plans for the future. What marketing activities have you decided to target at each group to encourage them to move one stage up the loyalty ladder? For example, you might decide to send a direct mail package with a money-back guarantee to the occasional attenders of one art form to encourage them to try another.

You do not have to target all the people in a box at once. You could divide them up according to the number of events for which you might need to send out direct mail. Send each sub-group a letter about a different show as you come to implement each campaign. By doing this, you can integrate your relationship building with your everyday marketing activities. (*See* p. 262.)

5 USING POSTCODES

The postcode is a vital piece of information and must be collected for every customer. It means that you:

- will save money on your postage bills because you can get a discount from the Royal Mail if your mailing is big enough
- can see easily where your customers come from and where they do not
- can look in the Area Profile Reports to find out what kind of people live there
- can find more of the same sort of people
- can avoid mailing people who live too far away to attend more than occasionally.

5.1 HOW POSTCODES WORK

This is the postcode for the Arts Marketing Association: CB1 2DG

This is the POSTAL AREA.
There are 124 postal districts in the UK

CB1 2DG

Each postal area is divided up into POSTAL DISTRICTS. There are an average of 8,197 addresses in a district

CB1 2DG

This is a POSTAL SECTOR.
There are on average 350 addresses in a postal sector. This makes it a useful bite-sized chunk for targeting. Area Profile Reports have information divided up by postal sector

CB1 **2**DG

CB1 2DG

This is a POSTCODE. There are 15 households on average in each postcode – roughly half the street. Sometimes a big business can have a postcode of its own. In inner city areas you could get up to 80 addresses in a postcode.

Postcodes relate to how the Royal Mail delivers mail, not to geographical boundaries. Grantham is in Lincolnshire, but the postal area is NG because mail is dealt with by the main sorting office in Nottingham.

OTHERS   SCHOOLS GROUPS INDIVIDUALS

☐			☐	*Donors of £50 or more*
☐			☐	*Donors of less than £50*
			☐	*Volunteers*
☐	☐		☐	*Very frequent, loyal attenders*
☐	☐	☐	☐	*Frequent attenders*
☐	☐	☐	☐	*Occasional attenders of different art forms*
☐	☐	☐	☐	*Occasional attenders of the same art form*
☐	☐	☐	☐	*People who have bought tickets for the first time in the past 12 months but only for one event in that time*
☐	☐	☐	☐	*People who have bought tickets at least twice but not in the past 18 months*
☐	☐	☐	☐	*People who attended once and never returned*
☐	☐	☐	☐	*People who have never bought a ticket*

6 TROUBLESHOOTING

You will find it difficult to use the information collected by your box office colleagues for effective marketing unless you set up some guidelines. Here are some suggestions:

- Always enter a title such as Mr, Ms or Dr, etc., otherwise some of your mailing labels will just have the surname on the first line.

- Decide whether you are going to collect first names or initials and then make sure that everyone sticks to it, otherwise your direct mail letters may start 'Dear I.J.' or 'Dear Green' and you may end up with duplicate records for everyone, one with initials and the other with the first name.

- Make sure that everyone enters the figure zero or the letter O in the right place, otherwise you will not be able to analyse or select by postcodes accurately.

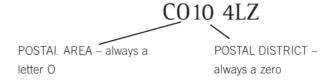

POSTAL AREA – always a letter O

POSTAL DISTRICT – always a zero

- Some people who have been trained to touch-type on a typewriter always type a lower-case L instead of a 1. Again, this means that you will not be able to analyse or select by postcodes.
- Agree whether you will enter house names when there is also a house number and stick to it, otherwise you will end up with lots of duplicate records.
- Always ask 'Have you bought tickets from us before?' at the beginning of the transaction and it will save time and effort for everyone.

7 THE DATA PROTECTION ACTS

This is an overview of some of the key points of the Data Protection Acts and how they affect arts organisations. Anything in this section is my opinion only on the implications of the Acts as at June 2000. Please check that you have accurate and up-to-date information by visiting the official website on **www.dataprotection.gov.uk**. The Theatrical Management Association and the Arts Marketing Association have published a guide to the Data Protection Acts which is essential reading.[2]

The basic idea behind the 1998 Act which came into force on 1 March 2000 is that you must tell every customer exactly what you want to do with their information and get their permission to do it. This permission must be specific, informed and involve active communication. They must 'opt in' rather than 'opt out' as under the previous Act. This applies even if you do not keep your mailing list on a computer.

[2] Roger Tomlinson *Data Protection: A Guide to the Data Protection Acts and their Implications for Managers in the Arts and Entertainment Industry* (Arts Marketing Association, 2000)

This is what you need to do:

1. Nominate a senior member of staff to be your data controller. They will be responsible for setting up guidelines for how data are collected in your organisation, and for making sure that everybody sticks to them. They should know exactly what data you hold, what you do with it and with whom you share it. Most arts organisations share their information with someone, perhaps a mailing fulfilment house or workshop leaders.

2. Check whether you need to notify the Data Protection Commissioner (this is similar to data protection registration under the previous Act). See Roger Tomlinson's comments below.

3. Customers can ask you to show them what information you hold about them. You need to set up systems for doing this quickly.

4. Look at the data you hold. Work out what data you hold that the customer has given active consent to you holding (e.g. by filling in a form to join a mailing list). Work out what data you do not have informed and active consent from the customer to hold.

5. Set up a procedure for getting informed consent from customers when they buy a ticket. When they first get in touch with you and you capture their details, you need to tell them:
    (a) the legal name of your organisation
    (b) exactly what you will be doing with their data
    (c) with whom you will be sharing the data.
    The customer needs to have the opportunity to say yes or no. See below for suggested wording for this.

6. You need to include this information on booking forms and in brochures so that people who do not telephone or come to the box office in person are clear about what you want to do with their information and have an opportunity to say yes or no. You must not use small print and customers should have two tick boxes, one for 'yes' and one for 'no'.

7. Get informed consent from the people on your database who have not yet given it. You can telephone them to update their records and while doing so give them the necessary information and get active informed consent as described below. You could also write to them, giving them the information and asking them to respond. This has the advantage that you can ask them other questions to collect additional information.

8. People can register with the Telephone Preference Service and the Mailing Preference Scheme to say that they do not want any direct mail or telephone calls from anyone they have not specifically asked for information. This means that if you have any customers who have not given informed consent, you will need to check their details against the Preference Services lists before you get in touch with them. You will be charged for checking these details.

9. Write a standard contract to use when you share your data, e.g. between touring companies and venues, or have it processed by someone else.

Roger Tomlinson has been keeping up to date with developments in data protection. Here was his view on the latest situation for arts and entertainment organisations in June 2000:

> Most not-for-profit organisations will not need to register/notify (though the Act still applies) and the Commissioner's compliance officers are being very relaxed about what venues have to do when data was collected before 1 March 2000 without proper compliance with the old Act, if it does not involve sharing and is only repeating mailing action done before. The guidance on what might be done without 'informed consent' seems to be stretched for arts venues, especially not-for-profit and non-data-sharing organisations. **Roger Tomlinson, Director of Business Development – Europe for Tickets.com**

7.1 GETTING CONSENT

This is the script that Roger devised for the Arts Marketing Association and TMA guide to data protection:

> 'Thank you for booking tickets to see the Touring Artists Company at the Any Town Venue. We would like to add your name to our marketing list so we can keep you informed about events and other developments at our venue.
>
> (Optional: 'Is this all right?' Await positive or negative response.)
>
> 'We are officially called the Any Town Venue Promotion Company Limited and we will give your details to the Touring Artists Company who trade as Actors Bank Raid Limited. Is this all right?'
>
> (Await positive or negative response.)
>
> 'From time to time we may also share your details with other (optional: arts and entertainment) organisations which we think you will be interested in. Is this all right?'
>
> (Await positive or negative response.)

7.2 GETTING HELP

Get up-to-date information about the implications of the Act from the Arts Marketing Association on 01223 578078 or the official website at **www.dataprotection.gov.uk**. Roger Tomlinson's guide to data protection is available from SAM's Books, 01883 345011.

27 YOUR ORGANISATION'S IDENTITY

1 HOW IT WORKS

Everything about your organisation contributes to its identity – your name and address, the way you answer the telephone, the prices you charge, the building from which you operate, your letterhead, your publicity material, what the press say about you and much more.

Your organisation's identity must spring from a sense of purpose and a sense of belonging, not just a logo or a slogan. Its artistic work, the buildings in which it works and performs, the way it tells people about what it does and the attitude and behaviour of its staff must all reinforce this sense of purpose and belonging.

STAFF ATTITUDE AND BEHAVIOUR

Eastern Touring Agency works with venues and companies to develop arts and audiences in the East of England. As well as a strong sense of purpose, it has developed a set of guidelines for how its staff go about their jobs. They call them 'Guiding Principles' and see them as an important part of their corporate identity:

- We strive for equity of provision for the East of England.
- We create, enhance and develop – not duplicate. We work in equal partnership with our colleagues regionally and nationally.
- We only work with people who actively want to work with us.
- We work imaginatively and in sustainable ways with existing resources.
- We are approachable, dynamic, flexible and fun.
- We encourage cooperation and collaboration between all arts organisations in the East of England.
- We trust and are trusted.
- We constantly strive to improve our own skills and knowledge.
- We monitor and evaluate all our work with good practice as our goal.
- We recognise that our staff are our best resource and we are committed to investing in them.
- We take the time to reflect upon what we do and to celebrate our successes.

The staff seem to live up to these standards as a recent review process by the funding body highlighted a strong sense of trust and mutual respect among the organisations with which they collaborate.

Your organisation's identity must be so strong that people feel that they know what to expect when they see a show, meet a member of staff or visit your office. This means that it can work for you or against you. This kind of strong identity, which creates a set of perceptions in people's minds, is also known as a brand.

An effective corporate identity will help you to get your message across to those around you: funding bodies, potential sponsors, other arts organisations and, of course, your potential audience. It is also a potentially powerful way of communicating what your organisation is all about to people who have no direct contact with your activities. Most importantly, it will tell everybody what makes you different from all the other arts organisations around.

A corporate identity means that you are instantly recognisable. **Marketing officer, national touring theatre company**

There are two aspects to your organisation's corporate identity: the way you want to be perceived by other people and the way that other people actually perceive you. Sometimes the two aspects do not match and this can have far-reaching effects on all your activities. One producing theatre was confronted by declining audiences. Staff felt that the underlying problem was that existing and potential audiences perceived the organisation as offering poor quality shows. Research into the attitudes of people who used to attend but did not do so any more showed that this was not the case. Lapsed attenders said things like 'The shows are fine, but it's hardly a welcoming place, is it?'

Corporate identity becomes a particularly important issue for organisations that are:

- starting up
- undergoing change
- in trouble.

STARTING UP

The identity of new organisations often develops naturally from the enthusiasm, energy and style of the people who set them up. But successful organisations usually develop lives of their own. They grow out of being one or two people's brainchild and become institutions in their own right, particularly when the founders move on to other projects. This is the point when the sense of purpose and belonging can evaporate unless the organisation consciously focuses on developing and reinforcing its corporate identity.

UNDERGOING CHANGE

Organisations evolve:

- They add new kinds of work to what they do already such as touring new writing alongside their usual productions of Shakespeare.
- They start to present their work in different environments and to

New Perspectives' corporate brochure

Established in 1972, New Perspectives creates original plays and theatre projects for the villages and towns of the East Midlands. Here you will find less structure and formality than might be expected.

The company has the people of Nottinghamshire, Rutland, Leicestershire, Derbyshire and Northamptonshire as its audience, participants and inspiration.

New Perspectives:

creates new plays for village halls and other spaces each spring, autumn and winter. These are stories for everyone shared with charm, humour, and originality;

develops projects in partnership with other organisations that encourage local people to make their own art;

runs the Old Library, a centre for the Arts in Mansfield, where the Company supports three thriving youth theatre groups, summer schools, a community choir, dance groups, writers workshops, and offers a variety of training and educational opportunities.

different audiences perhaps by developing a small-scale tour in winter alongside their performances at outdoor theatres in the summer or by adding an education programme in schools to their existing building-based programme.

- They change what they do altogether, maybe by concentrating on just one aspect of their programme – becoming a music venue rather than a mixed programme arts centre.
- A new creative leader arrives and wants to make their own, distinctive mark.

When this happens their corporate identity no longer expresses their sense of purpose. Audiences, funders or sponsors no longer get what they expect. The process of developing the corporate identity so that it expresses what the organisation wants to stand for can play an important role in helping everyone who works for it rationalise and understand the changes that are happening.

DEALING WITH TROUBLE

Organisations experiencing problems can find it difficult to escape from a downward spiral. Audiences, funders, sponsors and other arts organisations would rather be involved with an exciting, energetic and successful organisation. Too many headlines in the local paper saying that audience figures are down and your funding is under threat and people start to link the negative and depressing with your name. In this situation, the only solution is a planned and sustained campaign to ensure that the organisation's artistic work, the way it talks about it, the environment in which it is seen, and the way that staff behave all reflect positive values.

1.1 POSITIONING

A strong corporate identity should tell people what makes you different from other organisations offering the same sort of thing – perhaps 'a good night out'. This means that you and your colleagues need to make some decisions about:

- who you want to get involved in your events as audiences or participants
- what they think are important factors in deciding whether to get involved or not
- which of those factors both you and they think are part of your organisation's strengths
- which of these strengths you want to focus on to differentiate yourself from other organisations.

Use a diagram like the one below to help you understand better your organisation's positioning.

Each line represents one of the important factors that people use in deciding whether to get involved with your organisation. In this case the two factors are convenience and how comfortable they feel in the venue. You need to decide what are the opposite extremes of each factor – in this case it is the following:

- *right on the doorstep* as opposed to *we need to travel out of town to go there*
- *friendly and intimate* as opposed to *a grand and special occasion.*

It's important to think of these factors from the audience's point of view, not yours.

Mark how audiences would place you on the map and then add the other organisations that they might also choose to get involved with. Decide how you want to change your position on the map to emphasise what makes your organisation and its events special. You can now use these factors to build your brand. They will form the backbone of all your marketing communication. Arts organisations have a whole range of possibilities for positioning their organisation:

- the audience (e.g. The Junction as a venue for 16–30 year olds)
- the building (e.g. the Blackpool Grand with its beautiful art nouveau décor)
- geographical identity (e.g. Scottish Ballet or Hall for Cornwall)
- performers (e.g. Darcey Bussel and Viviana Durante at the Royal Ballet)
- a personality (e.g. Richard Alston at the Richard Alston Dance Company)
- programming (e.g. the Royal Court as a venue for new writing)
- the nature of the experience (e.g. Scottish Chamber Orchestra and the emotional impact of music)
- something for everyone (e.g. the South Holland Centre, Spalding, with 'a great night out on your doorstep').

However, it is essential that you choose a positioning option that your existing and potential audiences consider important. You can only do that by asking them about their perceptions through market research.

CASE STUDY

Exeter Phoenix corporate advertising campaign

The largest problems I face are limited resources and a public with little knowledge of what we do and where we do it. We have events on most nights so my budget is strictly event-based. There isn't the money to promote the centre itself with its café bar, gallery spaces and media centre as well as the performance spaces. This is why, rather than highlighting the product, I have chosen to highlight the customer. In a series of photographs, we have recorded a man walking around the city 'looking' for Exeter Phoenix. I want both the people who see him in town and the people who read the advert to ask themselves 'What is happening and why?' **Simon Whatley, Marketing Officer, Exeter Phoenix**

2 BRAND MARKETING

Brian Waring, a board member at Youth & Music, describes brand marketing as 'the development of an emotional bond between your customers and your brand'. He thinks that it is essential for arts organisations to think about the long term and not just market each event as it comes up. Marketing your brand rather than the show 'puts bums on seats and builds reputation and loyalty'.

Arts organisations tend to agree. They find it much easier to market their events if they are backed up by a strong brand. This gives their event a head start over all the others that their target group could choose because audiences:

- recognise the brand as something familiar
- connect the event with a particular set of perceptions such as good value or high quality
- feel a sense of connection with the brand.

The idea of the brand is important for the arts because what we are offering our audiences is an experience, not a tangible product. They cannot take a look before they buy and they cannot easily compare what one organisation offers with another. A strong brand will encapsulate the experience and help the potential audience member feel more confident about what they are buying.

CASE STUDY

SCOTTISH CHAMBER ORCHESTRA

Scottish Chamber Orchestra commissioned a qualitative research programme to look at their existing and potential audiences' perceptions of their organisation and classical music in general. They discovered that many thought that a chamber orchestra only had four or five players and that one of the most important elements of the experience of concert going was the emotional impact of the music. They used a poster campaign in the 1998/9 season to change people's perception of the brand by emphasising the size of the orchestra and telling them why they will enjoy classical music. The poster was used in displays in all of their venues before and during their visits, and some are still on view today.

Opposite

Photographer: Paul Hampton, The Picture House; Design: The Union

37 musicians, 1 conductor, endless emotions.

Scottish chamber Orchestra

25th Anniversary

Know the Score 0845 270 1812 for details of all concerts across Scotland. www.sco.org.uk

3 'WE OFFER SOMETHING FOR EVERYONE'

Organisations that offer a wide range of artistic activities to a wide range of target groups find developing an effective corporate identity particularly challenging. The organisation stands for a different sense of purpose and a different sense of belonging at different times and to different people. How is it possible to express all of them in a clear and simple way? If your organisation is like this, you and your colleagues have three choices:

1. Develop an identity that communicates a single, strong idea expressing the set of values that your activities and audiences have in common and use this as a consistent, global umbrella for the whole range.

2. Develop an identity that expresses a single, strong idea which is used in conjunction with separate subsidiary identities that reflect the individual nature of each type of activity. This means that each element of your organisation's activity is seen as different and distinct but also part of a much bigger whole. Some of the people interested in your organisation, such as funders, will be most interested in the whole organisation. Others, such as audiences and participants, can feel a strong sense of belonging to the facet of the organisation with which they are engaged.

3. Develop a series of completely separate identities that each express a single, strong and different idea about each activity. This means that the sense of belonging of the distinct group of audiences or participants engaged with each facet of the organisation will not have to be compromised. The disadvantage is that it will be more difficult for the organisation to communicate effectively with the stakeholders interested in the organisation as a whole.

4 YOUR LOGO

A logo, also known as a graphic identity, is a visual device that identifies your organisation and expresses its sense of purpose. This graphic identity can consist of your organisation's name set out in a particular way in a specific typeface (known as a logotype) or can include a picture or symbol.

It is important to have a logo that is both professional-looking, easy to reproduce and can be adapted for use in different places and on different materials, e.g. your letterhead, leaflets, T-shirts, badges, displays, the side of your van, etc. You must be able to photocopy it, use it in black and white, enlarge it to use on a banner and reduce it to head a newspaper advertisement.

You will want to keep using your logo for a long time to maintain a sense of continuity, so you will need a typeface that will stand the test of time and fashion. Trestle's logo is both powerful and enduring. (*See left*)

Trestle Theatre Company logo

CASE STUDY

Q ARTS

Q ARTS
GALLERY
PROJECTS
SIGHTINGS
STUDIOS
WORKSHOPS

Q Arts in Derby was created to bring together under the management umbrella of Derby Community Arts a range of different organisations that, at that time, had their own different names and different identities. They felt very strongly that if they were to forge enduring links between the people of Derby and artists of regional, national and international standing, they needed to maximise their impact. By packaging together with a single, strong idea all the facilities for creation, production, exhibition, participation and education, they could offer artists and audiences something very special.

Q Arts now consists of Q Workshops, Q Gallery, Q Studios and Q Sightings. This last element is a programme of art in public spaces.

The designers, De Facto in Nottingham, found it quite a challenge to incorporate all the different elements in a coherent way, but we think they did a great job. **Madeline Holmes, Director, Q Arts, Derby**

Q GALLERY

13 - 27 November

Tuesday to Friday
12.00 - 4.00pm,
Saturday & Sunday
10.00 - 4.00pm

Art House

Art House is a new unique exhibition documenting the relationship between people in Derby and art.

Representing a range of art forms - from framed photographs to a three-dimensional glass sculpture, twenty art works were "housed" with Derby people, chosen from a diverse range of life-styles, public and private, including a newsagent, a City Council Councillor and a solicitor.

The exhibition consists of the art works, shown alongside photographs of the pieces on location in their temporary home, and a video projection documenting the hosts' responses to, and feelings about, the work, art and their lives.

Gone To Ground

As we go about our lives we walk on, or come into contact with, an ever-growing mass of communication and disposal networks - sewers, gas mains, electronic links and now cable TV. Together, with the people who live in, or visit, Derby they make up the essence of the city, and the lives played out on this canvas of underground networks.

Gone To Ground is a large scale assemblage map, created by artist Joe Mahony, mapping out the trivial, and the not so trivial conveniences that characterise every-day existence.

Gone To Ground is also a reference map for the Q Arts launch programme, marking out places that have hosted Art House, art in public spaces and Q Arts' premises.

Q GALLERY

Digital Library

Browse the portholes of the Q Arts Digital Library to explore projects in images, video, text and sound.

Much more than a documentation the Digital Library, with its matrix of art forms, community groups and projects, and its print-off information sheets, is a "how to do it" resource for anyone wanting to undertake exciting, unusual and creative work or run workshop with community groups.

13 - 27 November
Q ARTS
Tuesday to Friday
12.00 - 4.00pm
Saturday & Sunday
10.00 - 4.00pm

Special Diets For Special People Cook Book

Take the imagination, talents and inventiveness of a group of disabled young people and mix well with artists from DCA/Q Arts, a strong partnership with East Midlands Shape, and funding from Glaxo-Wellcome and Dr Barnardos. Mix together the artists and the young people to devise new recipes for people with special dietary needs, and produce sculptural forms; take stunning full-colour photographs; design and layout the cook book format; prove and rise at the printers.

The Special Diets For Special People Cook Book has been made with students from St.Clares School, and copies are on sale throughout the Q Arts launch.

Ocean Sound Waves

Taken from work in progress by people with learning disabilities and First Movement in Derby, this interactive ocean of sound waves represents a major adventure into the use of new arts technologies.

Based on First Movement's "Live Room", a completely intuitive sound production environment, Ocean Sound Waves sees the project expanding into the creation and manipulation of visual arts technology to make an ocean of sounds, created by participants in the project, which they can animate themselves.

This projection gives you the opportunity to experience and gain an insight into the unique creativity of a group of people who are challenging and extending existing art forms and creating an evocation of their own ability and culture.

Q STUDIOS

Searching For Mr Marconetto
16 - 27 November
Tuesday - Saturday
12.00 - 4.00pm

Jack's Shed Artists' Collective - Jacob Tindall, Martyn Reed, Sarah Hicks and Conrad Smith - have specially curated Searching For Mr Marconetto, an eclectic exhibition of their work, to mark the start of their residency at Q Studios.

A small-scale venue redesigned their logo to fit in with their needs:

> It wasn't really a matter of changing it, it was just a matter of getting a
> strong identity that could go right across everything. Before we'd used a lot
> of different designers and things were a little bit disparate.

This kind of ongoing maintenance is important. You need to look at your graphic identity and how people perceive it every few years and carry out any running repairs that may be needed to keep it fresh and usable. This does not mean that you need to completely change it every few years. It is very tempting for marketers or directors newly in post to make a clean sweep and throw out the existing graphic identity. This underestimates the importance of continuity and can actively damage audiences' and participants' perceptions of the organisation. The only reason to change the graphic identity radically is if it no longer has any connection with the organisation's sense of purpose and belonging. Even then, it is often beneficial to keep some kind of visual link with the past in the new identity.

If you cannot afford to have a logo designed then make sure that everyone uses the same font, type size and layout on all their communications to set up a recognisable visual identity. You could even consistently use a particular coloured paper.

Just as the use of your logo will present a consistent image, it is equally important to use similar sorts of colours and typefaces and a consistent style in all areas of your organisation's communications.

Consistent design helps people to recognise your organisation immediately, so it is usually beneficial to use the same graphic designer for an entire project. For instance, for a touring show, a company will probably benefit from using the same graphic designer for a leaflet, poster, programme and any display advertisements.

> The logo and all the graphics are designed by the same person ... that's
> really important ... you can always tell it's one of our posters. **Marketing officer,**
> **national touring theatre company**

5 REVIEWING YOUR CORPORATE IDENTITY

1. Put together a small steering group to take responsibility for the process and involve people at all levels of your organisation.

2. Find out how the following groups of people currently perceive your organisation:

   (a) current audiences and participants

   (b) potential audiences and participants who choose not to get involved

   (c) other outside organisations such as funders and colleagues

(d) staff at all levels including the board of directors.

You, or specialists employed by you, will need to talk to people face to face, individually or in focus groups to find out what they really think. Ask about the strengths and weaknesses of the organisation, its reputation, what they think it's for and actually does, who they think it's for, what it's like to come into contact with it. How do they perceive the four elements of the organisation's existing corporate identity: its artistic work, the buildings in which it works and performs, the way it tells people about what it does and the attitude and behaviour of its staff.

3. Work with the steering group to take a close look at how the organisation communicates including who it communicates with, what methods it uses, how it presents itself and what it says. This includes testing how well the current graphic identity functions. What does it convey? Is it flexible enough to be used on all the different formats needed? How is it maintained? How consistently is it used throughout the organisation?

4. Work with the steering group to compare what your organisation says it does with what it actually does and what all the people who come into contact with it think it does. If there are any discrepancies, ask why. Can adapting, developing or changing the organisation's identity help to resolve any of these discrepancies? Make some broad recommendations.

5. Present the findings of the steering group to the rest of the staff at all levels. Sometimes, they may not like what they hear. Even so, ask them to endorse the broad recommendations.

6. Work with the steering group to put together a brief for the development of the graphic identity.

7. Work with the senior management team and board of directors to put together an action plan to implement the agreed recommendations about your organisation's artistic work, where it works and performs, how it communicates and the attitude and behaviour of staff.

8. Monitor whether your new corporate identity is working by continuing to talk to existing and potential audiences, outside organisations and your colleagues.

28  **PRICING**

SEE ALSO CHAPTERS
20. TALKING TO THE RIGHT PEOPLE
21. TALKING ABOUT THE RIGHT THINGS
25. AUDIENCE DEVELOPMENT
31. MONITORING AND EVALUATION

1 APPROACHES TO PRICING

Arts organisations approach pricing in many different ways. Some of the possibilities to be considered are as follows.

Across the programme:

- same price for all events
- different but consistent price structure for each art form
- different prices for each event, according to cost and popularity.

Level:

- low prices to enable access by as many members of the community as possible
- high prices for financial stability
- wide range of prices for the best of both worlds.

Number of prices:

- same price throughout the theatre
- different prices for different areas of the theatre.

Price rises:

- rise of 50p on all prices annually
- strategic price increases related to increases in costs
- a rise that brings the price to a level that people are used to paying.

Our venue in Edinburgh is the Queen's Hall which is a nice concert hall with comfortable seats in the city centre so we have five price bands and our top price there is £19. In Dumfries, where we only do two concerts a year in a multi-purpose hall, there are just two prices – reserved and unreserved – with a top price of £12. Glasgow is a bit cheaper than Edinburgh because the facilities for audiences are not quite so good. The top price at St Andrew's is £15 because the market is so much smaller and there are fewer professional classical music concerts so people aren't used paying high prices. In the Highlands we go into community centres and schools halls as well as beautiful little Victorian and Edwardian theatres but the top price is always £7. Everyone who tours the Highlands charges much less partly because customers have to pay so much more to travel to the venue. It's a question of what the audiences are used to. **Ann Montfries, Marketing Director, Scottish Chamber Orchestra**

The idea is to charge as much as the market will bear, but at the same time having the £1 concession so that we don't cut off people on very low incomes. **Administrator, metropolitan arts centre in England**

The administrator of a rural village hall touring circuit run by the county council comments that:

The village hall organisers tend to be community-spirited kind of people who want to keep prices low. We have set a minimum ticket price of £5 with a £3 concession. Some of the wealthier villages set higher ticket prices than this and do not give concessions to OAPs.

An arts centre in a small seaside town sets ticket prices according to the event. Higher prices are reserved for well-known small-scale national touring companies. Concessions, usually of £1 off, are offered to the low waged, UB40s, students and OAPs. Prices are increased in proportion to the venue's increased costs.

Most people see pricing as a purely financial matter. Their concern is 'How much do we need to charge in order to remain solvent?' Pricing can be much more than this. It can be a tool to persuade people to buy. Those responsible for marketing should always be involved in deciding how much tickets should cost. There are questions involved that only someone with a marketing viewpoint will have the information to answer. The case study at the end of this section provides a real-life example of this.

2 PERCEIVED VALUE

The kinds of prices charged by most arts organisations are not an important barrier to attendance for most people. Much more important is whether they are available to see the event. In fact, most people seem to decide that they want to see a particular event, then check their availability and if they are free, only then do they see what the ticket price is (see Chapter 21, 'Talking About the Right Things').

When faced with two similar items, people usually believe that the one that costs more must be of better quality.   They are willing to pay what they feel something is worth. Lowering prices does not usually mean increased attendances. If something seems cheap people think that it must be of low quality. Most promoters would agree that it is very difficult to get people to come to free events. An example of this is the city-based community theatre company which was funded by their local authority to give free performances in community centres. In spite of a thorough marketing campaign, audiences were very low indeed.

People will buy as long as the price is within their spending capacity. They may well include the whole cost of going to the theatre in their decision, taking into account what they will have to pay to park the car, have a drink in the interval and book a baby-sitter.

When prices are too high for them to afford the item is still regarded as desirable and of high quality; they just decide not to make the purchase. It is difficult to tell where this point is. A London fringe venue raised its prices by 20% with no reduction in attendance whatsoever. The only way to estimate at what point potential audiences will decide that they cannot afford to attend an event is to look at your competition. This consists of all the other ways that your audience could choose to spend their leisure time. The potential audience member will compare your ticket prices to the cost of going to the cinema, going to other performing arts events, hiring a video, spending the evening in the pub and so on, taking into account what they think each form of entertainment is worth.

> My husband goes to Nottingham Forest on Saturday and he has to pay an awful lot more for sitting not less than two hours in the cold. You come here and you get in for half the price and you have an interval and lots of people performing for you and have a jolly good evening. I think theatre is definitely good value. **Nottingham Playhouse audience member**

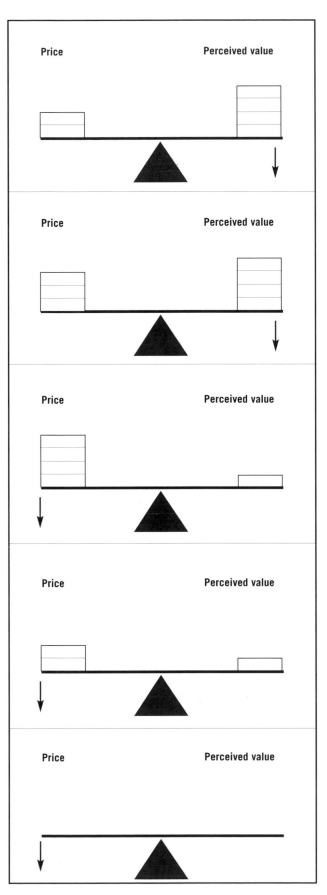

If the potential ticket buyer thinks that the experience of an evening out seeing your particular event is worth more than the price you are charging, then they will buy a ticket. This customer thinks that the experience is worth four units and the price is two units, so the seesaw tips in your favour.

But they would still have bought a ticket if the price had been three units.

This customer thinks that the experience of spending an evening seeing your event is only worth one unit. The ticket price is four units, so they will not be buying.

A hefty 50% discount will not persuade them otherwise. The price will still be two units and they only think your event is worth one.

For someone who is convinced that getting involved with your event is simply not the sort of thing they like to do, price is not an incentive. Even if you offered them a free ticket, they still have all the effort of getting there, so they are not going to accept. A much more effective strategy would be to persuade them that your event will be enjoyable, perhaps by adding value.

Price does affect frequency of attendance and choice. Audiences say that price does not affect their decision to attend something that they really want to see. A price that they perceive as high, however, makes the risk of going to a new or unfamiliar event greater. Sometimes potential attenders will choose a less risky event instead.

2.1 DISCOUNTS

People think of a ticket that has been discounted from £10 to £5 as more valuable than a ticket simply priced at £5. You can therefore use discounts to your advantage. You could set high prices with the intention of offering so many discounts that very few people will actually pay the top price. Aim the discounts at particular price-sensitive sections of the audience.

Offering a choice of prices for each performance works in much the same way. The tickets will assume a value relative to the highest ticket price. Some people will want to pay the highest price. Others will perceive the next price down as 'good value for money' while yet others will like to 'save money' by choosing the lowest ticket price.

It makes sense to charge as much as people are willing to pay.

2.2 MANAGING RISK

Most people when they go out want, not a cast iron guarantee, but they want to be pretty sure that they're going to enjoy it because you've got to get a baby-sitter and get the ticket and shave your legs and all that faffing about. You want payback.[1]

[1] Midlands Arts Marketing, Talking About Dance: Session 4 (Arts Council of England, 1998)

Like this participant in a focus group, most people talk about the time and effort they need to put into attending an arts event before they mention how much the ticket costs, but price does play a role.

Price does affect frequency of attendance and choice. Audiences say that price does not affect their decision to attend something that they really want to see. A high price, however, makes the risk of going to a new or unfamiliar event greater. Sometimes potential attenders will choose a less risky event instead. If they were offered a cheap ticket, they would be more willing to try it out as long as they thought that the event was interesting and they were available.

I looked at our database and found people who had bought tickets from us for the first time when they came to see *Passport to Pimlico*. I wrote to them about *The Provok'd Wife* saying that I was so sure they would enjoy the show, I'd give them their money back if they didn't. I targeted the offer very carefully to make sure I was only writing to new attenders and that they hadn't already bought tickets. This worked well and I only had one person who asked for their money back. They said that they hadn't understood what was going on. I wrote to them giving them their money back and saying that I hoped this hadn't put them off and that they would try something else next season. **Toby Oliver, Marketing Officer, Mercury Theatre, Colchester**

3 CONCESSIONARY PRICES

If you set your ticket prices at a level that reflects what the majority of your audiences are willing to pay, a section of the community that your organisation serves will not be able to afford to attend. Make provision specifically for these people when setting prices. The best way of doing this is to plan for generous concessions targeted at the appropriate people. These concessions could include standbys, sales promotions such as discount vouchers and concessionary ticket prices. These are subsidised by those who can and want to pay the higher prices associated with quality. The higher top prices make the concessions and any discounts you may offer even better value for money.

Concessionary prices are usually restricted to the unemployed (unwaged), people on Income Support, OAPs (senior citizens), students, registered disabled people and occasionally young people in general. Groups usually receive some kind of price reduction, although this is really a sales promotion discount rather than a concession. It is important to look at your classification of a group: a group of 8 is two car-loads, a group of 12 is three. You may find that the former is a more effective discount.

There is no point in charging £5 as the unwaged concession even if your top price is £12.50, as £5 is an impossibly high sum of money when you are living on around £27 per week! Charge a realistically low price in a way that does not cost your organisation money such as a UB40 standby where you offer any unsold tickets 30 minutes before a performance for £1. You are not going to get any money at all for an unsold seat, so your organisation is £1 better off for each of these tickets sold.

Incidentally, I am not sure that arts organisations should be using the term 'concession'. It sounds so begrudging and I've come across audiences in focus groups (students in particular) who simply do not understand that it applies to them. Why don't we simply use 'discount' instead?

4 TICKET YIELDS

A pricing system cannot be judged simply by looking at the ticket prices. Use ticket yields to get an accurate picture of what the system means in terms of income and attendance. This is the average amount of money that each attender pays for their ticket. You will be able to set income targets and budgets more easily using ticket yields.

CALCULATING TICKET YIELDS

Total income ÷ Total number of ticket buyers = Ticket yield

Estimate either the percentage or the number of attenders paying each ticket price.

How to calculate using percentages:

- multiply each price level by the relevant percentage
- add the results together and divide by 100.

For example:

56% at £9.50
37% at £8.50
7% at £1

56	x	9.50	=	532.00
37	x	8.50	=	314.50
7	x	1.00	=	007.00
100				853.50

853.5	÷	100	=	8.535

The ticket yield is £8.53.

How to calculate using numbers:

- multiply each price level by the relevant number of attenders
- add the results together and divide by the total number of attenders.

For example:

119	x	9.50	=	1,130.50
78	x	8.50	=	663.00
15	x	1	=	015.00
212				1,808.50

1808.50	÷	212	=	8.53066

The ticket yield is £8.53.

Ticket yields are important. A performance may have a bottom price of £1 – perhaps a standby for the unwaged. This may seem very low. However, if the top price is £9.50, and enough people are paying it, the ticket yield will be very healthy. Ticket yields are also a way of making allowances for any sales promotion discounts you may offer. It is best not to use ticket prices alone when setting income targets or judging pricing systems.

5 VAT

Most theatregoers do not realise that the money they pay for their ticket does not all go to the venue. The government takes 17.5% of it in VAT. Therefore with the ticket yield of £8.53 in the example above, the venue would only receive £7.26. If figures include VAT they are known as *gross*; if they do not they are *net*. You must make net, not gross income calculations because the VAT does not form part of your income.

HOW TO ADD VAT TO A PRICE

Net ticket yield £8.53

> 8.53 ÷ 100 = 0.0853
>
> 0.0853 x 17.5 = 1.49
>
> VAT is £1.49
>
> £8.53 + £1.49 = £10.02
>
> Gross ticket yield is £10.02

HOW TO WORK OUT HOW MUCH VAT IS INCLUDED IN A PRICE

Gross ticket yield £10.02

> £10.02 ÷ 117.5 = 0.0852765
>
> 0.0852765 x 100 = 8.52765
>
> round up to 8.53
>
> Net ticket yield is £8.53

You cannot just take 17.5% off the gross yield. Try it and see.

6 HOW TO SET TICKET PRICES

Before you can set ticket prices, you need to have read the previous paragraphs on VAT and ticket yields.

1. Work out your costs with your administrator or finance officer including such items as:

    (a) guarantee or fee to the company or the cost of staging the production

    (b) staffing costs for performances (attendants, bar staff, technicians, etc.)

    (c) proportion of overheads not covered by subsidy

    (d) marketing costs

    (e) income from programme and bar sales.

    This is in effect the income target – if the organisation's budget requires that the performance make a surplus, add this profit figure to the costs. Also look at the contract between the promoter and the company if this is appropriate. Your organisation may have arranged a deal involving a box office split where the promoter and company share the net income from the performance according to an agreed ratio. This can be anything between 70% and 80% to the company and 20% and 30% to the promoter.

2. Set an attendance target. Do this by examining the attendance at previous events of a similar nature at the venue and at other performances by the company. You also need to take into account the resources available for marketing.

3. Decide on the number of price levels you wish to have, including concessions and discounts.

4. Work out the proportion of tickets at each price likely to be sold, including concessionary tickets. Do this by looking at past performances or similar performances at other venues. Include discounted tickets from subscription schemes, etc.

5. Suggest some possible price structures and for each set of prices:

    (a) calculate the gross ticket yield

    (b) calculate the net ticket yield

    (c) calculate the total number of seats (no. of performances x capacity)

    (d) multiply the net ticket yield by number of seats to get total possible net income

    (e) calculate the percentage income using attendance target set in step 2.

    (f) subtract any guarantee to the company

    (g) calculate any box office split with the remainder.

6. Compare each figure with the income target in step 2. One set of prices will bring in more income than the others, but this is not necessarily the one to choose:

    (a) The high top price or the relatively higher concessionary price may make it difficult to meet the attendance target you set.

    (b) You need to look at how much you think the various sections of the audience would be willing to pay. Does the highest set of prices risk being seen as poor value for money?

    (c) Does the concessionary rate and the number of discounts allowed make it possible for you to attract the sections of the community for which you have planned?

You must balance all these issues in order to come to a decision. Once you have made that decision, stick to it. If you change ticket prices once they have been publicised, perhaps because a show is not selling as well as expected, you risk confusing customers, and those who have already bought tickets at the higher prices may demand refunds. Instead, offer targeted discounts which are only publicised to the target groups you select.

29 SETTING BUDGETS

SEE ALSO CHAPTERS
23. MARKETING PLANNING
24. MARKET RESEARCH
25. AUDIENCE DEVELOPMENT

Marketers prefer to think of marketing as an investment – the more marketing you are able to do, the more income you are likely to generate. Unfortunately, your colleagues may not see it like that but there is no harm in trying to persuade them.

1 HOW MUCH MONEY SHOULD YOU SPEND?

It is always hard to estimate how much an organisation ought to spend on marketing. The simplest method is to work out how much money you need to carry out your objectives. Then examine your resources and potential resources and try to match them with your needs.

Think of OSCAR:

- Establish **O**bjectives.
- Decide **S**trategy.
- **C**ost the programme.
- **A**llocate resources.
- **R**eview and consider.
- Action.

There are some other options:

- Add inflation to each item in last year's budget.
- Add a percentage increase to the total and allocate it to any new activity.
- Subtract a percentage decrease.

Funded organisations are usually expected to spend between 5% and 12% of their turnover on marketing excluding salaries.

1.1 TIME AND MONEY

For small-scale arts organisations the major cost of marketing is usually in terms of time rather than money. It is usually inappropriate for small-scale organisations to spend a lot of money on print and advertising (two of the most expensive areas of marketing activity), but it is vital that time is spent in marketing planning, especially when resources are few.

Time does, of course, usually cost money. You will probably have to channel time away from other tasks. But it may take as little as one week to draw up a marketing plan and this will almost certainly save you time in the long term. You can monitor the effectiveness of your marketing plan as you go along.

2 MARKETING EXPENDITURE

Here are some examples of marketing expenditure by small-scale arts organisations in 1999/2000.

Small-scale arts centre based in small regional town:

- turnover: £333,000
- marketing budget excluding staff costs: £37,000
- 11% of turnover.

Small/middle-scale touring company:

- turnover: £175,800
- marketing budget: £22,600 per year (£10,000 per show)
- 13% of turnover.

Middle-scale presenting venue:

- turnover: £1,813,527
- marketing budget: £180,000
- 10% of turnover.

Small-scale touring project company:

- turnover: £34,000
- marketing budget: £4,000
- 12% of turnover.

Large-scale presenting venue:

- turnover: £5,594,000
- marketing budget: £352,000
- 6% of turnover.

Regional producing theatre:

- turnover: £1,565,243
- marketing budget: £109,567
- 7% of turnover.

30 MARKETING TASKS FOR TOURING COMPANIES

SEE ALSO CHAPTERS

1. GETTING STARTED
3. HOW TO WRITE COPY
4. HOW TO PRODUCE PRINT
6. HOW TO USE PHOTOGRAPHS
12. HOW TO GET PRESS AND MEDIA COVERAGE
20. TALKING TO THE RIGHT PEOPLE
21. TALKING ABOUT THE RIGHT THINGS
23. MARKETING PLANNING
27. YOUR ORGANISATION'S IDENTITY
28. PRICING

This section looks at the details of the marketing tasks unique to touring companies.

1 BOOKING A TOUR

Booking a tour involves companies marketing themselves to promoters and uses many of the same strategies, skills and techniques as marketing to audiences and participants. The information needs and decision-making process of a promoter are very different to those of audiences, however.

The number of approaches that you, on behalf of your company, can make to promoters will be limited by your resources. Some promoters are more likely to book your company than others so you need to prioritise and focus your resources accordingly. You can do this by applying the principles already looked at in Chapter 1, 'Getting Started'.

To recap, first you need to identify the elements of both your company and the particular show you are selling that are likely to appeal to promoters, i.e. the benefits. You need to decide on which promoters to focus, i.e. the target groups, and which benefits are most appropriate for each target group. You then need to select the best method for communicating the benefits to the target groups.

> I'm very selective about the way in which I get in touch with promoters because there isn't much point in just blanket information. I do my research. For example, I would write to venues where I know from reviews I've read, or information I've had from one source or another, that dance activities have been successful. **Administrator for South Asian dance soloist**

1.1 PLANNING YOUR CAMPAIGN

Examine all aspects of your company's work. Work out its strengths and weaknesses, and the opportunities and threats that the outside world presents. For example:

- Strength: good financial administration
- Weakness: you have insufficient information about the forthcoming production
- Opportunity: two new arts festivals will open this year
- Threat: a company with a similar policy to you has recently been awarded project funding, giving it greater resources than you

How will you capitalise on the strengths and opportunities and reduce the risks associated with the weaknesses and threats?

BENEFITS

Decide what your company has to offer a promoter both in general terms and with reference to the particular production, for example:

- good marketing back-up
- regular tours to allow audience development
- a production that will attract young people
- growing audiences with many first time attenders.

Use any information you have collected about your audiences to help you identify the benefits your company can offer.

Decide what factors about your work make you different from other similar companies and put them in order of priority, for example:

- an unusual but very strong performance style
- the consistency of your past shows
- live music.

TARGET GROUPS

First, decide what scale of venue is appropriate for you. For example, can your organisation cope with performing in impromptu venues such as village halls or should you only tour to well-equipped small-scale venues that can meet all your technical needs?

Now make a close examination of the venues available at your chosen scale, e.g. policies, audience types, competition from other companies, geographic area, costs of touring at great distances, etc.

> The funding bodies have policies and they affect what venue managers will hire, so we also read all the current policies to find out what the demands would be. **Producer, unfunded theatre company, England**

Order the venues into similar groups and place the groups in order of priority. At the top of the list should be the promoters most likely to respond to your approach.

A suitable set of criteria for your target groups could be:

- promoters who book you regularly
- promoters who book you occasionally
- promoters who book similar companies
- promoters who book companies from other art forms with similar aims to your own
- venues and festivals that have audience types similar to your own.

These are similar to the criteria used in Chapter 20, 'Talking to the Right People', for identifying target groups of potential audience members.

MATCHING THE BENEFITS TO THE TARGET GROUPS

Match the benefits to the target groups of promoters.

1. List all the benefits you identified along the top of the matrix opposite.
2. List all the target groups you have selected down the side of the matrix.
3. Look at each target group in turn. Decide which of the benefits are most relevant for the target group and place a tick against it. You may find that several of the benefits are relevant for some target groups, but only select the three or four really important ones.
4. Put a circle round the tick for the benefit you think is most important to that particular target group.

This main benefit will become the headline in the letter you write to the promoter to accompany your information pack. You will talk about the other benefits you have ticked to back up your main benefit.

WHAT TO COMMUNICATE

Decide what you need to communicate to each target group, for example promoters who book you regularly will not need a great deal of general information about the company but the final three groups will.

You need to look at the level of understanding that each target group has of your art form. This will indicate the appropriate way to describe your organisation in both words and pictures.

It is important to remember that persuading a promoter to book your company and persuading a theatre-goer to buy a ticket are very different tasks although the marketing approach may be very similar. They are interested in different aspects of your organisation and so you need to give them different information. An

TARGET GROUPS/BENEFIT MATRIX
TARGET GROUPS

BENEFITS

overlap occurs only because the promoter needs to know that your show will appeal to their audience. You need to communicate this to them.

> We do have leaflets but we don't send them out very much because most of our work comes through word of mouth. For festivals, we tend to hand out material at the end of the show when people come along and ask. In schools, the same thing applies. Teachers move around a lot in schools, especially the special schools. It's a small world and people know each other and pass information on. **Administrator, cross-art form company touring to traditional and non-traditional venues**

HOW TO COMMUNICATE

Most promoters receive hundreds of approaches from companies each year. They will probably only give each information pack a few seconds of their time, therefore their first impressions of the information are extremely important. This will make the difference between your information staying on their desk and going in the wastepaper basket. You must therefore get your information across in a way that is immediately effective.

> The people who book us include schools, education advisers, arts centres and arts officers in local authorities. Our failure is that our marketing is mostly sending out some sort of flyer saying 'Our company's new show will be xyz. Contact us for further details' ... Flyers aren't successful at all because venues get millions of companies they've never heard of sending them ... We need another strand to our strategy which we are going to introduce ... We will identify a number of 'seeding' people who would act like unofficial travelling salespeople. Then we will bring together a number of agencies and talk to them. **Education officer, community dance company, England**

The method of communication that you choose will depend on the resources you have available. Inexpensive methods can be effective if the information is presented well.

The following are some possible methods.

Glossy brochures

These can be expensive to produce but enable you to communicate in a dramatic, visual way, This is particularly important for non-text based art forms like dance and mime. Brochures can range from single colour to full colour, and from A3 folded to A4 through to a 12-page booklet. They are expensive to update as the whole brochure has to be reprinted. If the brochures just contain information about the company, they can be sold to audiences.

> We put together a sales brochure very much like your typical double glazing advertising. We said something about the company, then a few things about what we are doing in particular, then a few sales points – for example, our cheap rates and quick get-in and get-out. Although it looks

[1] See Chapter 3, *'How to Write Copy'*, for more information.

like a very cheap and simple method of marketing it's actually quite a scientific document – it has Attention, Interest, Desire and Action[1]...Then it gives a few letters of recommendation from satisfied customers. **Artistic director, cross-art form company touring to non-traditional venues**

Information sheets

Information sheets about your organisation and the particular show you are selling can be produced inexpensively if they are photocopied onto good quality paper. Always illustrate the sheets in some way for maximum impact. You can update them individually.

Folders

These are expensive but give an impression of quality to less impressive contents such as the information sheets above.

Videos

This is the ideal way to give a clear idea of your show to promoters who are unable to see it live. However, videos are extremely expensive to produce: you may have to hire a studio; pay your performers for a day's work; hire an editing suite; and so on. You may be able to reduce your costs by finding college students to produce your video. They may have access to cheap college facilities. Your video need not be of a full performance. You could set up ten minutes of work to demonstrate the atmosphere of the production. Videos are almost always necessary to sell your company outside Britain.

Now that videos exist, all promoters (except, perhaps, the smallest of small scale) really take it for granted that you have a show-reel. It does seem essential for dance companies as people will often not listen to your verbal description of the work.

However, having a bad video is worse than not having one at all! Many people – particularly those unfamiliar with the dance world – expect the quality of a pop video. Something unedited, from a one-camera shoot, in performance lighting, from the back of the auditorium is not going to impress anyone unfamiliar with the work. Initially aim just to record a short piece or section – perhaps just ten minutes to give a 'flavour' and idea of the style. Try approaching students on TV and film courses such as the London College of Printing or Ravensbourne College of Art. For the best quality product try to make contact with anyone who is 'junior' in the TV or video editing world. The younger staff usually have access to the equipment and may well be anxious to produce their own show-reels out of working hours to help their own careers. Ideally the choreographer or company director should be involved in the editing, as what looks pretty to a video editor might look appalling to a dancer. To give a fair indication of your work, you will probably not require masses of video effects. If you are very lucky, you will only end up paying for copies of the tapes and perhaps a token fee. The 'real' cost of getting a 15-minute piece shot and edited in a professional situation could be around £20,000, taking into account fees and facilities, so you will definitely have to rely on good will. **Arts administrator, specialising in dance soloists and small dance companies**

Covering letters

These should accompany any of the communication methods you use. They will enable you to target each promoter individually by emphasising the particular benefits that they will find most appealing. Personalise letters and include clear details of the proposed cost of the production per performance, the dates that you propose touring and a contact name and telephone number. Include technical information if you have not done so elsewhere.

No available information

It is more difficult to get bookings if you do not have any information about the production you are selling or if your company is new.

Follow the planning process outlined above but focus on these areas:

- Place emphasis on the benefits of the company rather than the show.

- Talk about the sort of production that the company is likely to be presenting. Do this in the context of the artistic policy.

- Emphasise the company's track record. Include reviews, comments by audiences and other promoters and publicity material about previous successful productions in your information pack.

- It is rare for dance companies to have full information about productions when they are booking a tour. Remind promoters of this.

- Try to get the director/choreographer to give you a theme that the production will cover and indicate the ways in which this might be treated. This will give you something concrete to discuss with promoters without committing the company to anything.

- Find a striking visual image that is unspecific enough to be passed by the director/choreographer and use this on all the information you send out.

1.2 CARRYING OUT YOUR CAMPAIGN

Approach the promoter you have identified in order of priority, preferably beginning at least ten months before you plan to begin touring. Promoters work on widely different time-scales but if you do not make an early approach you risk missing out. Once a promoter has begun to select a number of possible companies for each available date, it is very difficult to persuade them to consider you.

Begin by sending your information to your target promoters. Follow up your mail shot with a telephone call about two or three weeks later. The purpose of this call is to ensure that the promoter has both read and remembered your information.

PROMOTER'S BRIEFING SHEET

Independent People adapted by Charles Way

What is the show about?

The play takes place in and around a small croft called Summerhouses in the hills of Iceland. Bjartur, a sheep farmer who has been fighting for 15 years to be independent, at last sets up home in the croft with his new wife and an abundance of sheep. But his relationship with his wife is far from harmonious as they constantly argue each other. Bjartur's inability to accept help from others finally sends his wife to an early grave, but not before she gives birth to a baby of somewhat questionable parenting.

With the help of the town elders, Bjartur is found another wife and her mother to look after the baby. He is equally as negligent of his second family but a special bond grows between himself and his eldest daughter, Asta. A bond that ultimately breaks as she proves to have inherited his stubbornness and to be as desperate for her own independence.

With great humanity and gentle humour, this beautiful tale is told against a backdrop of music and sound that evoke the clean air and rugged crags of the Icelandic hills. Superstition is a strong undercurrent in the play as the characters try to come to terms with the whole notion of being beholden to no man.

This play is an adaptation for stage of the Nobel prize winning novel *Independent People* by Halldor Laxness. This is the first time this novel has been adapted for stage in the English language and performed outside Iceland.

Set Design

The performance will be in formal theatre style with the set at one end of the venue and the audience facing. The set dimensions are approximately 16" x 20" x 9" high, but can be adapted for the smaller venues.

The show lasts for approximately two hours including a 15 minute interval, and is suitable for 10 years and over

Who will enjoy it?

Anyone who ever dreamt of being truly independent (i.e most of us!). Those that enjoy a good tale of rural life set against the atmospheric backdrop of Iceland. Lovers of Hardy and the great tradition of rural novels and people curious to learn more about Icelandic culture and superstition.

One sentence to sell the show?

Independent People – a beautiful tale of love, independence and stubborn sheep, told with gentle humour and set against the dramatic Icelandic countryside

I usually write a personalised letter to the director or administrator of wherever, and I usually leave it a while and then do a round of just checking up ... 'Did you receive the information? ... Perhaps I should reiterate that she's working here or there and perhaps you'd like to take the opportunity of seeing her while she's in that area.' If I know somebody is particularly interested in dance then I might emphasise that their dance programme is interesting – a bit of flattery! **Administrator for South Asian dance soloist**

Plan your telephone call carefully:

- Make a list of the benefits of particular interest to each promoter.

- If possible, have a new piece of information such as the name and past 'successes' of the director, or a particularly interesting aspect of the production like an unusual design concept.

- Be ready to counter, politely but firmly, any negative arguments that the promoter might put forward.

- Be clear about what makes your organisation different from similar companies.

- Be clear about the reason for your call and have a strong opening gambit. You are unlikely to gain the promoter's attention if you say that you are ringing to see if they have received your mail shot.

- Be prepared, however, for the promoter to have forgotten all about the information you sent and be ready to give a succinct and interesting summary of what it contained.

This is how the administrator of two solo mime performers gets bookings:

I send a two-colour, well-illustrated promotional brochure (which I can afford because they are also used as programmes at performances) and a covering letter, then follow it up in about ten days with a phone call.

If the promoter is out, then I try to talk to someone who can tell me when's the best time to contact them, and then make sure that I ring them then. It helps to have a contact – even if it's the receptionist or switchboard person – because you are more likely to get through to the promoter next time you call.

I keep a kind of visual checklist of progress: pink for 'yes', a booking; yellow for 'no'; and blanks with dates to call back for ones I'm working on.

When I'm speaking to them I keep it light and friendly, but not personal and always professional. You give an impression of this, but really it's a hard sell going on (although you don't show it). If it doesn't work, or if they're under pressure, then I ask, 'Can I call you back?' Sometimes, although they're interested, they're just not in the right frame of mind, and you can hear the panic ring in their voices when you start to speak!

I strongly believe that you need to give venues a chance to think. They may not know much about your art form. Just keep talking about what you're offering, think on your feet and respond to individual moves and pressures.

Sometimes you just can't get through to the right person, so I send a letter asking them if they're interested or not, and to let me know either way. Often they don't even respond to this.

If the promoter makes their complete lack of interest in your show very clear, do not pester them. This will only antagonise and jeopardise any future attempt to secure a booking.

If I speak to a promoter and really get a sense that they're not interested, they don't know about the subject ... I don't pursue it. I don't ever push it. I don't believe in coming back to promoters. I know one or two Indian dance soloists have reputations for being extremely pushy. You can say what you want to say, you can say it loud and clear, but pushing people I don't think helps. **Administrator for Indian dance soloist**

Aim to agree with the promoter that you are 'pencilled in' to their programme for a particular week. A pencil booking is not binding on either the company or the promoter. The dates will inevitably be juggled around until both sides have their season/tour schedule sorted out.

The promoter may agree to pencil in a booking straight away. It is more likely that they will ask you to ring back in a few weeks when the rest of their season is a little clearer. It is important that you do this, as the promoter is unlikely to contact you unless they are very interested indeed.

Once you have achieved a pencil booking, establish when you are likely to be able to 'firm it up'. Check periodically with the promoter on the progress of the season's programme. You should be able to exchange contracts to make the booking legally binding about four to six months before the performance(s).

PROMOTERS

Sometimes the shoe is on the other foot. A theatre in the extreme north of Scotland sends an information pack to touring companies to persuade them to accept a booking. The remoteness of its location means that it is very expensive for companies to travel there. To counter this the venue offers free accommodation to companies as well as a fee. In order to assist companies to set up tours in the area, it suggests other venues in the Highlands that might be interested in booking them. A venue with a well-equipped video workshop in a similar location offers a free promotional video to companies who tour there.

1.3 AFTER THE PERFORMANCES

Always ring the promoter shortly after your company's visit to discuss how the performances went. Discuss the quality of the production, the size of the audiences and their reaction to what they saw. This will give you useful information for the future and may form the basis for a repeat booking.

2 PROMOTER AND COMPANY WORKING TOGETHER

2.1 WHOSE RESPONSIBILITY?

An organisation that produces and promotes its own performance events clearly has to focus resources on marketing. There is often confusion, however, over who is primarily responsible for marketing an event produced by a touring company that is booked into a venue by a promoter.

Neither the promoter nor the company can be effective without input from the other. The promoter will have information about existing and potential audiences in the area (target groups) while the company will have information about the elements of the production that are likely to appeal to audiences (benefits) and experience of how audiences were obtained in other venues. The most successful marketing matches benefits to target groups by combining these areas of expertise and knowledge.

> I think it is very much a partnership. But we do much more work!
>
> **Administrator, arts centre, England**

Both the producing company and the promoter have a responsibility for marketing the show. A promoter purchases marketing input when they book a company. Conversely, if a company hires a venue, they expect marketing support. Make clear the extent of marketing input on each side in the contract.

> One dance company didn't tell me that the week before their visit they were going to be on TV. Why didn't they tell me? It takes a lot of weight off my shoulders to have that sort of information. **Theatre officer, local authority venue, Wales**

This concept of a partnership between company and promoter is still seen as unusual by some arts organisations. However, most realise that it is a logical and effective basis for success. Both sides of the partnership benefit. At the simplest level, a promoter is very unlikely to book a company again if they fail to reach their planned level of income from the box office. Likewise a company is very unlikely to hire a venue again if they do not get the level of help they expect.

2.2 PLANNING

Each organisation should have a marketing plan made up of aims, targets and broad guidelines for action as discussed in Chapter 1, 'Getting Started'. The marketing plans should identify ways in which resources can be used to bring the best possible results.

On the basis of these plans the company and the promoter should pool their specialised areas of expertise and knowledge to decide what resources they have available for the particular performances and what they are going to spend these resources on. This is a campaign plan.

> I think when I arrived two years ago, the companies weren't helpful, and I constantly had to get on to them for leaflets and photographs. But now I

> find people are much more aware that the marketing approach is not just
> off the venue's back. I think that people are a bit more professional in their
> attitude towards marketing. Rather than thinking 'We'll give 1,000 leaflets
> to this venue', people will actually sit down and say 'Who does this appeal
> to and what's the best way of reaching them?' **Administrator, arts centre, England**

The plan will include an agreement as to which target audiences to focus on and how to communicate with them. It will state clearly who is responsible for carrying out each element and what resources of staff time and money each side will provide.

Many touring companies make decisions about what they are going to provide venues with before they have entered into discussions with the promoters. Sometimes they decide before the tour has been booked. It is only after the benefits, target audiences and methods of communication have been agreed that you can decide whether you will be producing leaflets, posters, photographs, etc. Neither should you start commissioning designers and photographers until you are clear what images will communicate effectively with the chosen target audiences.

A campaign plan is essential to ensure that everyone has a clear idea of what will be happening. The likelihood of disputes between company and promoter will be reduced or eliminated, the performances will be more successful because your resources will be well focused and you will both get better value for the money you spend on marketing because your efforts will be coordinated.

> Our first point of liaison has been with theatre publicity officers. We will be
> visiting all the venues in advance to coordinate our marketing with theirs
> and to check up on the situation! In this way we can highlight the most
> needy areas and decide how to develop potential audiences. **Producer, unfunded**
> **touring theatre company, England**

It is tempting to wait until the other organisation gets in touch with you but someone has to initiate the contact. Get in touch the moment your organisation has made a firm booking, regardless of whether you are the promoter or the company.

2.3   DRAWING UP A CAMPAIGN PLAN

The best way to negotiate a campaign plan is in a face-to-face meeting. The company usually visits each of the promoters in turn but you may not be able to afford to do this. If you cannot spare the time or afford the train fares for individual visits, an excellent alternative is to hold a promoters' day in each of the regions to which you are touring. This involves inviting all the promoters who have booked your company in that region to meet. These sessions are often extremely helpful as particular promoters may have already identified ways of working that could solve problems faced by the others. But if you do not have the time for this either, make a lengthy telephone call to each promoter and/or publicist. If the promoter employs a marketing officer or publicist, speak to them rather than the administrator.

> Because we contact them in July for a November tour, we can work out whether we can help them with their marketing plan – how they're going to sell the show … Before I joined, I noticed that most venues were being sent publicity – posters and leaflets – but they weren't actually being visited or asked 'How will you go about selling [this production]?' **Marketing officer, Asian touring theatre company**

Write the campaign plan down once it is agreed and each of you keep a copy. Circulate it to all relevant staff on both sides, e.g. the box office staff, the administrators and even the performers, etc.

If there is an arts marketing agency in the area they will find a copy of your plan useful for their records. They may not be able to give you any direct help with the campaign, but they will have useful tips to offer.

2.4 THE CAMPAIGN PLAN STEP BY STEP

If your organisation has drawn up a marketing plan, you will find this process very easy. If it has not, a little more thought will be required.

1. Between you, set targets for income and attendances. They must be achievable. If the company has made previous visits to the venue then use these as a starting point.

2. Look at pricing. Discuss yield, range, perceived value, VAT, etc. Although the promoter usually makes the final decision on pricing, the company may have useful information about successful pricing structures for their performances elsewhere.

3. Review the resources that both sides have available. This includes both staff time and money.

4. Work out how the income and attendance targets are going to be achieved. This will involve selecting target groups and deciding how they will be reached.

   (a) Identify target audiences and decide how many people from each group you will be able to attract per performance. For example, a dance company that wanted to focus on young people, members of the theatre mailing list, audiences at dance events in other venues and those who had never visited the venue before, might set the following targets:

14–16 year olds	15 per performance
mailing list members	60 per performance
attenders at similar performances	30 per performance
new attenders	10 per performance

(b) Identify which benefits will appeal most to each target group. For example, for the 14–16 year olds, they might choose workshops in schools, a recent appearance on Saturday morning television, the pop music soundtrack to part of the performance and the subject matter.

(c) Identify methods of communication appropriate to each target group. For example, for the 14–16 year olds, they might choose selling tickets at workshops, direct mail to each member of the venue's youth theatre group, a discount offered to youth club members through the leaders and a competition on the music pages of the local listings magazine.

5. Work out who is going to be responsible for which element of the plan. Record this in the campaign plan, e.g. who is going to deal with the press, provide the direct mail letters, stuff envelopes, liaise with schools, etc.

We look at where the theatre's mailings go. We look at the postcodes and the interests of the people on the lists. Then we target areas not specifically covered by them. **Producer, unfunded touring theatre company**

6. Decide how the success of the plan is going to be measured. Work out how the response to each marketing activity can be monitored. This is very important because you will find out which methods worked for future reference.

7. Now review the targets you set in step 1. Are they realistic in the light of the plan you have set up?

They've had new audiences enter their venue … It's given the programmers enough confidence to say 'We can host this company in our main space because now we have that audience they've helped us develop and we can now also get to the main theatre-going audiences.' That's purely because we worked *with* the touring venue and created a long-term relationship.

Marketing officer, Asian touring theatre company

3 CAMPAIGN PLANNING MEETINGS

We have suggested that it is a good idea for companies and promoters to negotiate their campaign plan in a face-to-face meeting. This section looks at the further advantages of a meeting closer to the performance(s). Although many organisations do not have the resources to meet up, it must be stressed that a face-to-face marketing session near to the scheduled visit is usually extremely valuable.

No matter how comprehensive your joint campaign plan is, a face-to-face meeting will help both parties iron out any last-minute problems or capitalise on new developments. It is best if face-to-face meetings take place at the venue.

Companies can gain additional coverage by talking to the press and media themselves. They can also help the box office sell tickets by explaining the event further. Promoters can obtain instant answers to any queries about the company and production, which should help them focus their thoughts on the forthcoming performance. If sales figures are lower than planned, an emergency campaign plan can be quickly drawn up.

If you work for a small-scale company, you may not have the time or money to visit all the promoters on your tour schedule. Select the ones that would particularly benefit from a face-to-face meeting. These will often be new venues to which you have not toured previously. You can meet several promoters from the same region together, perhaps at the regional arts board.

> I visit the venues a couple of weeks before the performance, or even a week, just to see how things are going. I would check if they'd distributed the print ... and exactly who's going to be there on the night. I also check what the company actually has to do on the night. Normally you just turn up and perform but sometimes it's so small scale you actually need to be there to help tear the tickets. Administrator, regional touring mime company

3.1 WHEN TO HOLD THE MEETING

Face-to-face marketing meetings are best scheduled between ten days and four weeks before a performance. This timing is ideal for press and media interviews and for delivering foyer/front-of-house displays.

3.2 WHO SHOULD MEET

The person responsible for marketing the company should meet with the person responsible for marketing the venue. Just who these people are will depend on the size of your organisation.

3.3 PRINT

Companies can deliver extra print if it is needed. They can also make sure that sufficient print has been distributed to the agreed outlets. If necessary, they may want to help top up piles of print.

3.4 PRESS AND MEDIA

The person from the company can be interviewed by local journalists about the forthcoming performance. Most local press and media like the 'here's someone direct from the company' angle and the timing will probably be ideal for getting coverage in advance of the performance date. However, if any company members, e.g. performers, are well known, the press and media may not be interested in talking to anyone except them. You can provide local radio stations with a ready-made tape of an interview with different company members.

3.5 DISPLAY BOARDS AND MERCHANDISE

Companies can deliver ready-made display boards to the promoter for the foyer or elsewhere. They can liaise with the front-of-house manager about programmes and any merchandise they may have. They can even deliver programmes.

3.6 BOX OFFICE

Companies can speak to the box office staff and check that they are clear about the benefits of the show and target groups. This is especially useful for shows that are hard to describe in words like dance and mime performances and new plays that are unfamiliar to the public. The box office should have already received a box office pack from the company.

3.7 TALKS

Promoters can arrange for companies to talk to potential group bookers. For instance, the company could give a short talk to the youth theatre group about a particular aspect of the performance.

3.8 TROUBLESHOOTING

If the advance bookings are lower than targeted, both organisations can discuss emergency procedures for improving ticket sales.

4 COMPILING A MARKETING PACK

4.1 CONTENTS

Your marketing pack should contain:

- information, especially hard facts, about audiences
- information about your company
- information about the event
- a list of suggested target markets
- a list of suggested selling points
- appropriate copy and an image for the promoter's season brochure
- a sample direct mail letter for each of the target markets you suggest
- a sample press release
- a box office information sheet
- a tour schedule.

It can also contain:

- biographies of company members where the company is expecting the promoter to produce a programme
- images to help the promoter get a feel for the show
- press clippings and/or quotations about your previous work
- other supporting information.

But many promoters find it easier to use packs that avoid large quantities of supporting material such as biographies and photocopies of reviews. They need to find the essential information quickly.

4.2 INFORMATION ABOUT AUDIENCES

Include a brief profile of previous audiences for your company's work and a profile of audiences for dance in general.

4.3 INFORMATION ABOUT YOUR COMPANY

Aim to help your promoters understand more about the style of work your company creates and about its track record. Include any information that will help them convince audiences that your company will present high quality work. Listing the titles of previous productions is not helpful – you need to give them benefits, not features.

4.4 INFORMATION ABOUT THE EVENT

Use simple language, short sentences and lots of headings. Include:

- an initial brief summary of the plot or story
- the performance style
- the subject matter
- summary of the content
- key points about the choreographer
- sets and costumes
- likely audience reactions
- concise background information on the subject matter if appropriate
- information about contemporary dance in straightforward language if you think the promoter is likely not to be familiar with it
- whether it is part of an exam syllabus, its relevance to the National Curriculum, etc.
- suitability of the work for particular audiences including any bad language or nudity
- likely running time
- likely number and duration of intervals and pauses.

4.5 LIST OF SUGGESTED TARGET MARKETS

It is tempting to list as many target markets as possible. Stick to no more than ten best bets. Be as specific as possible: 'young people' is not a useful target market but 'young people aged 18–24 in further or higher education' tells the promoter exactly who to target and how to get hold of them.

4.6 LIST OF SUGGESTED SELLING POINTS

Think about what audience members will experience when they see your event. List the aspect that is most important to each marketing target, and then back this up with two or three other points. Make sure you list benefits, not features.

4.7 APPROPRIATE COPY
FOR THE PROMOTER'S SEASON BROCHURE

Write two versions, one of around 40 words and one of 100 words. Base your copy on the two or three most important selling points you identified earlier. Typically, between 40% and 50% of audiences hear about an event through the promoter's season brochure so it's important to get the copy and image right. See the separate section at the end of this worksheet for information about images.

4.8 SAMPLE DIRECT MAIL LETTER FOR EACH
OF THE TARGET MARKETS YOU SUGGEST

See Chapter 10, 'How to Create a Direct Mail Campaign'.

4.9 SAMPLE PRESS RELEASE

See Chapter 12, 'How to Get Press and Media Coverage'.

4.10 BOX OFFICE INFORMATION SHEET

This is a single sheet of concise information designed to enthuse as well as inform sales staff. Stiff, brightly coloured paper or card in a plastic cover will last longest in the box office. Include:

- a 20-word selling sentence about the event including the key benefit
- a 100-word synopsis of 'what it's about'
- a list of five selling points
- a list of 'the sort of people who will enjoy the show'
- the running time and number of intervals
- suitability – give the detail that the customer will ask for, e.g. 'there is one moment of nudity but it is not full frontal and is in low lighting'
- practical issues about which the promoter must inform the customer, e.g. strobe lighting, gunshots or other special effects
- very brief extracts from press reviews if available
- brief information about the company
- a list of tour dates with box office telephone numbers.

The box office staff may well read this information aloud to customers so make sure that it is in fairly informal language.

4.11 TOUR SCHEDULE

Promoters find it useful to keep in touch with other promoters on the tour to share information and ideas.

31 MONITORING AND EVALUATION

SEE ALSO CHAPTER
23. MARKETING PLANNING

The demands on arts organisations for information is increasing all the time. Best Value, applications for regional arts board project funding, applications to the Lottery for capital funds – they all demand information to demonstrate that there is a need for your work, that you can get new and different people involved in it and that it is of a high quality. Local authorities and the Lottery are increasingly looking at the relationship between the funding requested and the number of people who will benefit. As the funding pot begins to dry up, applications that do not have 'hard evidence' are turned down in favour of those that do.

This means that arts workers are beginning to equate 'evaluation' with 'bureaucracy'.

But there is a more important reason to monitor and evaluate your work. Eastern Touring Agency talked to around 350 arts organisations across all sectors about their projects to develop audiences. Just 15 of them could answer the question 'Did it work?' As resources get scarcer, each of us needs to make sure that we focus them on whatever gets us the results *we* want.

So how do marketers collect the evidence they need when they usually have so little time and no money to pay someone else to do it? Monitoring and evaluation begins with the setting of clear aims and objectives.

1 AIMS AND OBJECTIVES

An aim describes broadly what your project is trying to achieve:

> To bring 16–18 year olds into a theatre building and develop their understanding of how a dance work is created, staged and toured.

Objectives must be much more detailed – in fact, they are useless for monitoring and evaluation unless they are SMART: specific, measurable, actionable, realistic and have a time-scale.

Here are some examples of SMART objectives:

- To bring 3,000 people into contact with dance in performance for the first time during 1995.

- To achieve a 10% increase in the proportion of participants who describe themselves as 'white – other' in the questionnaire given out at workshops in the next three months. (NB: of course you will have to know exactly how many people fit this category at the moment.)

- To reduce the drop-out rate for the Rock School to 25% by the end of next term.

It may seem difficult to set objectives for long-term objectives. Try breaking down your long-term goals into a series of step-by-step objectives. It may be useful to base this on the idea that an attender or participant goes through a number of stages when they get involved in the arts.

First of all, they must be aware of what you have to offer, and have some positive feelings about it. Then they need to try it out for the first time. The next stage is for you to persuade them to participate or attend again. Now you can encourage them to get involved on a regular basis and then become an advocate who will persuade other people to try out your events.

This process can take a long time. Some organisations offer young people an experience of the arts in the hope that they will become attenders or participants when they are adults. Setting objectives for this kind of long-term project is not as difficult as it seems. You need to break down the process of becoming a regular participant into stages and work out what might signal future attendance now. One example of an objective like this might be:

> By the end of the workshop, 25% of the participants to say that they are not hostile to the idea of doing a music activity in the future and can describe some of the actions they would have to take to do so, e.g. to find out what is available in their area.

This is not ideal, but until we have the results of research that tracks the future arts attendance or participation of young people involved in arts education, it is the best we can do.

2 MONITORING PROJECTS

2.1 WHAT ARE YOU MONITORING?

These are the basic questions you need to answer:

- Did I achieve what I set out to do?
- How many people were involved?
- What kind of people were involved?
- How did they judge the quality of the experience?
- What would I do differently next time?
- Was it an effective use of my resources?
- Did I get any unexpected results?
- Is it worth doing again?

You cannot answer them unless you decided in detail what you were trying to do before you started.

2.2 COLLECTING INFORMATION

You will need to collect some information in order to get the evidence you need to monitor and evaluate your work. Chapter 24, 'Market Research', covers this area in much more detail, but here is a straightforward guide.

It is easy to waste time and perhaps money collecting information that you do not need. Too many people simply say 'It's time I did some audience research'. You need to ask yourself:

- What do I want to know?

- Why do I want to know it?

- What will I do with the information?

Asking these questions will also tell you how accurate you need your information to be – you will need to collect information from far more people to get hard evidence for a £150,000 capital lottery bid than for a £500 local authority project grant.

Collecting more facts does not mean that you end up with more useful information so you need to constantly weigh the value of information you are collecting against what it costs you in time, effort and maybe money to collect it. Information is useless if you do not use it.

WHO ARE YOU GOING TO COLLECT INFORMATION FROM?

You need to work out what kind of people you need to collect information from, e.g. are you going to approach everybody who attends classes, or just the people under 18 because they are your target group?

You need to work out how many of them you need to approach to get the level of accuracy you need, e.g. people at every class for a term or people at just four classes aimed at different abilities.

You also need to work out how you are going to choose the people to ask, e.g. do you need to make sure that you cover classes scheduled at different times of day because different sorts of people attend weekday afternoon and evening classes? You need to think about this so that you:

- collect information you can use

- avoid cheating (on purpose or by accident) by only collecting information from people who will give you the 'right' answers

- get the most accurate information you can, given the amount of time and effort you have available.

Most funding bodies scrutinise the information you give them to check that it gives an accurate picture of what is going on. They will discount it if they think that it is biased (i.e. that you have cheated when collecting it!).

If you are using questionnaires, you need to hand out a lot more than you want responses. You will get a response rate of 20–60% depending on the effectiveness and length of the questionnaire and how you distribute and collect them.

USING THE INFORMATION

You need to work out how you are going to analyse the information you collect now. This will save you time and effort later. You have two choices:

- *Tallying the answers by hand*: this involves counting the number of people who give each particular answer and will give you very basic results. It is time-consuming if you are collecting a lot of information.

- *Using a computer*: there is relatively cheap software available, or you can buy the analysis from a commercial bureau. If you have one in your region, a national marketing agency may offer you a better service for a better price. Some organisations have used the resources of their local tertiary education institution.

WAYS OF COLLECTING INFORMATION

Here are some ways of collecting the information you need:

- Talk to all your colleagues involved in organising and doing the activity.
- Talk to the participants or attenders after the event.
- Talk to the participants or attenders before and after the event and compare their expectations with what they think happened.
- Look at the information about your attenders or participants held on box office computer systems.
- Hand out and collect in questionnaires.
- Make available a comments book for people to write their impressions and suggestions.
- Analyse the information on booking forms.
- Ask individual people questions as they leave.
- Hand out suggestion cards.
- Hand out feedback forms.
- Analyse the information on theatre seating plans (box office staff often use different colours or symbols to record different concession prices so that you can count the number of tickets sold to children, or people with a disability, etc.).

Choose the method or methods that will tell you what you want to know most effectively.

CASE STUDY

THE ROADMENDER, a small but busy youth venue in Northampton, wanted to collect information about their audiences to prove to local and regional businesses that they were worth sponsoring. They wanted to show that lots of local young people attended their venue and that they had money to spend on the potential sponsors' products. They did not think that young people would want to fill in questionnaires.

First of all they got volunteers (mostly students) to collect the postcode of every single person who came into the building over a two-week period. This was evidence of the number of people who used the venue and where they came from. Then they talked to people at selected events and asked them just four questions designed to find out their age, attitude to spending money and what they spent money on.

Postcodes can tell you a lot about your audiences and participants such as:

- where they come from
- how far they travelled
- what kind of communities they come from, e.g. car ownership, age breakdown, likelihood to attend arts events and much more.

You will need a postcode map and maybe some expert help to analyse them. Try your region's national marketing agency (if you have one) or the person responsible for marketing or audience development at your regional arts board. They hold Area Profile Reports, information about your community broken down by postcode sector, which are available free to organisations funded by a regional arts board or Arts Council.

WHAT TO ASK AND HOW TO ASK IT

You need to work out how you are going to analyse the information before you work out what questions you are going to ask.

There are two basic sorts of question:

1. Closed questions ask the person responding to choose the most appropriate out of a set of answers you have provided, maybe by ticking a box on a questionnaire or choosing one of several options you have read out to them.

2. Open questions ask them to answer in their own words by writing in the space provided on a questionnaire or by telling an interviewer who then writes the answer down.

Open questions do not prompt the person responding who may give an answer you have not thought of. They take a lot of time and effort to analyse as you have to work out categories for the answers before you count how many people have responded like that. It is best to avoid open questions when you want to get a lot of people to give you information. You could ask a small number of people open questions and then use the answers they give to design a closed question to which you can get a large number to respond.

Types of question

There are many different ways of asking questions. You need to use the ones that will give you the type of answer you need. Here are some examples of ways of structuring closed questions. You will, of course, need to rephrase them to fit your situation:

- I think the quality of the performance I saw tonight was:

Excellent	Good	Fair	Poor	Very poor
❏	❏	❏	❏	❏

- I thought the performance I saw tonight was:

Exciting	❏	❏	❏	❏	❏ Boring
Easy to follow ❏		❏	❏	❏	❏ Hard to follow

- How likely are you to go to another workshop at the Centre?

Very likely	Fairly likely	Unlikely	Very unlikely
❏	❏	❏	❏

- Please say to what extent you agree or disagree with the following statements:

  I think the Centre should put on more events for people over 50:

Strongly disagree	Disagree	Neither agree nor disagree	Agree	Strongly disagree
❏	❏	❏	❏	❏

- Tick the words you think describe this event:

  Tiring ❏   Interesting ❏   Colourful ❏

  Easy ❏   Amusing ❏   Challenging ❏   Dull ❏

The fewer questions you ask, the more people will answer them so do not ask anything that you do not really need to know. Your questions should be in a logical order with the less interesting, personal questions, e.g. age, last.

Before you design your own questions, check that the work has not already been done for you by reading these two publications.

- Caroline Sharp and Karen Dust, *Artists in Schools: A Handbook for Teachers and Artists* (1997, National Foundation for Educational Research). This looks at how artists and schools can define quality and judge whether an experience has been of 'good' quality. It contains a list of questions to ask participants and organisers and is available from: Dissemination Unit, NFER, The Mere, Upton Park, Slough, Berks SL1 2DQ.

- Peter Verwey, *Sample Audience Questionnaires* (1995, Arts Council of England). This has a range of questions covering most eventualities suggested for audience surveys carried out by arts organisations presenting performing arts events. These have been tested so that they are unambiguous. You may want to compare your results with those from other organisations so you will need to make sure that you follow the standard ways of categorising age, ethnic origin, etc. that this booklet sets out. It is available free from the Marketing and Market Research Unit on 020-7630 9389.

Handing out questionnaires or feedback forms gets a better response rate than leaving them on seats. Talking to people gets a better response still. Ask for completed questionnaires or feedback forms as people leave. Very few people remember them once they have left the building, although a Freepost address (no stamp needed) may result in a few extra responses.

You will get even more people to answer your questions if you:

- explain why you need the information
- only ask relevant questions
- are friendly
- make sure that any questionnaires or forms look attractive.

GET HELP!

The people working with you may already be collecting the information you need (and analysing it, if you're very lucky). They may also want to know about your participants or attenders and so will help you with staff time, expertise and other resources. You should *always* collect information in collaboration with any companies, promoters or venues with whom you are working.

3 MARKETING CAMPAIGNS

The most appropriate method will depend on the nature of your campaign and its objectives. It will be more difficult to evaluate if your objectives are not SMART. Here are some options:

1. Monitor sales daily to observe the impact of particular elements of the campaign, e.g. the increase in sales after the direct mail letter hits the doormat.

2. Log financial information such as the total daily income, the take-up of discounted tickets, etc.

3. Ensure that discounts targeted at particular groups, such as people on income support, have specific concession codes allocated on your box office computer system and monitor the take-up over a period of time.

4. Install a special telephone line with a different number and log calls.

5. Use a coded booking form with a different code or colour for different target groups.

6. Use direct response methods, e.g. reply coupons, etc.

7. Tell respondents to ask for a named individual when calling the box office. Staff can say 'I'm sorry, Theresa isn't available but I can help you' and log the call.

8. Box office staff can ask customers how they heard about the event.

9. Measuring before and after, e.g.:

(a) do a postcode analysis of your database then implement your campaign focusing on a particular postcode area, then do the postcode analysis again

(b) hand out an audience questionnaire before and after a campaign targeting young people

(c) use a clicker to count the number of people coming through your doors before and after your campaign to promote the arts centre as somewhere to drop in for coffee and information

10. Ask people participating in customer circles how they hear about events and what makes them decide to come along.

11. Monitor the take-up of sales promotions.

12. Analyse box office computer data before and after your campaign, e.g. frequency of attendance, type of show attended, sales per performance by art form, etc.

3.1 ASKING TICKET BUYERS HOW THEY HEARD ABOUT THE SHOW

Most box office computer systems will have a facility for recording responses to this question. It can be an irksome task for box office staff, however. It is most effective to ask staff to ask absolutely everybody who buys a ticket for a period of a fortnight (yes, even for doors sales) to get a 90% + response rate. Reward them at the end of the period with a box of biscuits or a cake. If you get them to do it all the time, you will end up with a response rate of less than 50% and highly inaccurate results.

3.2 DIRECT MAIL RESPONSES

Most box office computer systems, notably Databox and PASS, also enable you to monitor responses to direct marketing. This involves saving and naming the mailing selection and, after the campaign, running a routine to calculate the volume and value of ticket sales to the ticket buyers in the selection. It is important to look at sales to an equivalent group who did not receive the mailing to assess what difference the mailing made, as this will give you an idea of how many people would have booked anyway.